FAST-TRACK
EXPORTING

FAST-TRACK EXPORTING

How *Your* Company
Can Succeed in the
Global Market

Sandra L. Renner
W. Gary Winget

amacom
American Management Association

This publication is designed to provide accurate and authoritative
information in regard to the subject matter covered. It is sold
with the understanding that the publisher is not engaged in
rendering legal, accounting, or other professional service. If legal
advice or other expert assistance is required, the services of a
competent professional person should be sought.

Library of Congress Cataloging-in-Publication Data

Renner, Sandra L.
    Fast-track exporting : how your company can succeed in the global
market / Sandra L. Renner, W. Gary Winget.
       p.   cm.
    Includes bibliographical references and index.
    ISBN 0-8144-5009-1
    1. Export marketing—United States. 2. Export marketing.
I. Winget, W. Gary. II. Title.
HF1416.5.R46 1991
658.8'48—dc20   90-56192
                                                          CIP

Printing number

10 9 8 7 6 5 4 3 2 1

Table of Contents

Preface and Acknowledgments

Fast-Track Exporting: How Your Company Can Succeed in the Global Market was written to help your company survive and thrive in the global economy of the 1990s and beyond.

The book is not a textbook. Rather, it presents a dynamic approach to exporting that follows the natural flow of the export process. It's a book based on the real-life experiences of the authors and of companies such as yours. It's a book with a point of view, and it redefines the classical approach to exporting.

We want to take this opportunity to thank the people who have helped make this book possible, including Becky Leisering, John McNab, Frank Rausa, Elisabeth Renner, Dale and Kelly Renner, Lisa Swenson, Mary Winget, and all our colleagues at both the Minnesota Trade Office and the U.S. Department of Commerce District Office in Minneapolis.

A thank you is also in order to the members of our Fast-Track Exporting review panel. The panel includes:

Frank Baeumler, International Marketing Manager, Mate Punch and Die Company
Lee M. Berlin, Chairman, LecTec Corporation
John Bondhus, President, Bondhus Corporation
William C. Dietrich, former Executive Director, Minnesota Trade Office
Dr. Ronald E. Kramer, Director, U.S. Department of Commerce, International Trade Administration, U.S. and Foreign Commercial Service District Office in Minneapolis
Duc Lam, Vice-President, International Banking Department, Norwest Bank Minnesota N.A.
William L. Sippel, Attorney, Doherty Rumble & Butler
Alan Verpy, Vice-President, Global Transportation Services, Inc.

We are especially grateful to the companies that shared their export success stories with us as well as to the state international trade offices and world trade centers around the country that recommended companies for inclusion in this book. We want to give a special thank you to Jeanette Colby, who conducted the case study interviews.

FAST-TRACK
EXPORTING

Introduction:

Internationalizing Your Company Through Fast-Track Exporting

If anyone ever doubted it, the 1990s are proving that the world is a global economy. We have gone beyond the point of no return, and businesses and governments in every country of the world are faced with the same reality: Internationalize your companies or you will perish.

Surviving and Thriving in the Global Economy

The world is moving competition out of the military and political arenas into the business arena. The barriers that artificially blocked the movement toward the world economy are falling everywhere, led by dramatic developments such as the Canada-U.S. Free Trade Agreement and Europe 1992.

The global economy based on business competition uses a worldwide system of production and distribution to deliver products and services to customers in every corner of the world. Those businesses that will survive and thrive in the global economy will produce the highest-quality product at the lowest cost and sell that product in every market on the face of the earth. The most efficient producer of a product in the world will dominate the market for that product worldwide.

This book was written to help you internationalize your company through Fast-Track Exporting, a proven step-by-step approach to quickly enter Trial Run export markets and proceed on to Market Penetration and profits.

Export is a frequently used term in today's government circles and business community. The rationale for exporting ranges *from* a moral obligation to help restore the balance of trade *to* a tax-free opportunity to travel to faraway places. And in between are the traditional reasons such as leveling out business cycles, increasing employment, selling surplus production, and extending the product life cycle.

The real reason your company will export, however, is to internationalize your company and prosper in the 1990s and beyond. There is a big market out there, and it could easily have the potential for doubling your sales. Exporting will help you develop your product or service into the world's highest-quality, lowest-cost product or service and then sell that product worldwide.

The world has seen many changes over the past several years. Communicating internationally is no longer a major problem with most countries. Fax machines, teleconferencing, and other instantaneous methods of communication enable you to interact with your customer abroad.

In short, these changes are creating opportunities for companies around the world. Whether you produce a product, provide a service, or have technology to sell, you must seize the global opportunities available to your company. Internationalizing your company through Fast-Track Exporting should be a driving force in shaping the way you do business in the future.

The Internationalizing of Two Companies

Throughout this book, we introduce you to companies that have successfully used the building blocks that form the foundation upon which Fast-Track Exporting was built. We begin by telling you about two of these companies, Northwestern Steel and Wire Company and Wahl Clipper Corporation, companies that overcame numerous hurdles in order to internationalize their operations. They also are a study in similarities, contrasts, and export successes, which should convince even the most skeptical among us that almost any product can be exported.

As for the similarities, both companies are located in Sterling, Illinois, a small midwestern town 200 kilometers (120 miles) west of Chicago and about 1,500 kilometers (900 miles) from the nearest coast. Northwestern was founded in 1879 and Wahl, in 1919; until 1988 when Northwestern's founding family sold its interest in the company to its employees, both companies were family-owned.

Northwestern Steel and Wire Company

Northwestern's mill in Sterling stretches eight kilometers (five miles) along the banks of the Rock River, employs 3,000 people, and has annual sales of $540 million. The company is a leading U.S. producer of raw and finished steel and finished wire products using the world's largest electric furnaces. The finished products range from heavy-section wide-flange steel beams weighing up to 380 kilograms per meter to the smallest finishing nails under the Sterling brand name. Until recently, the company's traditional market was the Midwest.

In the mid-1980s, at the depths of the steel crisis in this country, the global economy hit Northwestern, and Northwestern was not the highest-quality, lowest-cost steel and wire producer in the world.

In order to pull itself out of its crisis, the company set a goal of becoming the highest-quality, lowest-cost producer of heavy-section wide-flange steel beams in the world. The company and its employee-owners invested millions of dollars in new facilities, equipment, and training in order to achieve its goal. A jumbo caster was constructed to produce the required semifinished product. A closed rolling mill facility located on the port of Houston was purchased and renovated, turning it into a state-of-the-art facility. Top management, staff, and key employees from throughout the company set out to internationalize themselves, the company, and its products with an intensive eighteen-month export training and development program supported by the Illinois Department of Commerce and Community Affairs. To demonstrate its commitment to international markets and standards, Northwestern made a decision to roll steel that met international specifications and to pass the requirements of the major international standard-setting organizations.

Northwestern started exporting to Canada with a Trial Run at the market, moved on to Market Penetration, and established a successful export operation in the Canadian market. Then, it targeted certain markets in the Far East where it decided to use several export trading companies to launch its Trial Run in those markets.

Well over 100 years after its founding, Northwestern Steel and Wire Company became a successful exporter of heavy-section wide-flange steel beams as well as other structural steel products. To its surprise, Northwestern also found that it could successfully export certain of its wire products because of the unique design and features of these products.

Northwestern set out to internationalize its company, and through Fast-Track Exporting achieved its goal.

Wahl Clipper Corporation

Wahl's factory sits on the outskirts of Sterling, surrounded on three sides by cornfields, and employs 400 people. Wahl is possibly the world's largest manufacturer of electric hair clippers, and it has been an international company since the 1920s when it set up a distributor in Canada. Today, nearly 22 percent of its sales are generated by exports.

The company specializes in manufacturing hair clippers and facial hair clippers for the professional and consumer markets. It also makes pet clippers and grooming products such as curling irons, shavers, and massagers. One of its most popular consumer brands is the Groomsman line.

In 1919, Wahl set out to fill the niche for specialized electromagnetic hair clippers, and by 1920, it was the premier supplier to barbers all over the United States. As the reputation of the Wahl clippers began to spread abroad through English-speaking magazines and orders started coming in, Wahl recognized that the product had universal appeal. Thus, the company began manufacturing clippers in all the various voltages and cycles used around the world. As foreign sales grew during the 1930s, Wahl began to develop a foreign network of sales and service representatives and established an assembly factory in England. Today, Wahl has a worldwide network of distributors and wholly-owned operations in Canada and England. Wahl's products regularly carry their message in four foreign languages.

Wahl believes that people are not much different from country to country and that the key to success in exporting is finding the right representatives and developing long-term relationships with those representatives and their families. For example, the family that started the Wahl distributorship in Canada in the 1920s still represents the company.

Prior to 1975, Wahl's success in exporting happened because customers literally came to it, attracted by the company's reputation for a high-quality, low-cost, universal product. In 1975, however, the company made a conscious commitment to become an international company. To Wahl, this meant dedication to identifying the specific needs of customers around the world and filling those needs with the best possible product at the lowest possible price. Every product had to be a world-class product.

Wahl Clipper Corporation has always been an international company, but today it is striving to reach yet another international goal. "We want to sell in every country in Europe the way we sell in every state in the United States. That's our goal," states the company's chairman.

What Is Fast-Track Exporting?

Fast-Track Exporting is a proven step-by-step approach for internationalizing your company and achieving success in export markets now. With Fast-Track Exporting, your company can quickly enter Trial Run export markets and proceed on to Market Penetration and export profit.

We developed and used the Fast-Track Exporting process first during our years with Minnesota's international trade office and later in our own company.

We found that new-to-export as well as experienced exporters needed a *fast track* on which to run if they were to achieve timely success in new export markets. So we began to identify the techniques used by our most successful exporters and developed those techniques into a logical, manageable process—a process that achieves initial export sales in a relatively short time with minimal expense and creates opportunities to achieve market penetration and long-term profits in proven high-potential export markets (see Figure 1).

In addition to a fast track, we also found that companies needed a systematic set of export *tools* to assist them in quickly getting over some of the hurdles that they inevitably encountered on the track. This led to the development of a series of worksheets, many of which appear in this book.

Finally, exporters needed a synergistic export implementation *network* to help them increase their effectiveness in developing and implementing their export marketing program. This network consisted of the numerous already existing export promotion organizations whose purpose was to promote the export of U.S. products and services. By combining the limited resources and expertise of the exporter with those of the network, companies could effectively implement their export marketing programs without straining company staff and budget.

Fast-Track Exporting uses these key elements—the fast track, the

Figure 1. Fast-Track Exporting model.

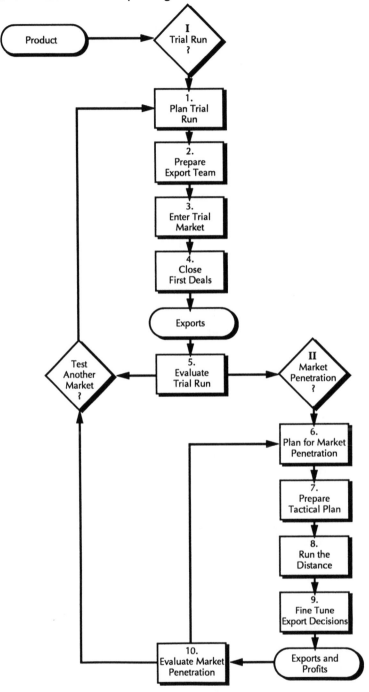

tools, and the network—to help companies achieve more export sales in more foreign markets in far less time than conventional export approaches.

From start to finish, your company will be on a visible, well-marked track. You will not get bogged down in the endless research, planning, and complicated pre-export activities, which become overwhelming hurdles to successful, timely, and profitable exporting. You will quickly move through the planning and preparation steps and on to successful and profitable exporting when you are on the fast track.

How to Get on the Export Fast Track

Fast-Track Exporting is a two-phase, ten-step program. We begin with Phase I, The Trial Run, which allows you to close your first export deals in your target country and worldwide markets by following five steps. We describe each of the steps in depth to ensure that you reach your initial export objectives effectively and quickly. Then we move on to Phase II, Market Penetration, where the discussion is widened to provide you with a strategic five-step framework to build your Market Penetration.

The combination of a Phase I "vertical" and a Phase II "horizontal" approach to Fast-Track Exporting takes your company straight from the Trial Run starting line to the Market Penetration finish line.

The Fast-Track Exporting model takes you through the natural flow of exporting and directly to the goal of internationalizing your company. It loops you back to the top of the process as you complete each phase. With each lap on the fast track, your company becomes more experienced and successful at selecting and penetrating high-potential markets for your products or services.

Phase I

The Trial Run

Test the Market's Potential With a Trial Run

Before setting off on the Trial Run, there are three preliminary questions you must ask yourself: (1) Do I have any products that I want to export? (2) Should I expand my markets through export? (3) Do I want to take a Trial Run at export markets?

If the answers to these three questions are yes, you are ready to launch the Fast-Track Exporting process and start the Trial Run.

Do I Have Any Products That I Want to Export?

In order to get on the export fast track, you need a commodity, service, or technology (hereafter, referred to as your "product") that you want to consider for introduction in foreign markets.

To start the Fast-Track Exporting process, prepare the Products With Export Potential Worksheet (see Worksheet 1) and list the current products you either want to consider for export or believe might have export potential. Beside each product listed, indicate why you want to export the product and/or believe that the product might be successful in export markets. This list should be based on your current knowledge; no research is required. Indicate why you are considering each for export.

After listing your products with export potential, select one or more products you believe might be your best-prospect products for export. Write these products and your rationale for selecting them at the bottom of the worksheet.

Assuming you have at least one product with export potential, you can answer the product question with a yes.

- -

CASE EXAMPLE: Northwestern Steel and Wire Company produces structural steel and fabricated wire products in hundreds of shapes and sizes. Although the company was willing to export any product for which there was an order, it identified two products that it felt had a high potential for export. The

WORKSHEET 1. Products With Export Potential

PRODUCTS WITH EXPORT POTENTIAL	≡*FASTRACK*™
	Success Through Fast-Track Exporting

Purpose: To initially identify products with export potential. Directions: Prepare a preliminary list of the products (commodities, services, technologies) you want to consider for export. Indicate why you want to export the product and/or believe the product will be successful in export markets. Choose the products you believe have export potential and indicate your rationale.

Company Name/Division

Product	Why Being Considered for Export

Products with Export Potential:

Rationale:

DECISION: Do I have any products that I want to Export?   Yes   No

Completed by	Date

Copyright Export Resource Associates, Inc., 1990

steel division selected heavy wide-flange steel beams as its most exportable product because it felt that recent capital investments to modernize its facilities and the current value of the U.S. dollar in world markets meant that Northwestern could be a high-quality, low-cost producer of this product line in domestic and international markets. The wire division selected its plastic-coated flower garden fence as its most exportable product because it felt the product was unique in international markets and that the margins were such that Northwestern could profitably sell it in export markets.

Should I Expand My Markets Through Export?

To help you decide whether you want to expand your markets through export or whether you want to step aside and forgo the export opportunity, prepare the Market Expansion Through Exporting Worksheet (see Worksheet 2) by writing down a list of market-expansion-through-export pros and cons. The pros and cons should be based on your current knowledge and assumptions about your product, the industry, domestic and world market potential, and so forth. The objective is to determine if you believe that sales could be expanded by exploring export markets.

If you believe that sales could be expanded through exporting, enter your rationale at the bottom of the worksheet. You are now in a position to answer the market expansion question with a yes.

Do I Want to Take a Trial Run at Export Markets?

Now you are ready to make the Trial Run decision—Do you want to take a Trial Run at export markets?

The decision to launch a Trial Run at export markets is an important one and must be supported by top management and those people in your organization who will be involved in the export process. Success in exporting is very directly related to a company's commitment to properly planning, preparing, and implementing the export program.

If you decide to launch the Trial Run effort, you and your company will be affirming your commitment to carrying out the Trial Run phase of

WORKSHEET 2.   Market Expansion Through Exporting

MARKET EXPANSION THROUGH EXPORTING	**≡FASTRACK** *Success Through Fast-Track Exporting*

Purpose: To decide whether or not to expand markets through exporting. Directions: List the pros and cons of expanding your markets through exporting based on your current knowledge and assumptions about your product, world markets, etc. Decide whether or not you believe sales will expand through exporting to foreign markets. Decide whether or not you want to expand your markets through exporting.

Company Name/Division

Pros	Cons

Will sales be expanded through exports to foreign markets?   _____ Yes   _____ No
DECISION: Should I expand my markets through exporting?   _____ Yes   _____ No
Rationale:

Completed by	Date

the Fast-Track Exporting process. This process has been designed to allow your company to achieve significant results with a limited allocation of company resources. Don't be scared off by the erroneous assumption that exporting is too difficult for your company. You can do it.

If it is a "go," you are now ready to launch Step 1 of the process—planning the Trial Run.

Step 1:

Plan the Trial Run

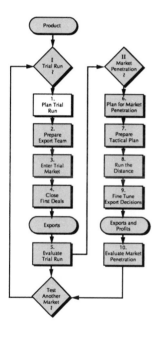

In Step 1, you will make the final selection of the product to be considered for export, synergize your resources with those of the appropriate export promotion organizations, set up an export center, conduct your initial market research and select your target market, select your market entry method for the Trial Run, assess your company's readiness to export, and finalize strategic export decisions for the Trial Run.

Your strategic plan for the Trial Run will include a proactive campaign to test a single target market as well as a general campaign to attract inquiries worldwide. At this stage of the process, your decisions will be based primarily on your existing knowledge of your product and the international market, supplemented by a limited amount of market research.

Select the Trial Run Product

Assessing the Product

At this stage, you are making a worldwide assessment of your product to identify hurdles which might prevent your product from being exported from the U.S. and from selling in foreign markets. This initial assessment is designed to determine likely regulatory issues that will be encountered such as governmental approvals and standards, necessary export licenses, if any, and product features or characteristics that may require a certain degree of alteration. Ideally, your Trial Run product can be exported as is, since one of your objectives will be to successfully sell your product in export markets with a minimum of expense and complication. Use your experience in the U.S. market and your intuition to start the assessment process.

There are five questions you will want to address to initially determine the exportability of your product:

1. What hurdles might I have to overcome in order to *export* my product?
2. What hurdles might my foreign customers have to overcome in order to *import* my product?
3. What hurdles might my foreign customers have to overcome in order to *sell or use* my product in foreign markets?
4. What other hurdles might I have to overcome?
5. Are there other issues that I might have to address in order to export my product?

The Product Assessment and Selection Worksheet (see Worksheet 3) will help you select your most exportable products. Start with the best-prospect products you selected for your Worksheet 1 from the previous section.

Enter *Worldwide* for the target country. The information you currently have about your product and your potential worldwide customers should be based on your existing knowledge and perceptions. For each product you are considering for export, write down the hurdles you believe you will have to overcome or about which you have questions. This list does not have to be long. The number of questions will, of course, depend on the type of product you want to export.

One of your first export hurdles may be that a product under consideration will need a special validated export license which will restrict its export to certain countries. Whether or not a special export license is required depends on the type of product you are selling abroad and to which country. Products or equipment with military applications are likely to have some export restrictions although the number of these restrictions has been greatly reduced in recent years. However, the vast

WORKSHEET 3. Product Assessment and Selection

PRODUCT ASSESSMENT & SELECTION   ≡*FASTRACK*™
                                                                    Success Through Fast-Track Exporting

---

Purpose: To select the products that will be introduced into export markets. Directions: Start with the products listed on the Products with Export Potential worksheet. Assess each product by itemizing the known or possible hurdles you anticipate in exporting the product from the U.S., importing the product into the foreign country, selling/using the product in the foreign country, and other types of hurdles/issues to be addressed. Then idenfity your most exportable products and select the specific product to be used in the Trial Run.

Company Name/Division _____
Target Country

Product	Export Hurdles	Import Hurdles	Sales/Use Hurdles	Other Hurdles/Issues

Identify the Most Exportable Products:

DECISION: Which product will be selected for the Trial Run? _____

Rationale:

Completed by   Date

Copyright Export Resource Associates, Inc., 1990   090 majority of products are exported under one or more general export licenses, which requires no special approvals and is not an export hurdle.

In many countries your customers may have import hurdles such as tariffs, restrictive quotas, or other formal and informal barriers to importing. If you are exporting electrical, medical, food, or certain other types of products, your customer may not be able to import the product until it has passed inspection and meets the standards of the importing country. For example, if your product requires U.S. Food and Drug Administration approval in the United States, chances are there is a comparable agency in most other countries from which you or your foreign customer will have to obtain approval. Obtaining import approvals is not necessarily an obstacle because there are a number of ways to work through the approval processes. The important thing at this time is to raise the questions that will have to be answered by you or your customer at some later step in the process.

Your initial product screening should also include an assessment of sales and usage hurdles such as product features and characteristics. Are there things that would obviously need some modification in order to make the product marketable and, if so, how difficult would it be to implement the changes? Because all but three countries of the world uses the metric system and many parts of the world use different types of electrical power, your foreign customers may have problems selling and/or using your product without modification. Also consider foreign sales and usage problems such as the need for training in the use of the product, frequent after-sale support or maintenance, and so forth.

During the initial assessment you may identify other hurdles and issues about which you are unsure and which must be considered as you progress down the export fast track. For example, if your product is competitive with imports in the U.S. market, will it also be competitive in foreign markets? Are there patents or trademarks that will have to be protected? By starting a list of these unresolved issues now, you are more likely to address all the potential areas of concern that must be resolved before you take your product into foreign markets.

Remember, the assessment of your product will be an ongoing process as you progress through the Trial Run, move into the Market Penetration phase, and target new markets for export.

Selecting the Most Exportable Product

The assessment of your best-prospect export products has identified some of the potential hurdles you and/or your customers will have to overcome in order to get your product on the export fast track. In addition, you have raised other issues that have to be considered along the way.

At this point, you should be able to determine the exportability of your products. List the product or products which you believe to be most exportable at the bottom of the Product Assessment and Selection Worksheet. Then, decide which product (or products) you are going to select for the Trial Run, and write in the product name at the bottom of Worksheet 3.

Multiply Your Resources

Using Export Promotion Organization Networks

Since it can be very difficult to do everything alone as a new exporter, we recommend that your company utilize the unique support services of export promotion organizations (EPOs). Their mission is to help U.S. companies promote their products abroad. These EPOs include a broad range of federal, state, local, educational, and private entities. By using the right EPO at the right time, your company can move more quickly and effectively through the export fast track.

The help provided by EPOs falls into three general categories: (1) help to companies, (2) help to targeted export industries, and (3) help to foreign buyers.

How EPOs Help Companies. EPOs can play a major role in helping your company get on the export fast track. Each EPO possesses some of the specific tools that can assist your company in achieving its full export potential.

Specific services that you can expect from EPOs include: Export readiness assessment to help you identify export strengths and weaknesses; export publications such as how-to manuals, a list of export service organizations, and market data information; a research library with export manuals, extensive country marketing data, and industry export information; educational programs on the export process and current opportunities in high-potential markets; counseling services that provide one-on-one assistance in working through problems and taking advantage of opportunities; export sales leads that match your product and interests; sales contacts in foreign markets such as agents, distributors, retailers, and end users; participation in foreign trade shows and missions;

meetings with foreign buyers visiting the United States; export finance and insurance programs to help you fund your export effort and protect you from the unique risks that you will face in export markets.

CASE EXAMPLE: Murdock, Inc., got into exporting in 1980 quite by chance—a Japanese company wanted to buy one of the company's machines. Murdock makes custom aircraft parts and hot press machines. After that sale, the company made a conscious decision to develop exports and it started using the services of EPOs. One of its first planned export activities was to participate in the California State World Trade Commission's pavilion at the Paris Air Show. This step helped move Murdock's export program forward and led to participation in other shows. Today, exports account for 10 to 19 percent of the company's sales.

Systematic cooperation among EPOs enables you to develop a well-defined track upon which to run and assists you in taking your first strides in the race for exporting success. By synergizing your resources with those of the EPOs, you will be able to maximize the speed at which your company runs its first lap and successive laps on the export fast track.

How EPOs Promote Targeted Export Industries. The EPO can also be an invaluable asset to your company if you are a member of an industry sector that the EPO has targeted for promotion in international markets. The promotion of target export industries in foreign markets is important to your company because it increases the foreign buyer's awareness of companies and products, including your own, in an industry which has a high potential for export. EPO services available to an industry sector include target industry export readiness assessment, trade association support, industry and product publications, direct promotion campaigns, and industry-specific trade shows and missions.

How EPOs Bring the Foreign Buyer to the Finish Line. The third role of the EPO is to actually bring foreign buyers to your door step. In this case the EPO becomes a sourcing vehicle for the foreign buyer, matches the foreign buyers with your company's product, and refers the buyer directly to you.

Finding the EPOs

There is a support network of hundreds of both private and public EPOs that offers a wide variety of services to help your company get on the export fast track and with which you can start synergizing your resources.

A good place to start is with a copy of the *International Trade State and Local Resource Directory* for your state (see Appendix B for information on how to order your free copy). This U.S. Small Business Administration (SBA) publication has a very comprehensive list of international trade services for your state. In addition to the SBA directory, consult your local or nearby metropolitan Yellow Pages. Some of the most important EPOs to identify include the following:

> U.S. Department of Agriculture (USDA) Foreign Agriculture Service
> U.S. Department of Commerce (USDOC) District Office
> U.S. Small Business Administration (SBA) District Office
> Your state's international trade program office
> Your state's export finance program office
> Your state's department of agriculture
> Your nearest world trade center
> Your nearest port authority
> Your national trade association
> Your city's export promotion programs, local Small Business Development Center (SBDC) program, community college, or vocational school

Establishing Continuing Relationships With EPOs

Start developing your relationship with local EPOs by calling them to set up appointments. The purpose of your visits is to introduce your company and product and to assess the network of specific services offered by the EPOs. It is important to establish a long-term relationship with representatives of these organizations. The more they know about your company, your goals and objectives, and your resources, the better service they can provide.

When you meet with the EPOs, tell them that you are interested in Fast-Track Exporting, ask to be listed on their exporter/product database and to be included in their export sales lead notification program, provide them with information on your business and your product, and collect any information and materials that they have available for exporters.

You will provide the EPOs with the following information: Background information on your company, including your annual report; key company contacts; your export experiences and the state of your planning and preparation for exporting; and the products you want to export, including your product literature. Your product information should include the proper Harmonized System (HS)/Schedule B and Standard Industrial Classification (SIC) codes for your products (if you do not know the codes, your USDOC District Office will help you identify the correct codes) as well as why you believe the products are exportable in terms of the competitiveness of the product with domestic and imported goods on price, quality, service, and technology; the customer segments and distribution channels you anticipate using in foreign markets; some of the export markets that you would like to consider; potential hurdles your product may have in being exported and imported (Worksheet 3); and any market research that you have conducted to date.

CASE EXAMPLE: James Clem Corporation is a classic example of how establishing a continuing relationship with EPOs can result in export success. The company invented a geocomposite clay liner system for landfills and other situations where waterproofing is necessary. Clem went to the USDOC District Office and the State of Illinois' International Business Division where they were introduced to four promotion activities—the Agent/Distributor Service, advertising in *Commercial News USA*, a trade show in Europe, and a USDOC Matchmaker delegation to Italy. Within three years export sales reached $1.2 million and the James Clem Corporation received the President's "E" Award for success in exporting.

Since one of your purposes in meeting with the EPOs is to inventory the specific services each EPO offers in relation to your current and expected export assistance needs, be prepared to ask questions. At this stage of the export process your most immediate interests will probably be the services that will help you set up your export library, conduct market research, assess your company's readiness to export, and obtain export training for your staff. Use the Export Promotion Organization Inventory Worksheet (see Worksheet 4) to keep track of the specific services offered by each EPO, and use the bottom of the inventory form to list the key services that you want to utilize during the Trial Run. Ask each EPO to help you develop a service plan that will assist your company to utilize the key services that they have to offer more fully.

In your initial meetings with the EPOs, you should also discuss the potential hurdles (Worksheet 3) that you expect you will have to overcome in order for your product to be successful in export markets. Specifically, you should discuss the issue of export licenses with the USDOC District Office to determine if a validated export license will be required in order to export your product from the United States and, if so, to which countries. If a validated license is required, ask the District Office to help you determine the specific rules that apply to exporting your product under the *Export Administration Regulations.*

In summary, your meetings with the EPOs should result in the following:

- ▲ The EPOs should be aware of your company and its exportable products.
- ▲ Your company should be in each EPO database so that you will receive sales opportunity leads, timely information on upcoming events, and other important export information.
- ▲ You should know your product HS/Schedule B and SIC code numbers.
- ▲ You should have inventoried and selected the specific services of each EPO that you will want to use in the future, and the EPOs

WORKSHEET 4.   Export Promotion Organization Inventory

EXPORT PROMOTION ORGANIZATION INVENTORY					≡FASTRACK℠ Success Through Fast-Track Exporting	

Purpose: To identify the EPO services that will be used. Directions: Inventory the specific services offered by each EPO and assess their usefulness. Select the key services to be used during the Trial Run.

Company Name/Division _____

Service	USDOC District Office	SBA	State Trade Office	World Trade Center	Natl Trade Association	
Contact and Telephone						
1. Export Readiness Assessment						
2. Publications						
3. Market Research Resources						
4. Education Programs						
5. Counseling						
6. Sales Leads						
7. Market Contacts						
8. Foreign Trade Missions/Shows						
9. Buying Mission Visits						
10. Financing and Insurance						
11. Promotion of My Industry Sector in Export Markets						
Most Useful Services - List Number for Key Service to Be Used During Trial Run						

Completed by	Date

Copyright Export Resource Associates, Inc., 1990

090

should have developed a service plan for providing your company with the assistance it will need during the Trial Run.

▲ You should have collected how-to information and other publications and materials from each EPO.

▲ You should have determined if a validated export license is required to export your product from the United States and the specific limitations that apply.

The key to your company's success with any EPO is to clearly determine and define what you want them to do for you or with you and keep them appraised of your progress and results. It is important to remain highly visible so they keep your company in mind for the many opportunities that come across their desks. You must view them as an ongoing resource and one that has the potential of saving you lots of time and money.

It is common for experienced and successful exporters to continue using the services of EPOs long after they have gone beyond the Trial Run stage of the process. Therefore, maintain your relationships with the EPOs and continue to reap the benefits they have to offer.

Set Up an Export Center

Collecting How-To Resources

With the resource publications you have collected from your visits with the EPOs and the SBA directory you previously requested, you have the start of an in-house library for your export center. These resources will include an array of helpful how-to resource publications, on-line services, computer software packages, and videos available without charge or for a nominal fee. Many of these resources will be useful to you now and other resources will become useful as you progress down the export fast track.

In addition to the materials you have already collected, we recommend that your company initially invest about $350 to obtain the following startup export resources. (Ordering information for these and all subsequent resources suggested in this book can be found in Appendix B.)

A Basic Guide to Exporting. A summary of various export topics.

Correct Way to Fill Out the Shipper's Export Declaration. Instructions for preparing the SED.

Discover Dollars in Drawback. An explanation of the drawback benefit and how to use it.

Foreign Sales Corporation. An explanation of the FSC and tax benefits for exporters.

Incoterms 1990. Trade/shipping terms used in international trade and the responsibilities of buyers and sellers.

Schedule B. The Harmonized System (HS) codes used to classify exports from the United States.

Foreign Economic Trends. A subscription service that summarizes the current economic and commercial trends in each country.

Overseas Business Reports. A subscription service that periodically provides updated information on how to do business in each country.

Background Notes. Background information such as people, government, and the economy on each country.

Culturegram. Information on the people and culture of most nations.

Business America and/or *AgExporter.* A magazine for exporters.

Export Administration Regulations. Order only if the USDOC has indicated that your product requires a validated export license.

Exporter's Guide to Federal Resources for Small Business. A summary of federal international trade programs and contacts.

Foreign Consular Offices in the U.S. A listing of the locations of the consular offices.

International Trade State and Local Resources Directory. A listing of EPO and export service organizations in your state.

Key Officers of Foreign Service Posts. A directory of U.S. government export contacts in foreign embassies and consulates.

Metrification for the Manager. An introduction to metrics.

The World Is Your Market. A summary of export topics and the service programs of the U.S. government and other organizations.

Traveler's World Atlas and Guide. A quick reference guide to the world and major cities.

USDOC Telephone Directory or *Food & Agriculture Export Directory.* A directory of USDOC and USDA contacts and telephone numbers.

Unz & Co. Catalog for International and Domestic Shippers. A catalog of useful forms for exporters.

If your company has a personal computer with a CD-ROM reader, you may also want to order a single issue of *The National Trade Data Bank.* This resource has such information as trade data, market research, and foreign buyer contacts for fourteen federal agencies in a very economical and compact form. In addition to the above materials, you will want to collect existing in-house resources that can be added to the export library and subscribe to international publications for your industry. Such materials might include copies of trade publication articles on imports/exports, trade association data on imports/exports, and books with chapters on international trade.

CASE EXAMPLE: Benfield Electric Supply Company distributes the electrical materials of over 300 U.S. manufacturers to foreign engineering and construction companies. The company uses its in-house library as a major source of market research and sales lead information. Industry publications, for example, announce major foreign construction projects and name the companies that were awarded the contracts. These leads, along with leads received from New York State's International Division, provide Benfield with the information needed to close many of its export sales.

At the start it will be helpful to physically organize your library materials into separate sections so that as they begin to accumulate, you will be able to easily locate the needed information. The following section scheme has proved useful:

- ▲ How-To Resources
- ▲ Market Data General
- ▲ Industry Information
- ▲ Country Information
- ▲ Regional Information
- ▲ Other Information

The Country Information section of the library should consist of a set of files for each country on which you have country-specific information. This section of the library will become invaluable as you begin to target your initial and follow-up Trial Run markets.

Building the Country Information Files

Prepare a set of eleven file folders for each country market that you are considering for your Trial Run or in which you have a potential future interest. The country files will help you organize the market research materials you will build during the course of the Trial Run and thereafter. The eleven file folders should be labeled as follows:

1. General Information
2. Business Practices
3. Competition
4. Cultural/Social Information
5. Demand
6. Demographic/Economic Information
7. Distribution Contacts/Characteristics
8. End-User Contacts/Characteristics
9. Import/Use Hurdles
10. Legal/Political Information
11. Travel

To start your country files, ask your USDOC District Office for a copy of the following documents for each of your potential target markets: *Background Notes, Foreign Economic Trends* reports, and *Overseas Business Reports* country marketing reports.

The USDA Foreign Agriculture Service produces a *Market Backgrounder Reports* country series that describes the prospects for U.S. food and farm products in specific countries.

Contact the Overseas Private Investment Corporation (OPIC) and order its *Country Information Kit* for your potential target countries.

There are several export manuals with extensive country information to which you will want to refer as you progress down the export fast track. You should find a copy of these manuals in a public or EPO library. Review the information they provide on each potential target country. The manuals include *Exporter's Encyclopaedia, International Trade*

Reporter: Export Reference (Shipping) Manual, Official Export Guide, and *Reference Book for World Traders.*

Write to the U.S. offices of the foreign governments in which you are interested and ask for travel and market information and publications that will help you gather information for each of your files. The embassy and consular offices are listed in the *Foreign Consular Offices in the U.S.* publication.

The major accounting firms frequently publish a series of country information guides that would be appropriate for your library. For example, contact Price Waterhouse for a copy of its *Doing Business In* publication for your target market.

When you complete your initial country files, you will have gathered much of the information you will need to complete your next task— selecting the Trial Run market.

Select the Trial Run Market

During the Trial Run, you will be reacting to sales inquiries from around the world and taking a proactive position in a single, high-potential country market where you want to test your initial success at exporting. The immediate task is to select this target market.

The road signs along this stretch of the fast track will help you target a country market for the Trial Run. This task will not only open the opportunity for immediate export sales during the Trial Run, but it will give you much of the information you need to determine whether or not to proceed with the Phase II, Market Penetration, process in the test market.

Selecting your target market involves surveying the worldwide demand for your product and identifying the high-potential markets, assessing each of the high-potential markets using several market indicators, and reaching a decision.

Surveying Worldwide Demand

Collect and summarize data, expert opinion, and market intelligence in order to survey the worldwide demand for your product and to identify high-potential markets. Use the Markets With Export Potential Worksheet (see Worksheet 5) to compile the following summary indicators.

WORKSHEET 5. Markets with Export Potential

MARKETS WITH EXPORT POTENTIAL	≠ASTRACK
	Success Through Fast-Track Exporting

Purpose: To initially identify markets with export potential for your product. Directions: Enter primary data sources and product codes used for the data in each column. Use the worldwide line to record total data for all countries. List countries with highest potential in left column and data or information for country in appropriate columns. Choose the countries that appear to have the greatest export potential and indicate your rationale.

Company Name/Division _____

Product _____ HS/Schedule B # _____ SIC # _____

Country	Imports from US	Exports to US	Imports from World	Exports to World	Foreign Inquiries	Competitors' Exports	Unique Factors	Expert Opinion
Primary Data Source								
Product Code								
Worldwide Total								

Top 5 Export Markets with Export Potential:

1.   2.   3.   4.   5.

Rationale:

Completed by	Date

Copyright Export Resource Associates, Inc., 1990

▲ *Imports from the United States*—the top importers of your product from the United States.

▲ *Exports to the United States*—the primary exporters of your product to the United States.

▲ *Imports from the world*—the top importers of your product from all sources including the United States.

▲ *Exports to the world*—the primary exporters of your product to all countries of the world.

▲ *Foreign inquiries*—the top countries from which your company has received quality foreign inquiries.

▲ *Competitors' exports*—the primary countries to which your product is exported by known U.S. and foreign competitors.

▲ *Unique factors*—other factors that indicate the potential for your product, e.g., gross domestic product and per capita income.

▲ *Expert opinion*—the primary countries which experts in your industry and others believe to be the markets for your product.

Collecting Historical Industry Data. If you are lucky enough to have a product that fits neatly into a standard product classification code, collecting your data will be easy since the most accessible data is reported by one of the following four product classification systems:

1. Standard Industrial Classification (SIC) codes
2. Harmonized System (HS)/Schedule B codes
3. Standard Industrial Trade Classification (SITC) Revision 1 codes
4. Standard Industrial Trade Classification (SITC) Revision 2 codes

The SIC codes are an old U.S. product coding system. The Harmonized System (HS)/Schedule B codes are the new international product classification system which the United States adopted for exports in January 1989. The SITC codes are the United Nation's classification and reporting system.

It's likely, however, that your product does not fit neatly into one of the SIC, HS, or SITC product classification codes. Instead, it will probably fall under a product code and be mixed in with many products in the general category. If you have a service or technology that you want to export, finding data becomes even more difficult because the product classification systems either do not cover or inadequately cover these types of exports.

If you have not already found the HS/Schedule B and SIC codes for your product, this will be your next task. It will also be necessary to identify the SITC Revision 1 and Revision 2 codes for your product. Refer to the *Schedule B* manual in your export library for the HS/ Schedule B code. Your USDOC District Office will help you determine your SIC and SITC Revision 1 codes, and your SBA District Office will help you with the SITC Revision 2 codes.

Let's start off assuming that your product can be classified with some accuracy by the above product codes and that there are meaningful data on foreign market demand. There are four primary EPOs from which you will want to collect data: (1) the SBA, (2) the USDOC, (3) the USDA, and (4) your industry trade association.

1. *SBA.* The first data you will want to collect are available through your SBA District Office. Request that the office prepare a computer-generated *Export Information System (XIS) Product Report* for your product's SITC Revision 2 product code. The report is compiled using either a three-, four-, or five-digit SITC product code depending on the product involved. The *XIS* report is a good summary source of information on your product and will provide you with the initial information for Worksheet 5. The report includes the following data: (a) the top importing countries of your product from the world (insert this data in the Imports from the World column of Worksheet 5); (b) the top importing countries of your product from the United States based on the U.S. share of the markets; and (c) the top importing countries from the United States based on the U.S. sales volume in the markets.

2. *USDOC.* The second place to visit for historical export data is your USDOC District Office. You established your relationship with the office earlier and obtained information about the services it could provide. Now you want to use its *National Trade Data Bank* and other data services. Order three computer reports on your product using its *Custom Statistical Service.*

The first USDOC report you will want is a search for the top ten U.S. export markets for your product. You will most likely want a five-year time series based on export volume and/or U.S. dollar value. Because the data reporting system is in the process of switching from SIC codes to HS/Schedule B codes, you may want to request the data using both types of codes, since the pre-1989 data were compiled using SIC codes. The data from this report should be entered in the Imports from U.S. column of Worksheet 5. At this point, you might find that for some countries you have duplicate data from the USDOC and SBA reports and that the data do not match! If this is the case, there are numerous reasons (for example, the SITC and SIC codes define the product differently and the SBA data come from the United Nations database and are much less accurate than the USDOC data) for explaining the difference.

The second USDOC report you want is a list of the top ten markets from which the United States imports your product. Enter this data in the Exports to the U.S. column on Worksheet 5.

The third USDOC report you need will be compiled from the United Nations Trade Data System. Review Worksheet 5 and identify five to ten countries that appear to be of the greatest export potential; order a printout for each country for imports to and exports from these markets. The report can be presented with a five-year time series and be based on either U.S. dollar value or quantity. As mentioned above, the U.N. data are frequently inaccurate because of internal inconsistencies and incomplete reporting by many countries. Therefore, the absolute amounts presented in the reports may be of limited value. The real use of the U.N. data, however, will be to identify the import and export flows and the relative magnitude of those flows.

While you are at the USDOC District Office, you can also use the microfiche data bank, *U.S. Exports of Domestic and Foreign Merchandise FT545* (data through 1989), and the hardcopy export data reports, *U.S. Exports: Schedule E Commodity by Country FT410* (data through 1988) and *U.S. Merchandise Trade FT925* (data beginning 1989), for a detailed search of U.S. exports to each of the high-import companies you have identified to date.

CASE EXAMPLE: Little Giant Pump Company makes all kinds of small pumps—e.g., sump pumps, pumps for air conditioners, and pumps for medical use. The USDOC District Office has been one of the company's first stops in locating and developing new markets. The company starts with USDOC trade statistics to determine if similar products sell in a target market. Next, it does an ADS search to identify interested local representatives. Depending on the circumstances, it visits the market and the interested representatives. While in the country, Little Giant may visit with the USDOC commercial officer at the embassy or consulate, the local and American chambers of commerce, and local trade associations and publications. Today, the company sells in fifty-one countries. While in the market looking for representatives, Little Giant also identifies its competition and runs a credit check on them in order to determine the volume of their business (and thus, their market share).

----

3. *USDA.* The third data source is the USDA. *Foreign Agriculture* and *Foreign Agriculture Trade of the U.S.* are comprehensive data sources available from USDA. *Outlook for U.S. Agriculture Exports* and *Situation and Outlook Reports,* the USDA Economic Research Service's timely product market intelligence reports, are available on a subscription basis. Special *U.S. Trade Reports* can be prepared by the USDA Foreign Agriculture Service (FAS). The FAS and its AgExport Services program can either compile reports or refer you to a variety of resources that will assist you in targeting export markets (see Appendix A for information on how to contact USDA agencies).

4. *Industry Trade Association.* Frequently, industry trade associations collect data from the USDOC and other primary sources. If these types of data are available, they can be extremely helpful to your company. Data generated by trade associations are easier to understand and evaluate than data obtained from generalized public sources such as the SBA and the USDOC because the trade association data have been sorted and organized specifically for use by companies such as yours.

Collecting Foreign Inquiry Data. Among the data that you collect on export demand for your product, be sure to include any inquiries you may have received from foreign buyers and distributors. Often these inquiries are good indicators of potential demand for your product and provide valuable information on potential target countries, the types of buyers, the anticipated quantities, and other specific information. Enter the number of quality inquiries for each country in the Foreign Inquiries column of Worksheet 5.

Collecting Competitors' Export Destinations. One of the best sources of information on market demand will be information on the countries to which your competitors, both U.S. and foreign, are exporting. The easiest way to find this information is to ask your competitors. Other methods of obtaining this information include asking trade association officials or other people in the industry and reviewing industry trade journals for articles on your competitors. If your product is usually transported by ship (as opposed to air, rail, or truck), it is possible to use the *P.I.E.R.S.* service (see Appendix B) to get a detailed printout of your U.S. competitors' export shipments. The cost of this service is relatively high and very likely impractical during your first Trial Run.

Using Unique Market Indicators. Now, let's go back and discuss what you can do when your product cannot be easily coded and/or the above data sources do not produce meaningful information on the potential markets for your product. This calls for a more creative approach to data collection. You may have to develop a data-gathering strategy unique to your product.

It is also possible that the more creative approaches to the collection of data can end up being much easier methods and provide a higher quality result than the methods described above.

For example, if your product piggy-backs on the demand for another product and the demand for the other product can be determined, use the data on foreign market demand for the other product to identify the demand for your product.

- -

CASE EXAMPLE: ARTIST Graphics, an industry pioneer in the design and manufacture of high-resolution graphic display controllers, tends to sell its products to purchasers of the leading CAD software. When the company initiated its export activities, it identified those foreign markets into which the software was selling and targeted those markets for exports. Today, ARTIST Graphics' products are sold on a worldwide basis.

- -

If your product sells into a specific industrial sector that can be easily identified, look for historical data that will give you the primary producing countries for that sector. Then, select those countries for follow-up market research.

CASE EXAMPLE: Mate Punch and Die Company produces punches and dies that are used by fabricated metal manufacturers. When the company decided to aggressively pursue exporting, it could not find data on the demand for its product. So, the new international marketing manager decided to look for data that would identify the countries that were the major producers of fabricated metal products. The manager's assumption that those countries would be the most likely markets for the company's products proved to be correct. Export sales are now a significant percentage of the company's total sales.

There are times when export and import data will provide misleading information and paint an inaccurate picture of the market potential for your product. For example, if a local manufacturer dominates a specific market and does not export, this foreign market will not appear to have export potential if your analysis uses only export-import analysis. In such a situation, it will be necessary to look for more unique market data such as gross domestic product or industrial production.

CASE EXAMPLE: Bondhus Corporation, a manufacturer of non-power fastener tools, uses three types of data to create a simple but effective weighted market demand indicator for its product in each country worldwide. The data are gross domestic product (GDP), the percentage of gross domestic product generated by industrial production (%IND), and per capita income (PCI). The GDP and %IND factors address the size of the market, and the PCI factor weights the market (that is, countries with higher labor costs are more likely to buy Bondhus's product than those of its competitors). The formula (GDP × %IND × PCI) / (USGDP × US%IND × USPCI) produces a percentage—the percentage of the specific country market demand to that of the U.S. market demand. The countries with the highest percentage ratings are the high-potential export markets.

It is always a good idea to ask yourself, How do I identify market demand in the United States? Then, determine if the same procedures that you use in the U.S. market can be applied in identifying demand in overseas markets.

Using Expert Opinion and Market Intelligence. All data need to be weighed against the test of common sense. For that reason, it is imperative that you use your own judgment as well as seek out the opinion of experts in your field. For example, the data may show that a market has been a big importer of your product for the past five years, but two months ago the foreign government may have imposed stiff import restrictions on your product. Data will not tell you this.

Thus, use expert opinion to further narrow your potential markets. Review your trade journals and contact your trade associations for current information. Discuss your most promising markets with the USDOC District Office and other appropriate EPOs and export service organizations such as your international banker. Talk with known exporters in your industry, including competitors. Discuss potential export markets with foreign visitors at trade shows. Go to your public library and search the computer databases for recent articles on your product, the industry, and selected foreign markets.

Market intelligence should also be collected on your potential Trial Markets in order to further assess your product's prospects. Ask the USDOC District Office to use its *Foreign Market Research Service* to search for marketing reports that will provide further insights into the demand for your product in each of your potential markets. Using product codes, product keywords, and country codes, the District Office can print a copy of report titles from which you can select and order the reports that are of interest to you.

The primary conclusions that you draw from the expert opinion and market intelligence research should be entered in the Expert Opinion column on Worksheet 5.

After completing the collection of data, expert opinion, and market intelligence tasks, your Markets With Export Potential Worksheet should be filled with data and comments. You should now be in a position to narrow down the list of potential target countries. From the information on the worksheet, select the five country markets that you believe represent the high-potential export markets for your product. List these five countries at the bottom of Worksheet 5.

Assessing the High-Potential Markets

You are now ready to assess the five high-potential markets. The market assessment indicators that you will use are divided into world indicator and country indicator categories.

The worldwide indicators help you know if you're in the right place at the right time. They provide the international context for your Trial Run. For example, if a general expansion of the world economy is expected, you might expect that conditions in your target market would also be expanding. The worldwide indicators are categorized as either direction of the economy or direction of the industry.

The country indicators address the environmental, product, and other factors in each of the high-potential country markets. The environmental indicators are useful in identifying the general business environment and the basic need potential of the market. Some of the environmental indicators must be considered independent of your product. For example, the availability of U.S. dollars to foreign buyers is an important factor. If the foreign buyer cannot convert his or her currency into U.S. dollars, you may not be interested in the market. If the government and economy of the country are very unstable, you may determine that the country risk is too great for your company. Depending on your product, there may be key pieces of information that can be used to identify the potential need for your product. For example, if you sell a consumer product, you may be interested in private consumption data, such as total private consumption, private consumption for household items, or number of television sets. If you sell an industrial product, you may be interested in industrial production data. The environmental indicators are grouped as follows: demographic, economic, political/legal, social/cultural, business, and industrial sector.

The product indicators point directly to your specific product and include a detailed assessment of hurdles and other indicators of your ability to be successful in the markets. For example, some countries may have barriers to entering the market that would slow down your entry into the market, or significantly increase the cost of your product to the end buyer while other countries may have no effective barriers. The data and information needed to complete the product indicators may not be readily available to you at this early stage of the Trial Run. The effects of cultural factors on the use and acceptability of your product, for example, may not be easily determined at this point. The product indicators include the following groups of indicators: export hurdles, import hurdles, use hurdles, demand, customer distribution, and competition.

The final category of market indicators includes other factors that may influence your decision in selecting the market. These might include climate or the availability of good in-land transportation.

Use the Market Assessment and Selection Worksheet (Worksheet 6) to start your assessment. Enter the five high-potential export markets from Worksheet 5 on Worksheet 6. Review the market characteristics listed on the worksheet. Place a check by the characteristics that are important indicators of demand for your product and insert additional characteristics that are unique to your product or that are important to your company.

When selecting the foreign market indicators, you should consider that the indicators of demand used in the U.S. market are also likely to be among your best market indicators in foreign markets. The assumption is that the conditions affecting market demand for your product in the United States are to some degree similar to those in foreign markets. However, the foreign environment will add a new dimension to your assessment of market demand and, during the course of your planning, you may need to identify some new indicators that are unique to foreign markets.

Once you have selected the specific market indicators to be used in the assessment, collect the data and information needed to complete the assessment. Start by reviewing the materials in your export library. You will probably find that some of the subscription materials in the library have not been received on the five markets. Since many of the items may be available through your USDOC District Office, call this office to see if it can send you copies. Otherwise, you will have to order back-

(text continues on page 43)

WORKSHEET 6. Market Assessment and Selection

MARKET ASSESSMENT & SELECTION	═FASTRACK₌
	Success Through Fast-Track Exporting

Purpose: To select the target country for the Trial Run. Direction: Summarize worldwide indicators of demand. Complete the country indicator section. (1) Start by inserting the countries listed in the Markets With Export Potential worksheet at the top of the columns. (2) Check the market indicators in the left column that are important for your product. (3) Insert and check additional market indicators in the left column that are unique to your product. (4) Collect and insert the selected data/information for each country. (5) Score each indicator on a 0-10 scale with 0 for poor (or do not know) and 10 for good. (6) Select the target market and indicate your rationale.

Company Name/Division _____

Product

WORLDWIDE INDICATORS	Data / Information
Direction of Economy _Expanding/Contracting _Other:	
Direction of Industry _Expanding/Contracting _Other:	

COUNTRY INDICATORS	Country & Data / Information								
		Score		Score		Score		Score		Score
ENVIRONMENT									
Demographic _Population _Population Growth Rate _Other:									
Economic _Stability _GDP _GDP Growth Rate _Private Consumption _Balance of Payment _Favorable Exchange Rate _Currency Convertibility _Other:									
Political/Legal _Stability _Patent/TM Protection _Other:									
Social/Cultural _Education _Other:									

Market Assessment & Selection Worksheet	Page 1

Copyright Export Resource Associates, Inc., 1990

Country / Score		Score		Score		Score		Score		Score
Business										
__Business Practices										
__Other:										
Industry Sector										
__Production										
__Production Growth Rate										
__Number/Size of Producers										
__Strengths/Weaknesses										
__Other:										
PRODUCT										
Export Hurdles										
__US Validated Export Lic.										
__Other:										
Import Hurdles										
__Tariff Barriers										
__Non-Tariff Barriers										
__Standards										
__Other:										
Use Hurdles										
__Culture										
__Lifestyle										
__Technical										
__Product Life Cycle										
__Other:										
Demand										
__Stability										
__Size										
__Size Growth Rate										
__Sales/Quantity										
__Sales/Qty Growth Rate										
__Other:										
Customer										
__Need Product										
__Afford Product										
__Market #1 Segment/Sze										
__Market #2 Segment/Size										
__Market #3 Segment/Size										
__Other:										

Market Assessment & Selection Worksheet
Page 2

Worksheet 6 (*continued*)

Country / Score		Score		Score		Score		Score		Score
Distribution										
__Channels										
__Termination Restrictions										
__Other:										
Competition										
__Price										
__Quality										
__Service										
__Technology										
__Promotion										
__Coverage										
__Market Share Domestic										
__Market Share Import NonUS										
__Market Share Import US										
__Other:										
OTHER										
Physical										
__Climate										
__Other:										
Infrastructure										
__Ports										
__In-Land Transportation										
__Other:										
Total Score										
Number of Indicators Scored										
Market Potential Index										
Rating = (Score) / (# Indicators)										

Note: Critical market indicators can be given double weight by: (a) multiplying the indicator score by two and (b) increasing the Number of Indicators Scored by one for each indicator given double weight.

DECISION: Which country will be selected as the target market for the Trial Run? _____

Rationale:

Completed by	Date
Market Assessment & Selection Worksheet	Page 3

issues of the publications for each of your five markets.

The most useful materials from your library will include the *Foreign Economic Trends, Overseas Business Reports, Background Notes,* and *Doing Business In* series publications for the five high-potential markets.

Contact the USDOC District Office and order the *Country Marketing Plans* for each of the five markets.

Other sources of summary data that might be very useful include: *Business International: Indicators of Market Size, Statistical Yearbook, World Market Atlas,* and *World Tables.* Other sources of data are listed in Appendix B and include publications such as *European Marketing Data and Statistics* and *International Marketing Data and Statistics.*

Since you have now focused your market research on five countries and have selected the market indicators that are of interest to you, you might again want to contact the embassies or consulates of these countries for more detailed marketing information.

Your search for market assessment data and information could go on endlessly. However, your primary purpose at this point is to obtain enough information about the countries to decide which one of the five countries will be your target market for the Trial Run.

Once you have collected enough data and information to satisfy your current needs, summarize your findings for each market indicator on Worksheet 6. Then, one by one, compare each of the countries on each market indicator. For each indicator use the boxes in the country columns to enter a score of zero if the country indicator is very negative (or if you have no information), ten if the indicator is very positive, or a number between zero and ten. After you have rated each country indicator, total the column of scores for each country, count the number of indicators beings used, and enter the amounts at the bottom of the worksheet. Divide the total country score by the number of indicators used in order to determine a summary rating for each country. This summary rating is your market potential index for your product in that market.

Selecting the Target Market

You now face the decision of selecting the single country market on which you will focus your efforts during the Trial Run—the target market.

The country with the highest market potential index on Worksheet 6 is most likely your best market for the Trial Run. Before making your final decision on the Trial Run market, however, consider two optional market assessment methods—the weighted market potential index and a series of indexes by various groups of indicators.

The weighted market potential index assessment option recognizes that there are undoubtedly some market indicators on your worksheet that are much more important than others. These critical indicators can be given double or greater weight by (1) multiplying the indicator score for each country by two or whatever additional unit of weight you want to give the indicator and (2) increasing the number of indicators scored at the bottom of the assessment by one for each additional unit of weight you give to the score for the critical indicators. The resulting weighted market potential index will now give greater weight to the critical market indicators and may change the country with the highest market potential on your worksheet.

Rather than creating a single index for each country, the series of indexes allows you to break your indicators down into logical sub-groups for analysis. For example, the *Business International: Indicators of Market Size* publication creates three market potential indexes for each country— market size, which provides a measure of the relative dimensions of each market; market intensity, which measures the richness of each market; and market growth, which uses a five-year time series to determine the average growth of each market. You might, for example, group the environmental- and product-related factors and create an environmental index and a product index.

Once you have determined which of your markets appears to be the most likely candidate for the Trial Run, review each of the indicators for that country and assure yourself that there is no single indicator which is so negative that it would prevent you from selecting that country for the Trial Run. Remember, this worksheet is a tool to help point you to your target. In the end, you must use your own judgment.

Based on your assessment, you can now select the target market for your Trial Run and summarize your rationale for selecting this market.

CASE EXAMPLE: Bondhus Corporation selected its initial target markets by looking for mid-size markets with the weakest competitors. Its rationale was that the largest markets had the most aggressive competitors and that it could not compete effectively in these markets until it had more export experience.

Select the Export Market Entry Method

It is time to make a critical decision: Do you want to enter your target export market *directly* or would you prefer to enter it *indirectly*?

The direct export entry method implies that your company will sell its product directly into foreign markets, usually through your own sales operation or through a foreign representative such as an agent or distributor. You will be the exporter, control the introduction of your product into the export market, and, if you use your own sales operations, control the channel of distribution right to the end user.

The indirect export entry method involves the use of U.S. domestic export intermediaries. These companies are commonly either export trading companies or export merchants. The intermediary buys your product, exports it to the foreign market, and controls the introduction of your product into the market. Frequently, the company will resell the product under its own name. Your sale is strictly a domestic sale.

CASE EXAMPLE: The Witt Company, the holder of the patent on the original corrugated steel trash can and manufacturer of high-quality trash receptacles, got into exporting because it was receiving foreign inquiries. Rather than develop the in-house expertise needed to sell its product abroad, Witt set up a relationship with an export trading company to handle its exports. The trading company takes title to the shipment, accepts the credit risk, and handles the shipping and export paperwork. Having established that there was a significant export market for the product, Witt was then in a position to review its market entry options and determine if it wanted to market the product more aggressively through direct exports.

You should be aware that there are other types of U.S. export intermediaries that offer a middle ground between direct and indirect exporting. For example, organizations frequently called export management companies may assume the responsibility for introducing your product in foreign markets and controlling the distribution channel to the end user, but you will remain the exporter. You should also be aware that there are *nonexport* market entry methods for introducing your product into foreign markets, such as licensing the production of your product to a foreign manufacturer or establishing your own foreign manufacturing operations. (We will not be pursuing these options during the Trial Run, so they will not be discussed in any detail until you reach the Market Penetration phase.)

There are many factors to be considered in assessing your export market entry method options, and the Export Market Entry Method Worksheet (Worksheet 7) helps you sort out the advantages and disadvantages of each method based on your own product and organization and the target country you have selected.

We expect that if your company has made the decision to enter export markets, you will select the direct export market entry method. If this is the case, skip to the next stage of the export process, assessing the company's readiness to export.

CASE EXAMPLE: Las Americas International, an exporter of Upper Midwest holstein dairy cattle, is an intermediary between foreign buyers and U.S. cattle raisers. Because of Las Americas, hundreds of dairy cattle producers are able to export to foreign markets. The business thrives because of the unique nature of the dairy industry and the high level of trust and expertise the company has developed with both its buyers and sellers. Producers are scattered on farms all over the Upper Midwest and the number of holsteins any one producer has for sale is small. But the buyer wants a large number of animals. Las Americas links the needs of sellers and the buyer, and that makes the export of U.S. dairy cattle possible.

WORKSHEET 7.   Export Market Entry Method

EXPORT MARKET ENTRY METHOD	**≡FASTRACK** *Success Through Fast-Track Exporting*

Purpose: To select the direct or indirect export market entry method for the Trial Run. Directions: (1) For each of the two market entry methods, evaluate each advantage and disadvantage and enter a score on a scale of 0 to +10 for each advantage and a scale of -10 to 0 for each disadvantage. (2) Total the scores and number of items scored for each column; add the advantage and disadvantage scores and number of items scored amounts in the Total Score column; determine the Net Advantage / Disadvantage by dividing the total score by the total number of items scored. (3) Determine whether the direct or indirect market entry method had the highest positive score, select the method, and summarize your rationale.

Company Name/Division _____

Product _____   Target Country _____

Mkt Entry Method	Advantages 0 = None. +10 = Significant Advantage.	Score	Disadvantages -10 = Significant Disadvantage. 0 = None.	Score	Total Score
Direct	Develop market knowledge in-house.	+	Must train/hire staff.	-	
	Develop customer knowledge in-house.	+	Must pay sales costs.	-	
	Gain export experience/expertise in-house.	+	Must learn export documentation/shipping.	-	
	Control distribution channels, promotion,	+	Export sales could be slower to develop.	-	
	after-sale service, quality.		May compete with domestic sales resources.	-	
	Control priority given to exporting product.	+	Management commitment required.	-	
	Profit margins could be higher.	+	Financial risk of foreign sales.	-	
	Price to end user could be lower.	+	Other:		
	Other:				
	Score	+	Score	-	+ -
	Number of Items Scored		Number of Items Scored		
	Net Advantage/Disadvantage of Direct Entry Method = (+ - Total Score) / (Total Number of Items Scored) =				+ -
Indirect	No staff to train/hire.	+	Lost sales because foreign customer wants	-	
	Need not learn export documentation/shipping.	+	to buy directly from manufacturer.		
	Export sales could develop more quickly.	+	Develop no in-house knowledge of markets.	-	
	No competition with domestic sales resources.	+	Develop no in-house knowledge of customers.	-	
	Management's commitment is not required.	+	Gain no experience/expertise in exporting.	-	
	No financial risk other than those of a	+	Loss of control over distribution channels,	-	
	domestic sale.		promotion, after-sale service, quality.		
	Other:	+	No control over priority given to exporting	-	
			product and/or conflict of interest.		
			Profit margins could be lower.	-	
			Price could be higher for the end customer.	-	
			Other:	-	
	Score	+	Score	-	+ -
	Number of Items Scored		Number of Items Scored		
	Net Advantage/Disadvantage of Indirect Entry Method (+/- Total Score) / (Total Number of Items Scored) =				+ -

Which market entry method has the most positive score (the higher advantage)? ___ Direct.   ___ Indirect.

DECISION: Which export market entry method will be used during the Trial Run? _____

Rationale:

Completed by	Date

Copyright Export Resource Associates, Inc., 1990

If, on the other hand, you decide to use the indirect export market entry method, you will have to find and select an export trading company, export merchant, or other type of export intermediary. To start your search for an export intermediary, look to these sources: *International Trade State and Local Resource Directory, The ExportYellow Pages,* the Yellow Pages of your local or nearest metropolitan area, and your state international trade office and nearest world trade center. Interview several companies and assess their qualifications to sell your product in your target export market as well as in worldwide markets. How does the company handle its current product lines and how satisfied are its current suppliers? Does the company have the capacity to introduce and promote your product in the target market and elsewhere? Will you offer the company an exclusive or nonexclusive right to a limited or worldwide market and for how long? Will you establish minimum performance objectives?

The agreement you sign with an export intermediary is a potential hazard zone—an exclusive agreement with an ineffective intermediary can cut off future export opportunities. So don't be in a rush. Select your export intermediary well and negotiate an agreement that gives you the flexibility to switch to direct exporting at a later date.

Assess the Company's Readiness to Export

An important part of the planning step is to make a realistic assessment of your company's readiness to export and to develop an action plan to strengthen it.

Identifying Strengths and Weaknesses

The objective of the export readiness assessment is to assess the current state of your company's export readiness in relation to factors that are associated with successful exporting and to identify specific areas of strength as well as areas of weakness in your organization and product that will require further attention. The Export Readiness Assessment and Action Plan Worksheet (Worksheet 8) can be used as a tool to assist you in this task.

The readiness factors are ideal states that your company should seek

(*text continues on page 53*)

WORKSHEET 8.   Export Readiness Assessment and Action Plan

EXPORT READINESS ASSESSMENT & ACTION PLAN	

Success Through Fast-Track Exporting

Purpose: To make a summary assessment of your company's export readiness in relation to factors that are associated with successful exporting. Directions: (1) The Readiness Factors represent an ideal state which your company should seek to achieve as it progresses through the Trial Run and Market Penetration phases; evaluate your company against the stated Readiness Factor; note areas of strength and areas that require additional development; rate your readiness in the Score column using a 0-10 scale with 0 for no progress toward achieving the factor, 10 for full achievement of the factor, and NA when a factor is not applicable in your situation. (2) Use the Readiness Action Plan column to identify the tasks you will undertake during the current phase to achieve a higher level of export readiness. (3) Total the Scores and Number of Factors used for each set of factors in the Readiness Rating section. (4) Compute the Export Readiness Rating for each Set of Factors; compute the Summary Export Readiness Rating Index. Note that your readiness scores and ratings will probably be low when you start your first Trial Run; as you implement your Readiness Action Plan your readiness scores will rise.

Company Name/Division _____

Product _____ Target Country _____

Readiness Factors	Strengths/Weaknesses	Score	Readiness Action Plan
A. Planning Factors			
A1. Company			
___ The company has achieved a level of U.S. sales that supports an export effort and demonstrates in export markets that the company is a credible organization with a viable product.			
A2. Management			
___ Management has decided to explore export markets and to allocate a portion of its time to the export effort sufficient to launch and direct the export effort.			
___ Management has identified the business reasons and benefits for entering export markets sufficiently to sustain a long-term export commitment.			
A3. Product Selection			
___ The product has been determined to be competitive on price, quality, service, and technology with foreign products being imported and with domestic products being exported sufficiently to support a decision to export the product.			
___ The product's after-sale training and support can be provided sufficiently to service the product and train users in export markets.			
___ The product's patent, trademark, copyright, or trade secret rights can be protected sufficiently to allow shipment to the export market.			
___ The product has been determined to be acceptable in export markets or can be modified to make it acceptable at an affordable cost.			
A4. Market Selection & Market Entry Method			
___ The market has been determined to have a demand for the product sufficient to support a decision to export.			
___ The market has been researched and sales volume and sales growth potential have been projected.			

Export Readiness Assessment & Action Plan   Page 1

Worksheet 8 (*continued*)

Readiness Factors	Strengths/Weaknesses	Score	Readiness Action Plan
__ The market has no obstacles that will prevent the product from being competitive in the export market including tariff, **nontariff, standards, or cultural barriers.** __ The market has no U.S. export licensing restrictions that will prevent the product from being shipped to the markets in a timely manner. __ A market entry method has been decided.			
A5. Strategic Plan __ The companywide plan has incorporated exporting, defined the scope of the export effort, and provided the resource necessary to assure success. __ The export plan has stated the assumptions, goals, objectives, tasks, budget, and evaluation criteria sufficiently to guide the implementation of the program.			
A6. Organization __ The authority required to implement the export plan has been assigned. __ The intracompany coordination required to implement the export plan has been committed. __ The policies and procedures that guide the business activity have been adjusted to accommodate the export plan.			
A7. Resources __ An in-house export information center has been developed. __ Export promotion organizations have been utilized to the maximum extent possible. __ Export service organizations have been utilized to the extent needed.			
B. Preparation and Implementation Factors B1. Export Team __ The Export Team has been identified, assigned their export tasks, and trained. __ The team has knowledge of foreign cultures, business practices, and languages sufficient to conduct business and avoid pitfalls. __ The team has experience in export transactions and documentation sufficient to understand the export steps and to process export sales and shipments.			
B2. Distribution __ The distribution channels have been selected in the export market in order to match with the buying patterns of each export market segment to which the product is to be sold.			
B3. Product Position __ The product has been positioned in the export market in order to differentiate it from competing products.			

Export Readiness Assessment & Action Plan   Page 2

Readiness Factors	Strengths/Weaknesses	Score	Readiness Action Plan
B4. Production ___ The company has adequate production capacity and/or available capital sufficient to make the investment necessary to produce and promptly fill the export orders.			
B5. Price and Terms ___ The price and terms of payment have been set in order to achieve the export plan objectives and to reflect tax and other governmental benefits available to exporters.			
B6. Contacts and Promotion ___ A database of potential foreign customers and promotion materials have been developed to promote the product and generate an adequate number of prospects in the export market. ___ A marketing and sales process has been put in place to promote the product, to screen and qualify inquiries, to respond to qualified customers, and to close the deals in order to achieve the export plan objectives. ___ Agreements have been developed to state clearly the expectations of the exporter and customer, to be consistent with U.S. and foreign law, and to avoid pitfalls. ___ Major customers in the export market have been visited and evaluated to verify their credibility, to establish relationships, and to minimize the chance for misunderstandings due to unfamiliar customs, language, and business practices.			
B7. Ship and Collect ___ A shipping system has been put in place to efficiently process export documentation and to assure timely delivery to the customer. ___ A collection system has been put in place to limit the risks associated with export.			
C. Evaluation Factors ___ Planned results have been compared to actual results in order to determine the effectiveness of the export effort, to identify adjustments needed in the implementation of the export process, and to develop future export plans. ___ Current events have been monitored to identify developments in export markets that may change the demand for the company's product.			

Worksheet 8 (*continued*)

Readiness Rating	Score	# Factors	Readiness Rating
Sets of Factors			
A. Planning Factors	_____	+ _____	= _____
A.1. Company	_____	+ _____	= _____
A.2. Management	_____	+ _____	= _____
A.3. Product Selection	_____	+ _____	= _____
A.4. Market Selection & Market Entry Method	_____	+ _____	= _____
A.5. Strategic Plan	_____	+ _____	= _____
A.6. Organization	_____	+ _____	= _____
A.7. Resources	_____	+ _____	= _____
B. Preparation and Implementation Factors			
B.1. Staff	_____	+ _____	= _____
B.2. Distribution	_____	+ _____	= _____
B.3. Product Position	_____	+ _____	= _____
B.4. Production	_____	+ _____	= _____
B.5. Price and Terms	_____	+ _____	= _____
B.6. Contacts and Promotion	_____	+ _____	= _____
B.7. Ship and Collect	_____	+ _____	= _____
C. Evaluation Factors	_____	+ _____	= _____
Summary Export Readiness Rating Index	_____	+ _____	= _____

The Company's Summary Export Readiness Rating Index is: ___Low (<4) ___Medium (4 - 7.5) ___High (>7.5)

Areas of strength:

Areas of weakness:

Major Export Readiness Action Plan steps to be undertaken:

Completed by	Date
Export Readiness Assessment & Action Plan	Page 4

to achieve as it progresses through the Trial Run and on into Market Penetration. If you are a new exporter, your assessment will identify many areas of weakness and undoubtedly produce a low readiness score because you are still in the early stages of the export process. However, as you progress through the Trial Run your strengths will grow and your readiness rating will increase. Worksheet 8 will be used on a regular basis to reassess your readiness for export and help you identify continuing areas of weakness that need to be addressed.

The readiness factors include:

- ▲ *Planning factors.* Company readiness, management readiness, product readiness, market selection and market entry method readiness, strategic plan readiness, organization readiness, and resource readiness.
- ▲ *Preparation and implementation factors.* Export team readiness, distribution channel readiness, product position readiness, production readiness, price and terms of payment readiness, contacts and promotion readiness, shipping and collection readiness.
- ▲ *Evaluation factors.* Comparing results to plan and monitoring events.

For each readiness factor identify your company's strengths and weaknesses and rate your readiness on that factor. There may be certain factors that will not apply to your company, and you may identify additional readiness factors that you will want to include on the worksheet. You may also identify critical readiness factors that are more important than others.

Once you have completed the readiness assessment and rated your company on each factor, complete the readiness rating section at the end of the assessment worksheet.

If your export readiness rating index is less than 4.0, you have received a low rating. However, a low rating is normal for a new exporter and what is important at this stage of the process is that you have effectively identified your strength and weakness for each readiness factor. If you have a clear understanding of your areas of strengths and weaknesses, you are in a position to determine what is necessary to achieve a higher state of readiness. That is the purpose of the readiness assessment process. As you work to prepare your company to enter export markets and reassess your readiness at a later date, you will see the rating increase into the medium and high readiness categories.

Developing a Readiness Action Plan

It is now time to develop your export readiness action plan. Use the right column of Worksheet 8 to list the steps you will take to address the areas of weakness you have identified. For convenience, you may create a separate action plan document and add target dates for completing each task, the resources that will be used, the person in your organization responsible for the task, and a place for recording the date the task was satisfactorily completed.

As you progress down the export fast track, you will use the resources of your EPO network to assist you in implementing the readiness action plan and in strengthening your organization's and product's readiness for export.

Finalize the Trial Run Plan

You are now ready to create a pen-to-pad strategic plan for the Trial Run. First, summarize the decisions you have made to date. Then establish your goals and objectives, state your assumptions about the markets, and allocate and organize the resources that will be devoted to the export program.

Before proceeding with finalizing the strategic plan, the issue of top management's commitment to the Trial Run needs to be stressed. When you make the decision to take a Trial Run at export markets, the decision to launch a Trial Run must be supported by top management if it is to be successful. When you undertake your export readiness assessment, one of the critical factors for successful exporting is management's commitment to providing the leadership and resources needed to launch and direct the effort. It is imperative that your company's top management be committed to the export program. During the course of the Trial Run, demands will be placed on various parts of the organization, and top management's leadership will be needed to ensure that the entire organization is responsive to the new demands that exporting will bring to your company.

- -

CASE EXAMPLE: Murdock, Inc., a quality maker of custom aircraft parts and hot press machines, believes that the commitment and involvement of top management is an essential ingredient in a successful and profitable export marketing program. Top management's support is crucial to convincing foreign customers that the company can and will support the customer's requirements from a continent away. "The most important thing top management can do is go see the customer, no matter where the customer is," states the director of international sales. Top management's commitment helped make Murdock competitive in export markets even when strong national preferences existed.

- -

Reviewing the Decisions to Date

You have made five major decisions up to this point in the planning process:

1. Whether or not you have a product you want to export
2. Whether or not you want to expand your market through exporting
3. Which product you want to select for the Trial Run
4. Which country you want to select as the target market for the Trial Run
5. Whether or not you will use the direct or indirect export market entry method

You have also determined your export readiness rating index and identified your areas of readiness strength and weakness. Finally, you have developed an export readiness action plan to address your areas of weakness and improve your company's overall readiness to export.

The Trial Run Plan Worksheet (Worksheet 9) should be used to summarize these decisions and the rationale for each.

(text continues on page 58)

WORKSHEET 9.   Trial Run Plan

TRIAL RUN PLAN	**≡FASTRACK**™
	Success Through Fast-Track Exporting

Purpose: To summarize the strategic decisions made during the planning step of the Trial Run.

Company Name/Division _____

Period: Start _____ End _____

Worksheet 1. DECISION: Do I have a product that I want to export? ___Yes ___No
Rationale:

Worksheet 2. DECISION: Should I expand my markets through exporting? ___Yes ___No
Rationale:

Worksheet 3. DECISION: Which product will be selected for the Trial Run? _____
Rationale:

Worksheet 6. DECISION: Which country will be selected as the target market for the Trial Run? _____
Rationale:

Worksheet 7. DECISION: Which export market entry method will be used during the Trial Run? ___Direct ___Indirect
Rationale:

Worksheet 8. Export Readiness Strengths.

Worksheet 8. Export Readiness Weaknesses.

Worksheet 8. Major Export Readiness Action Plan steps to be undertaken.

Trial Run Plan   Page 1

Company/Division Mission Statement: (Your current company mission statement, stated or implied)

Trial Run Export Goal: (A summary statement of the Company's expectations for the Trial Run.)

Trial Run Export Objectives: (Specific, quantifiable results to be achieved during the Trial Run.)
1. In Worldwide Markets.

2. In the Target Country Market.

Assumptions: (Mix of facts, judgements, and assumed states upon which decisions, goals, and objectives are based.)
1. In Worldwide Markets.

2. In the Target Country Market.

Completed by   Date

Trial Run Plan   Page 2

Establishing the Goals and Objectives

The goals and objectives for your strategic export plan should, at some point, be integrated into the companywide mission and strategic plan. This means reviewing the company's statement of mission and its goals, and adjusting or expanding them to incorporate the export effort. It may be premature to tackle this task during the Trial Run, but you should consider when and how you will address the integration issue if you proceed to the Market Penetration phase and develop your current strategic export plan accordingly. For now, insert your company's current mission statement, stated or implied, on the worksheet.

For purposes of the Trial Run, develop an initial statement of your export goal(s). This goal should not be in conflict with your company's current statement of mission and goals and should be reviewed by and have the support of top management. The goal should be an expression of some future state you want your company to achieve in export markets. It should be stated in such a way that it can be evaluated, but it need not necessarily be stated in quantitative terms. Your export goal will normally have a horizon of five to ten years, although you may want to establish a more tentative and short-term goal that is related specifically to this Trial Run effort. For example, a longer-term goal might be "to establish the company as a reliable supplier of quality widgets to the world." Or, a more tentative goal limited to the Trial Run might be "to test the company's product in worldwide markets, as well as a specific country market, to determine if there is a potential demand which the company could profitably supply."

The next task is to establish your objectives for the Trial Run. Your objectives should clearly state the specific results you want to accomplish, in quantifiable or measurable terms, and the date by which they are to be achieved. Your objectives may also include a "cost not to exceed" statement to indicate the limits that will be placed on the resources devoted to accomplishing each objective. The horizon of your Trial Run objectives will usually be from six to twelve months.

For purposes of the Trial Run, we recommend that you consider stating objectives for worldwide markets as well as your target country export market. This will assist you when you reach Step 5, Decide the Next Steps, because your two critical decisions during these steps will require two different sets of information.

Each of your objectives may need to be supplemented by a set of performance criteria that state more precisely the conditions that will constitute achievement of the objective. For example, your sales objective may contain a specific dollar amount, while your performance criteria spell out specific conditions such as the quantities by product type, expected terms of payment, expected profit margins, and so forth. The combination of the quantifiable objective and the performance criteria for each objective provides a sound basis for developing and implementing your analysis and evaluation activities in Step 5. Remember, the time and resources your company invests in the Trial Run may be largely wasted if, after several months of effort, no one knows what constitutes a successful or unsuccessful Trial Run.

After completing your goals and objectives, enter them on the worksheet.

Stating the Assumptions

Assumptions are a mix of facts, judgments, and assumed states that you have sifted out of the planning step and upon which you have based your planning decisions. The purpose in summarizing these assumptions on the worksheet is to document why decisions were made and why certain actions were taken. Your assumptions will also serve as a guide in preparing for and implementing the next steps in Trial Run, as well as analyzing the Trial Run and planning your next steps.

As your research and planning become more sophisticated in future Trial Runs and the Market Penetration phase, you will obtain information that can be measured against the assumptions made during this Trial Run. Obviously, the more acquainted you become with the worldwide and specific markets, the more accurate will be your assumptions.

Your assumptions should be organized into the following general categories: internal assumptions relating to the readiness of your organization and product for export; external assumptions relating to the worldwide economy, industry, and customer; and the target country assumptions related to the country's economy, industry, and customer.

(text continues on page 60)

CASE EXAMPLE: Mate Punch and Die Company's initial export "plan" consisted of a long-term sales goal and an outline of the company's marketing strategies and policies covering such things as pricing, distribution, product return, currentness of payment, promotion, and protection of intellectual property. The outline represented enough of a plan to successfully launch the export program yet offer flexibility for adapting to unique market conditions in different target markets.

Allocating and Organizing the Resources

Additional resources over and above the company's normal budget will have to be allocated to implement the Trial Run. These costs may range from as little as a few hundred dollars into the tens of thousands of dollars depending on your company's approach to the Trial Run. Worksheet 10 is an example of a basic Trial Run Budget for $6,500.

The Trial Run budget reflects the costs you have incurred to date in the planning step and those that you might expect in the following steps of the Trial Run. One major cost factor that needs to be considered during the Trial Run is a visit to the target market. While it is usually advisable to include a visit in your budget, the significant cost of a trip has to be weighed against several factors, including the potential sales volume your company might expect from the market. Ideally, there would be resources for one visit to the Trial Run country, although such a visit is not essential to the success of the Trial Run.

In addition to financial resources, people and time must also be allocated in order to implement the Trial Run. Staff will have to be assigned to visit with EPOs and export service organizations, prepare promotion and response materials, respond to foreign buyer inquiries, and learn how to prepare export documentation forms. Someone will also have to assume the responsibility for leading and/or coordinating the Trial Run. Many organizations believe that they have been more successful in exporting in the long-run because they used an export team or project approach rather than assigning a single person to be the export expert. Organizations using the project management approach have involved top management, several managers, and other staff in the export

WORKSHEET 10. Trial Run Budget

TRIAL RUN BUDGET	*FASTRACK*
	Success Through Fast-Track Exporting

Purpose: To plan the budget for the Trial Run. Directions: The Basic column is a "low" budget estimate of what your Trial Run will cost. Use the Medium and High columns to estimate more aggressive Trial Run budgets.

Company Name/Division _____

Product _____ Target market _____ Period: _____ to _____

Item	Explanation	Basic Budget	Medium Budget	High Budget
Advertising	Commerical News USA	250	_____	_____
Communications	Telephone/Fax/Postage	600	_____	_____
Computer Software	Databases	350	_____	_____
Contact Lists	ADS/Export Contact Lists	350	_____	_____
Insurance: Product Liability	Foreign Exposure	_____	_____	_____
Legal Services	Review Documents/Patents/Marks	500	_____	_____
Market Research	Custom Statistics/Studies/Kits	300	_____	_____
Product Packaging & Modification	Labeling/Standards	_____	_____	_____
Promotion Materials	Media/Direct-Mail	600	_____	_____
Resource Library Materials	Start Up	500	_____	_____
Trade Show	Booth/Travel/Etc.	_____	_____	_____
Translation Services	Materials	300	_____	_____
Travel: Foreign	Visit Potential Customers & Trade Shows	1,500	_____	_____
Travel: In-State	Visit EPOs & ESOs/Training	250	_____	_____
Training	CEO/Marketing/Transportation/Credit	1,000	_____	_____
Other		_____	_____	_____
		_____	_____	_____
Total		$ 6,500	$	$

Notes:

Completed by _____ Date _____

090

process and as a result have internationalized their entire company, thereby better positioning the company to deal with the long-term changes that have to be made when the company develops a more significant commitment to international markets.

CASE EXAMPLE: The International Diabetes Center was a national nonprofit educational and service organization that decided to change its missions and name in order to expand its area of concern to include the world. In the early stages of its expansion, the Center assigned one person to deal with international program activities. After several years that person left the organization, management found that it was without any international expertise, and that, in fact, the Center had never *internationalized* its operations—it merely had a program that included international operations. As a result of this experience, management made a strategic decision that in the future it would use a project management approach to direct its international operations. The result has been that every manager and department of the Center now thinks "international" and is prepared to take advantage of opportunities to improve the lives of diabetes patients no matter where they are in the world.

Now let's stop and retrace Step 1 to see just how far you've come on the export fast track. Your initial efforts helped you to select both your export product and target market, to collect and organize the in-house export center, and to synergize the company's resources with those of the EPO network. This enabled you to pick up speed on the track and rapidly obtain the information and assistance needed to complete the planning tasks. You selected the company's export market entry method, assessed your readiness to export and prepared an export readiness action plan, and developed a pen-to-pad Trial Run Plan and Budget. You are now positioning yourself to pursue Trial Run opportunities in a single targeted market as well as to react to opportunities on a worldwide basis.

Step 2:

Prepare the Export Team and Organization

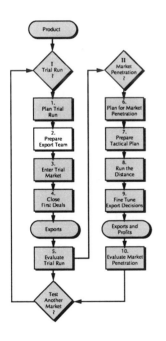

Step 2 explains the pre-export tasks required to get your export team and organization ready for entering the trial markets. You will then be in a position to smoothly implement the Trial Run when you reach Step 3.

Develop the Export Team

Identifying the Export-Related Tasks and Positions

As you prepare for and implement the Trial Run, new or expanded demands are going to be placed on almost every operating unit in your company. In order to identify your in-house export team (different from an export department) and develop the skills each member will need to effectively and efficiently carry out the Trial Run, inventory each organizational unit in order to identify the export-related tasks in the unit and the current positions that will

63

be assigned the responsibility for carrying out the tasks or positions that will be created to carry out the tasks.

When the export readiness assessment and action plan was prepared in Step 1, some of the units involved in the export program were identified. To start your inventory, use the Export Team Inventory Worksheet (see Worksheet 11) to list each of your company's operating units and the export-related tasks that will be performed by the unit. The following units and tasks are suggested to get you started:

▲ *Executive.* Committing the organization to entering export markets; defining the business reasons and benefits for entering export markets; developing the export plan; allocating the financial and organizational resources required to implement the export program; evaluating the export program.

▲ *Marketing and sales.* Selecting the export product; establishing EPO relationships; selecting the target export markets; researching foreign market demand; projecting sales volume and growth potential; identifying export, import, sales, and use hurdles; selecting market entry method; setting market entry prices, shipping terms, and payment terms; understanding export documentation; understanding foreign cultures and business practices; speaking foreign languages; selecting the channels of distribution; identifying foreign contacts; negotiating foreign sales agreements; screening foreign representatives and negotiating agreements; exhibiting at foreign trade shows; visiting foreign customers; hosting foreign customers; avoiding pitfalls.

▲ *Finance.* Establishing relationship with international banker and accountant; utilizing drawback and foreign sales corporation benefits; establishing foreign payment terms, credit policies, and credit checking procedures; understanding export documentation; collecting from foreign buyers.

▲ *Shipping and traffic.* Export packaging; export documentation; establishing relationship with international freight forwarder.

▲ *Engineering.* Adapting product to export market standards, conditions, uses, and preferences.

▲ *Communications.* Internationalizing printed materials; translating materials; understanding foreign cultures.

▲ *Legal.* Protecting intellectual property rights; drafting representa-

WORKSHEET 11. Export Team Inventory

EXPORT TEAM INVENTORY		FASTRACK™	
		Success Through Fast-Track Exporting	

Purpose: To identify the export team tasks, positions, and training needs.

Company Name/Division

Operating Unit	Export Related Tasks	Position Assigned	Training Needed

| Completed by | | Date | |

Copyright Export Resource Associates, Inc., 1990

090

tion agreements; reviewing sales acknowledgment forms; reviewing warranties; reviewing product liability risks and insurance coverage.

▲ *Production.* Scheduling production of export shipments; modifying production process to meet export market standards, conditions, uses, and preferences.

▲ *Service.* Providing after-sales training, support, repairs, warranty service, and replacement parts.

▲ *Librarian.* Collecting the hard-copy, on-line, video, and other resources.

▲ *Data processing.* Adjusting files to accommodate foreign contacts and sales, and converting to metric.

Once you have developed a list of your company's units and the export-related tasks that will be performed by each unit, list the specific positions that will be assigned the responsibility for carrying out and providing backup for each task on the worksheet. This is your export team.

CASE EXAMPLE: Northwestern Steel and Wire Company set out to internationalize the company and become a major U.S. exporter. Every department in the organization had to buy into internationalization and adjust its operations in order to achieve the company goal. Northwestern brought every member of its senior management team into the process and created an export team composed of about thirty key employees ranging from clerical staff to senior managers—the people who had to work together to achieve a smooth export operation. All team members participated in an intensive eighteen-month Fast-Track Exporting Training and Development Program provided through the Illinois Department of Commerce and Community Affairs' Division of Job Training Programs.

Determining the Training Needed

Your export team will already possess much of the knowledge and many of the skills that will be required to implement your export program. However, there will undoubtedly be gaps that will have to be filled in order to ensure a smooth export operation.

Therefore, it will be necessary to identify the specific knowledge and skill needs of each member of the export team and to determine the types of training that will be required to bring each team member's knowledge and skill level up to the level required to complete his or her work.

Training needs will fall into the following general categories:

▲ *Start-to-finish export process training programs.* These provide your export team with a thorough understanding of the export process and how each member's tasks fit into the overall process.

▲ *How-to training programs.* These provide specific members of your team with the particular skills they need to carry out their export-related tasks such as identifying foreign markets, selling your product overseas, selecting and qualifying foreign distributors, modifying the product and product sales literature for export, responding to a foreign sales lead, exhibiting at a foreign trade show, negotiating letters of credit, preparing export documents, using international forwarders, and financing and insuring export sales.

▲ *Market-specific training programs.* These increase your team's knowledge of your target market, including cultural characteristics, business practices, language, up-to-date market information, and market opportunities and hurdles.

▲ *Industry-specific training programs.* These provide export marketing, regulatory, and other information specific to your product line.

▲ *Special-topic training programs.* These address timely topics such as exporting to the European Community and changes in export regulations.

Your company's mid- to upper-level management, for example, will be interested in programs that provide it with the knowledge and skills needed to operate successfully in the global marketplace; the marketing staff will need to learn how to develop and implement successful international marketing strategies; those involved in finance will need an understanding of payment methods and terms; and shipping/transportation people will need to understand export documentation as it relates to shipping procedures, customs requirements, and conforming to the terms of the sale. In addition to each functional area understanding its role in the export program, it must learn to coordinate its activities to ensure the smooth flow of the overall export operation.

Training the Export Team

Most of the members of your initial export team will come from your current staff and will need to participate in some aspect of the export training program.

Depending on the time staff have available and the financial resources budgeted for training, you will be able to choose from a wide range of training programs and resources. Some of the programs will be more suited to your immediate needs while others should be considered as preparation for the Market Penetration phase.

There are numerous sources of training that you will want to use for training your export team. Start with the EPOs that you visited with in Step 1. Review the inventory of EPO services you prepared on Worksheet 4 and identify those EPOs that offer the specific types of training your team members need. Every USDOC District Office and state EPO, for example, either provides or cooperates in sponsoring export training sessions for new-to-export companies, and most of these EPOs provide a variety of country and topic-specific seminars and workshops.

A number of colleges, universities, and technical institutes offer training in many areas of international trade. These programs address both managerial and technical aspects of export development. You can use the SBA's *International Trade State and Local Resources Directory* or local directories to identify other EPOs that offer training in your locale.

While most training will be out-of-house, you might prefer to have some training conducted in-house and customized to your company's special needs and interests. Many of the EPOs can provide this service as can private consulting and training organizations. Videos can be used for in-house training sessions; for example, there may be videos on your target market available through the country's consulates located in the United States. The *Going International* Video Series has two videos which will help orient your staff to cultural differences around the world.

It is advisable to work with your local EPOs to identify the appropriate training for each of the export team members involved in the

Trial Run, including top management and personnel from marketing, shipping, accounting, and engineering. Training should be viewed as an ongoing process and all members of the export team should be encouraged to participate.

In addition to the information obtained from the presenters at training programs, team members will have an opportunity to meet and share experiences with other new-to-export or new-to-market companies, as well as experienced exporters. This networking is a very important part of the education process and should be used extensively.

Working as a Team

You have invested a lot in your export team. Now you have to make sure the team actually works together as it progresses down the export fast track in order to assure a smooth and successful export operation.

While the initial steps in the Trial Run will fall largely on management and the sales department, these units cannot operate up until the last minute in isolation from finance, engineering, production, shipping/transportation, and other units in your organization. For example, don't let your sales organization quote a price and close its first sale without involving finance ("We can't collect on that letter of credit!") and shipping ("We can't get that product there by those dates or at those costs!").

The export team should meet on a periodic basis to review the progress each unit is making in implementing the export readiness action plan, update each other on new developments in the Trial Run, raise potential problems and highlight developing successes, fine-tune inter-departmental coordination, and so forth. As the Trial Run moves closer to Step 4 and closing the first deals, the export team will have to be an effective coordinating unit that identifies the broad as well as the detailed issues that must be addressed and resolved.

Select the Export Service Organizations

There are a wide range of export service organizations (ESOs) designed to support exporters. It is important for your company to become acquainted with these support services and to determine whether or not to seek their advice during the Trial Run. ESOs differ from EPOs in that ESOs support your company in carrying out specific export-related implementation tasks while EPOs focus on helping you promote your products in export markets and train your export team.

To find a list of export service organizations in your locale, consult the *International Trade State and Local Resources Directory* for your state, the Yellow Pages in your nearest metropolitan area, your state EPO, and your nearest world trade center. The primary ESOs that you will want to consider using are an international freight forwarder, a banker, an attorney, and an accountant.

By involving the ESOs you select in the preparation process, you can save your company time, insure a more successful Trial Run, and frequently keep yourself out of a lot of trouble.

International Freight Forwarder

The international freight forwarder acts as your company's agent in moving your product to your foreign buyer and is the middle person between you and the carriers that will transport the product. The services of an international freight forwarder may be critical to the success of your Trial Run and are available for a minimal fee. The services of the international freight forwarder fall into three general categories:

1. Arranging for the handling and transportation of your product from your company's dock to the foreign buyer
2. Completing the documents required to get your product out of the United States and into the foreign country
3. Presenting the documents upon which you will be paid

Examples of specific services provided by the international freight forwarder include reviewing a letter of credit to determine if the terms can be met, advising you on export regulations and foreign import requirements, advising you on special circumstances such as port facilities and clearing through customs in specific foreign countries, applying for export licenses, consolidating small shipments into container shipments, containerizing shipments, researching and negotiating with carriers, arranging bookings on vessels and aircraft, arranging for export packaging and markings, arranging for loading and unloading, issuing delivery orders, preparing the export declaration documents, preparing consular invoices and legalizations, preparing the bill of lading, arranging for insurance, seeing the shipment through customs, assembling all the required documents, preparing collection drafts, forwarding documents to the bank for collection, arranging for warehousing or delivery to the foreign buyer's location, filing damage claims with carriers and insurance companies, and tracking shipments.

Whether or not your company will need an international freight forwarder depends on factors such as these:

▲ *Size of shipment.* Small products may not require complex shipping arrangements and can frequently be shipped through the U.S. Post Office or air couriers, although they will not provide the full services of a freight forwarder. Large shipments, however, can involve complex shipping arrangements and documentation and require the services of an experienced international freight forwarder.

▲ *Value of shipment.* Low-value shipments may require little paperwork and be sold cash-in-advance or on open account, thus minimizing the number and complexity of the documents that need to be prepared. High-value shipments, on the other hand, will frequently involve a letter of credit and extensive export and shipping documentation and, thus, the need for the services of a freight forwarder.

▲ *Delivery time.* If the delivery date of a shipment is critical to the terms of the transaction and the shipment is by ocean vessel, then the services of the international freight forwarder with extensive ocean shipping may be required.

▲ *Nature of product shipped.* Extremely heavy products, products requiring special packaging for export shipment, hazardous materials, and other physical characteristics of the product may require special attention in order to ensure that the shipment arrives in good condition and complies with shipping and documentation requirements. A freight forwarder may be the only efficient and effective method of handling these types of product shipments.

▲ *Nature of foreign market.* Some foreign markets are relatively easy to enter and require little expertise. Other markets, on the other hand, have formal and informal barriers and pitfalls that require the expertise of a very experienced freight forwarder.

▲ *Experience of shipping/traffic department and other personnel.* If your company is large and has an experienced traffic department, you may not need the services of a freight forwarder or only use a forwarder for specific aspects of the transportation and documentation process. However, a company without such experience will frequently need to use the international freight forwarder as its full-service international traffic department in order to get the shipments to the foreign buyer without a hitch.

▲ *Control company wants to maintain.* There are probably certain shipping and documentation tasks over which you will want to have control or which your personnel are better qualified to perform than is the freight forwarder. If this is the case, then you will want to maximize the use of your in-house resources rather than relying on the services of the forwarder.

▲ *Frequency of shipments.* For destinations to which your company makes frequent shipments, it may be cost effective to develop the in-house expertise required to ship to the markets. On the other hand, a freight forwarder may be the most cost-effective method for shipping to markets where there are infrequent sales.

▲ *Cost of freight forwarder.* While the freight forwarder's fees are relatively low, you may find that you can get better shipping rates than the freight forwarder.

Now is the time to make a preliminary decision as to whether or not you want to use, or at least explore using, the services of an international freight forwarder.

You will find that freight forwarders come in a variety of types. For example, there are ocean freight forwarders licensed by the Federal Maritime Commission; ocean freight consolidators, also known as Non-Vessel Operating Common Carriers (NVOCC), which are required to file their tariffs with the Federal Maritime Commission; air freight forwarders approved by the air carriers' Cargo Network System (CNS, formerly IATA); and air freight consolidators. Many international freight forwarders perform several or all of these services.

Obtain a list of freight forwarders from the sources mentioned above. Narrow down that list based on your company's needs and the services offered by the forwarders. Since not every freight forwarder can be expected to be fully versed in every aspect of the business, it is important to locate those freight forwarders that can do the best job for your company's products in your target export markets. The following criteria will help you screen, qualify, and select the international freight forwarders that will best serve your needs:

▲ Does the forwarder specialize in your type of product, the type of carriers you will need, and your target market?

▲ Has the forwarder been in business long enough to develop the expertise required to handle your business?

▲ Is the forwarder financially sound? What is the forwarder's reputation with the carriers, its clients, and its bank?

▲ What licenses and approvals does the forwarder have? If the forwarder offers ocean freight forwarding, is it in fact licensed by the Federal Maritime Commission? If the forwarder offers ocean freight consolidation, does it in fact file its tariffs with the Federal Maritime Commission? If the forwarder offers air freight forwarding, is it in fact approved by the air carriers' Cargo Network System?

▲ Is the forwarder located in and well represented in your area? Does the forwarder have sufficient staff to serve your needs in a timely and accurate manner? Will it assign a key contact person and are you satisfied with that person? Does the forwarder take the time to help you understand the requirements, costs, and other specifications?

▲ Can the forwarder get you favorable shipping rates and delivery schedules?

Once you have selected one or more international freight forwarders with whom you want to work, visit with them. Orient the forwarders to your company, product, and service needs, and supply them with your company profile and product catalogs. Since the forwarders' interest in you will be related to the quantity of business you will generate, be prepared to provide them with a projection of the quantities of product you expect to export.

CASE EXAMPLE: nView Corporation manufactures an innovative liquid crystal display panel and wireless keyboard. The company describes its international freight forwarder as its most valuable export service. Its forwarder prepares the documents, presents all the documents and letters of credit to the bank for payment, and evaluates transportation and other shipping matters. Even though 20 to 40 percent of the company's business is exports, the company does not plan to bring any part of the forwarder's services in-house.

- -

International Banker

An international banker that can assist you with your international transactions is another important support service that needs to be identified early in your planning process, since your domestic banker may be ill-prepared to provide you with the services you will need for an export transaction.

An international banker should be able to provide you with these services:

- ▲ Financing of your export sales
- ▲ Collection of foreign drafts, letters of credit, and other foreign receivables
- ▲ Credit checks on potential foreign representatives and customers
- ▲ Access to private and government payment guarantee programs and other methods of getting paid
- ▲ Guidance in structuring competitive payment terms in your target market and other specific markets
- ▲ Wire transfers of funds from your foreign customer
- ▲ Information on your target market such as risk factors and economic data
- ▲ Trade promotion services and introductions through correspondent banks in your target market

If your current bank offers the above package of services, visit with the international division to discuss your needs and become acquainted with its staff. If your current bank does not provide the services you need, establish an account with another bank for your international transactions. If for some reason you cannot obtain the type of international banking services you need, determine if your state has an export financing agency and, if so, ask it for assistance.

International Attorney

An attorney experienced in international trade can keep you from being derailed by one of the legal hazards that you may happen upon as you progress down the export fast track.

When and how you use an attorney is something you will have to decide based on your specific situation. One case when an attorney should be involved is the finalizing of an agent or distributor agreement in your target market and other important foreign market. In many countries, the laws defining these arrangements are radically different from U.S. laws, and it is important to have legal counsel before entering into any final agreement. Other types of counsel provided by an international attorney include:

- ▲ Review of order acknowledgment and sales confirmation forms
- ▲ Protection of intellectual property rights including patents, trademarks, copyrights, and trade secrets
- ▲ Evaluation of product warranties, liability, and other legal requirements

If your company currently has legal counsel, determine whether or not this counsel is adequate to meet your needs as an exporter and in your target market. If not, ask your attorney for a referral, consult the resources listed above or your state bar association, or inquire about the Export Legal Assistance Program, a program jointly sponsored by the Federal Bar Association, the SBA and the USDOC, which provides a free, one-time consultation to new exporters. Don't let your fear of attorney fees keep you from exporting. Remember, your biggest risk will usually be that a legal problem could keep you from exporting to that country again.

International Accountant

The international accountant's services will be limited during the Trial Run since there are few situations that require their advice and counsel. However, it is advisable to inquire into the services of firms providing international accounting services. Many of these firms have free publications on subjects such as the benefits of a foreign sales corporation, how to use drawbacks, and the tax laws in your target market.

Select the Channels of Distribution

The next decision you have to make is whether to use a direct-to-end-user or representative channel of distribution in the worldwide and target export markets.

Direct-to-End-User or Representative

Use of a direct-to-end-user channel means that your company will sell directly to the end user or retail establishment through one of several methods such as direct mail, company sales agents operating out of the United States, or a company sales office or subsidiary in the foreign market. The representative channel of distribution involves the use of a foreign sales agent or distributor.

With instant communications, more timely and predictable transportation, just-in-time delivery and inventory minimization strategies, customer satisfaction programs, and other related developments, the role of middle persons such as agents and distributors has become not only less necessary than in the past but also an impediment in the distribution process. Producers are increasingly going direct to the end users of their products. However, the movement is not progressing at the same pace for all product lines and in all markets. Thus, the question you face is how to set up your distribution channel in your target market and other worldwide markets.

The best channels of distribution for your company will depend on a combination of several factors:

- ▲ Price of the product
- ▲ Margin on the product
- ▲ Nature of the product
- ▲ Number of end users
- ▲ Sales potential in the market
- ▲ After-sales service requirements
- ▲ Customary distribution channels in the market
- ▲ Your company's preferred method of distribution
- ▲ Your Trial Run budget
- ▲ Whether the market is your target country or worldwide market

For example, if you are selling a low-cost, mass-produced product into your target market, if there are a large number of end users and a high sales potential, if your product requires extensive on-site training and support, and if the product is normally sold through local distributors, you might decide that selling directly to foreign end users is not an attractive option. Some of the reasons why a direct-to-end-user channel of distribution would not be attractive include: Transportation and import costs for small retail shipments will drive your price up and place an extremely heavy burden on your shipping department; your sales organization is unlikely to maximize your potential in the market; your service organization cannot provide the after-sale support customers require; you are bucking the accepted way of doing business in the market by not using a distributor. In this case, it would be to your advantage to use a distributor to whom you can make large volume shipments, who can capitalize on the potential in the market, and who can provide good customer support services.

Some of the advantages of selling directly to the end user or retailer include a lower mark-up for the customer and/or higher margins for your company. Some of the disadvantages are that you will have to sell to more people and the more people you sell to the more resources you will have to invest in serving your customers.

- -

CASE EXAMPLE: LecTec Corporation is a state-of-the-art manufacturer of medical electrodes, tapes, and transdermal drug delivery systems, always searching for new distribution methods that will get it closer to the end user of its products. In one market the company used graduate business students in the country to research the market and introduce its product as part of their course work. The students earned commissions and the company learned a lot more about the market, its customers, and the suitability of its product than it could have ever learned from a distributor. The company is now in a better position to determine the channels of distribution it wants to use in the market.

- -

The channels of distribution your company uses in the U.S. market, and the reasons you use those channels, should serve as a starting point for making your export market channel decisions. However, you will find that the United States tends to have fewer middlemen than do many other countries.

For your first few worldwide and target market sales during the Trial Run, we suggest that you consider making several trial sales direct to your end users if it is at all feasible. This approach will allow you to make some initial sales and establish person-to-person relationships with end users and retailers. End user and retailer contact is very important as you start down the export fast track because they provide you with first-hand knowledge about your ultimate customers and eliminate the filters that representative channels of distribution place between you and the ultimate customer.

However, in your target market you may find that a representative channel of distribution will be the most effective channel during the Trial Run (and the early stages of the Market Penetration phase). One of the main factors in favor of a representative channel is that it limits the investment you have to make to establish your product in the market. In most cases it would take a major cash outlay to establish your own sales and service facilities in your target market.

In your worldwide markets you will probably follow a mixed pattern of direct and representative channels of distribution based on the opportunities that develop in various markets during the course of the Trial Run.

Sales Agents or Distributors?

If you decide upon a representative channel of distribution, your next decision will be to determine whether you prefer a sales agent or a distributor. There are several important differences between the typical sales agent and a distributor.

Sales Agent. A sales agent can be an employee or independent contractor, might be paid either a commission or a base plus a commission, and is financed by your company. The agent sells at the prices you set and does not stock your products (although the product may be carried on consignment in some cases). The risk of loss, nonpayment, liability, and responsibility for service and warranty remain with you, the exporter.

Termination of a representative will frequently be more difficult and costly than terminating a distributor.

Distributor. The distributor is an independent contractor who typically purchases your product at a discount and stocks the product locally, sets the selling price, provides buyer financing, handles service and warranty needs, and assumes certain risks and liabilities. However, with a distributor you give up control over pricing and marketing methods and have limited or no contact with the final customer. Because the distributor usually handles several product lines, you cannot be assured that your product or service will get the attention you want in the market.

At this point, you may have developed a preference for your channels of distribution in your worldwide markets and target country markets. If not, or if you are open to either type of representative depending upon the circumstances, you can wait until you have learned more about the market and received inquiries from potential agents and distributors before making a final decision as to which channels will best serve your company's needs.

The channels of distribution that you select for the Trial Run must allow you to test the worldwide markets and a target country market within the limits of the resources you have allocated for the Trial Run.

Establish the Market Entry Export Price

Your initial market entry minimum order, transportation mode, payment terms, shipping terms, and price need to be established for worldwide markets and for your target market. This information will be necessary in order to prepare specific price lists and pro forma invoices for potential customers in the next step of the Trial Run.

If you are selling a service, determining a market entry export price will not require as much pen-and-pad calculation as with a commodity. Also, if your product is shipped through one of the express air services, you will find that determining your market entry export price will be less difficult than if you are shipping by vessel.

Setting the Minimum Order

The size of an order will influence your shipping costs and, thus, your price. Therefore, you need to determine what your minimum order will be for test sales and regular sales.

Your domestic minimum order may be appropriate for test and regular export sales. However, it is likely that the minimum order size will have to be larger for export sales. For example, your domestic minimum order may be twenty-four cases of product, but you may decide to increase your export minimum order to a container load in order to obtain good shipping rates, cover the additional paperwork involved in an export shipment, prevent the shipment from being damaged during shipment, and protect the product from being stolen in transit.

In order to make the determination on your optimum minimum shipment, assess the factors and consult with your international freight forwarder or potential carriers.

Selecting the Transportation Mode

The mode of shipment that you select will influence your costs and shipping terms. Therefore, it is necessary to determine which mode will be most appropriate for your export orders.

Factors that will influence your decision include your product size, product value, minimum order quantity, delivery time versus delivery cost trade-off, and country of destination of your shipment. Your most common options include containerized and break-bulk ocean vessel carriers; courier, container, and freight air carriers; intermodal carriers; truck carriers; and rail carriers.

Once again, your international freight forwarder may be needed to determine the most appropriate mode of shipment for your product.

Selecting the Payment Terms

The terms of payment that you quote will be a factor in determining how competitive your product is going to be in foreign markets and what your costs will be. The terms of payment also affect your collection risk, how long you have to wait for payment, your ability to obtain financing for your export sale, and other financial matters.

You will want to establish an initial set of general payment terms for your worldwide sales and another set of specific payment terms for sales in your target market. Your international banker will be invaluable in helping you make these decisions because your banker is in a position to assist you in assessing the risks you will face and to know the methods of collection being used in specific foreign markets. You may also want to consult with your trade associations and other exporters for advice on the most appropriate terms of payment for your target market.

During the start-up of your Trial Run and before you have developed a relationship with your foreign customers and established their credit worthiness, your decisions on payment terms will be influenced by several factors. These factors include the value of your product/shipment, whether you have made special modifications to the product for the buyer, the country risk, the buyer risk, your company's financial condition, and your competitors' payment terms. Your export payment terms will be designed to provide protection against the risks common to your domestic sales as well as against those risks unique to export sales.

You and your international banker will consider several common payment terms during the start-up of your Trial Run. After you have established a relationship with a specific buyer, your international banker may advise you to adjust your payment terms. A list of options follows.

▲ *Cash in advance.* Your customer pays you either with the order or before the product is shipped.

▲ *Letter of credit (LC).* The LC substitutes the credit of your customer's bank for that of the customer. Your customer obtains an LC from a bank in the customer's country issued to you and advised through your bank. Payment under an LC will usually be at the time of shipment and your presentation of the documents specified in the LC to your bank with a sight draft, or within a given period (usually up to 180 days) with a time draft. You are required to submit the specified documents listed in the LC to your bank and perform your responsibilities in absolute adherence to the specific terms of the LC. Otherwise, any discrepancies will prevent you from collecting on the LC, and you will have to rely on your customers to waive the discrepancies on your documents in order to get paid.

The LC must be an irrevocable LC, which means that there can be no cancellation or modification of the conditions stated in the LC without the consent of all parties involved. Depending on the country involved, your banker may advise you to require a confirmed LC, whereby the LC is confirmed by your bank—your bank guarantees payment by the customer's bank. The bank fees in the customer's country are paid by your customer and can have a significant effect on the customer's total cost. The fees outside of the customer's country are your cost, unless otherwise specified.

It should be noted that an LC is frequently ineffective with air shipments if there are seller performance discrepancies that prevent you from collecting on the LC. The reason is that, even though you cannot collect on the LC, possession of the products shipped by air passes to the customer when you deliver the product to the air carrier at the airport. You are now in effect trying to collect on open account.

▲ *Collection.* There are two collection methods: Documents Against Payment (D/P) and Documents Against Acceptance (D/A).

The D/P is a sight draft documentary collection instrument (similar to a promissory note). Your bank's services will be required to collect payment, but there are no guarantees associated with the D/P, and the buyer may cancel his order prior to accepting the shipment, leaving you with your product sitting in a foreign port and no way to collect. A draft drawn on the buyer and payable to your company is prepared by you and is forwarded to your bank with the bill of lading and other documents. Your bank forwards the draft, bill of lading, and other documents to its correspondent bank in your buyer's country, and the correspondent bank collects from your buyer. The D/P works only with a negotiable ocean bill of lading, since your buyer needs the bill of lading to obtain the goods. However, the D/P provides little protection for a shipment made by air or for a consigned ocean bill of lading, since, in many countries, one may not need the airway bill or consigned bill of lading in order to obtain the shipment. Payment of the bank fees for the D/P services must be stipulated in your agreement with the buyer.

The D/A is a time draft and is processed like the D/P. However, the terms allow the buyer to receive the shipment and make payment within a given period, for example, ninety days. The primary advantage of the D/A over open account terms is that you may also be able to discount the acceptance draft and receive immediate payment if the buyer's credit is strong and is known to the bank.

▲ *Open account.* The bill of lading and a commercial invoice are forwarded directly to your buyer. Depending on local business practices, open account terms can vary from net in 30 days to net in 180 days.

When your buyer is paying you directly as in the cash in advance or open account methods, require that the funds be wire transferred from your buyer's bank account to your bank account. Foreign checks take a long time to clear.

Selecting the Shipping Terms

The shipping or trade terms define how the functions, costs, risks, and other aspects of an international transaction are distributed between your company and your buyer and must be determined in order to set your market entry price.

Since international shipping terms are different from those used in the United States, it is important to not only establish what your shipping terms will be but to also use the proper international terms in order that you and the buyer will have a common understanding of your respective responsibilities. The internationally accepted shipping terms are called Incoterms and are defined in the book *Incoterms 1990*. The following is a summary description of selected shipping terms:

EXW   "Ex Works" (named place). You deliver the shipment to the buyer at your premises.

FCA   "Free Carrier" (named place). You clear the shipment for export and deliver the shipment to the carrier appointed by the buyer at the named place.

FOB   "Free On Board" (named port of shipment). You clear the shipment for export and deliver the shipment "over the rail" of the vessel appointed by the buyer at the named port. Note that *FOB* as used in export differs from *FOB* used in domestic trade.

CIF   "Cost, Insurance and Freight" (named port of destination). You clear the shipment for export, deliver the shipment "over the rail" of the vessel selected by you, and pay the costs, freight, and insurance necessary to bring the shipment to the named port of destination. The buyer assumes the risk of loss or additional cost due to events occurring after the shipment is delivered over the ship's rail at the port of shipment.

CIP   "Carriage and Insurance Paid To" (named place of destination). You clear the shipment for export, deliver the shipment to the carrier selected by you, and pay the costs, freight, and insurance necessary to bring the shipment to the named place of destination. The buyer assumes the risk of loss or additional costs due to events occurring after the shipment is delivered to the carrier.

DDP   "Delivered Duty Paid" (named placed of destination). You clear the shipment for export, pay the cost of shipment, bear the risk of loss, clear the shipment for importation, pay all duties, taxes and other import charges, and deliver the shipment at the named place of destination in the country of importation.

These are only a sample of selected shipping terms. Refer to *Incoterms 1990* for a complete definition of these and the other Incoterms.

In order to establish your export shipping terms, you must consider two factors: (1) your transportation mode and (2) the point at which you want to deliver the shipment to your buyer. The transportation mode has already been established. The points of delivery from which you can choose are as follows: (a) at your premises, (b) to the carrier appointed by the buyer, (c) to the carrier selected by you (with you paying the shipping costs), or (d) at the foreign destination.

The Shipping Term Selection Worksheet (Worksheet 12) can be used with the above definitions and *Incoterms 1990* to select the specific shipping terms that you will use for your market entry export price.

While you may prefer to minimize your work and risk by establishing your price with delivery to the foreign buyer at your premises (Ex Works), this is not an attractive price quote for your foreign buyer since he or she does not know how to estimate or arrange inland U.S. transportation. The most reasonable shipping terms, ones that balance your desire to minimize risk and your buyer's need to determine his or her total costs, will be FCA or FOB for your worldwide markets and CIP or CIF for your target market.

Determining the Price

You will be determining the market entry export prices for a single unit of product (e.g., the price for a case of your product) not only for your target country but for worldwide markets as well. Your prices will be calculated for a distributor or end user depending on the channel of distribution and type of representative you have selected in a market. In later steps you will use these calculations to prepare price lists and pro forma invoices for individual customers.

Determining the export price involves excluding some costs included in the calculations for a domestic price and adding other costs that are unique to shipping products abroad. Although there are several ways to determine price, for the Trial Run you will use the following method:

1. Start with your U.S. price ex works for a unit of product.
2. Determine your export price ex works. Subtract your U.S. mar-

WORKSHEET 12. Shipping Term Selection

SHIPPING TERM SELECTION	**FASTRACK**
	Success Through Fast-Track Exporting

Purpose: To select the shipping terms for the Trial Run market. Directions: Select and circle the transportation mode in the top row. Select and circle the point of delivery in the left column. Use the matrix to identify the appropriate shipping terms; if more than one shipping term may be used, select the desired term. Note: Shipping terms are <u>Incoterms 1990</u>.

Company Name/Division _____

Product _____ Target Market _____

Point of Delivery	Transportation Mode			
	Sea	Rail	Air	Intermodal or / Other
"E" Destinations: Seller delivers shipment to buyer at seller's premises.	EXW - EX Works	EXW - EX Works	EXW - Ex Works	EXW - Ex Works
"F" Destinations: Seller delivers shipment to carrier appointed by buyer.	FCA - Free Carrier FAS - Free Alongside Ship FOB - Free On Board	FCA - Free Carrier	FCA - Free Carrier	FCA - Free Carrier
"C" Destinations: Seller delivers shipment to carrier selected by seller who pays shipping cost to the foreign destination.	CIP - Carriage and Insurance Paid to CPT - Carriage Paid to CIF - Cost, Insurance & Freight CFR - Cost and Freight	CIP - Carriage and Insurance Paid to	CIP - Carriage and Insurance Paid to	CIP - Carriage and Insurance Paid to
"D" Destinations: Seller delivers shipment to foreign destination.	DAF - Delivered at Frontier DDU - Delivered Duty Unpaid DDP - Delivered Duty Paid DES - Delivered Ex Ship DEQ - Delivered Ex Quay	DAF - Delivered at Frontier DDU - Delivered Duty Unpaid DDP - Delivered Duty Paid	DAF - Delivered at Frontier DDU - Delivered Duty Unpaid DDP - Delivered Duty Paid	DAF - Delivered at Frontier DDU - Delivered Duty Unpaid DDP - Delivered Duty Paid

DECISION: What transportation mode will be used? _____ (From Above)
Rationale:

DECISION: What point of delivery will be selected? "_____" <u>Destination</u> (From Above)
Rationale:

DECISION: What specific <u>Incoterms 1990</u> shipping term will be selected _____ / _____
Rationale:

Completed by	Date

Copyright Export Resource Associates, Inc., 1990

090

keting costs and export drawback and foreign sales corporation tax benefits from the U.S. price ex works, and add your export marketing and financing costs.

3. Determine your export price FCA or FOB. Add the cost of getting the shipment to the carrier to the export price ex works.

4. Determine your export price CIP or CIF. Add the carrier's freight and related costs and insurance costs to the FCA or FOB price.

5. Determine the import price DDP for your distributor and import price to the end user. Add the costs required to import your product into the foreign market to the export price CIP or CIF.

6. Compare your calculated import price with your competitors' prices.

7. Determine the desired import price per unit that will allow you to be competitive in the market, that will cover your costs, and that will meet your desired profit margins.

8. Recalculate the unit cost to meet the desired import price, and restate your market entry export price and terms.

The Market/Entry Export Price and Terms Worksheet (Worksheet 13) can be used to help you arrive at the right price. Prepare one worksheet for your worldwide markets and another for your target market.

You may need the assistance of your international freight forwarder, international accountant, international banker, and international attorney to complete the unit price worksheet. For example, your freight forwarder will be indispensable in identifying the most appropriate modes of transportation and numerous costs that are involved in moving your product to the export market. Cost factors that may require consultation with your other ESOs include drawback benefits, foreign sales corporation tax benefits, financing fees, risk insurance, foreign taxes, and banking fees.

In order to determine the import tariff on your product in your target market, contact the USDOC District Office and request that they look up the tariff on your product in *Douanes Duty Books*. The import customs tariffs, which are paid by the buyer, will influence your competitiveness in the export markets. The type of tariff your customers must pay—ad valorem tariffs (based on a percentage of the values of the goods) and specific (based on units of weight and measure or number of items)—may eventually have an influence on your packaging methods.

(text continues on page 89)

WORKSHEET 13. Market Entry Export Price and Terms

MARKET ENTRY EXPORT PRICE & TERMS	*FASTRACK*ₛₘ
	Success Through Fast-Track Exporting

Purpose: To determine the market entry export single unit price and terms for a specific target country. Directions: (1) Complete the unit, order, transportation, and terms information. (2) Start with the U.S. Price EXW or factory price. (3) Subtract/add costs not related/related to exporting for the Export Price EXW. Adjust for the distributor's discount. (4) Add the shipping and related costs necessary to deliver the product to the carrier for a FCA/FOB price. (5) Add the freight and insurance costs for a CIP/CIF price. (6) Add the importer's costs for a DDP price. Adjust for the distributor's markup. Determine the Import Price to the end user. (7) Identify competitive prices and terms in the market. (8) Set the Import Price at which you want your product to sell. State your Market Entry Price and Terms for a unit of product. Note: This price will be used later in preparing your Customer Export Quotation worksheet. Shipping terms are <u>Incoterms 1990.</u>

Company Name/Division _____

Product	HS/Schedule B Code	Target Market

Product Unit _____

    Shipping Basis: __Weight or __Measure? __US Tons or __Metric Tons? __Lb or __Kg? __Foot or __Meter?

    Unit: Net Weight _____ Gross Weight _____ Dimensions _____ Cubic Measure _____

Minimum Order Export Crated _____ Total # Units _____

    Points of Origin _____ Delivery _____ Destination _____

    Total Net Weight _____ Total Gross Weight _____

    Total Dimensions _____ Total Cubic Measure _____

    Explain Crating, Etc. _____

Transportation Mode: __Ocean __Rail __Air __Intermodal __Truck Delivery Time Constraints _____

    Freight Rate _____ Based on: __FCL __LCL __BBLK __Deck __Under Deck __Ventilation __Refrigeration

    Container Dimensions _____ Container Cubic Measure _____

Payment Terms: __Cash in Advance __LC __DP __DA __30 days __60 days __90 days __days __Open Account __Other:

    Explanation _____

    Currency _____ Assumed Exchange Rate _____

Shipping Terms: FCA   FOB   CIP   CIF   Other: Explanation

Pricing Factors	Named Place	Notes on Costs	Unit Cost	Recalculated Unit Cost
U.S. Price EX WORKS	_____		_____	
US Marketing/Sales Costs			- _____	
US Warranty/Service Costs			- _____	
Drawback on Imported Components			- _____	
Foreign Sales Corporation Tax Savings			- _____	
Other Subsidies/Savings			- _____	
Export Product Modification Costs			+ _____	
Export Product Packaging/Etc.			+ _____	
Export Marketing/Sales Costs			+ _____	
Export Warranty/Service Costs			+ _____	
Export Financing Fees			+ _____	
Export Risk Insurance Fees			+ _____	
Banking Fees			+ _____	
Other Costs:			± _____	
Export Price EX WORKS	_____		_____	
Distributor's Discount @ _____ % of EXW			_____	
Market Entry Export Price				Page 1

Copyright Export Resource Associates, Inc., 1990

Worksheet 13 (*continued*)

Pricing Factors	Named Place	Notes on Costs	Unit Cost	Recalculated Unit Cost
Distributor's Export Price EX WORKS			————	
Export Crating/Marking Costs			+ ————	
Freight Forwarder Fees			+ ————	
Loading			+ ————	
Cartage			+ ————	
Inland Freight by _____ to	————		+ ————	
Unloading Costs at	————		+ ————	
Terminal Costs			+ ————	
Demurrage Costs			+ ————	
Special Ship Loading Costs			+ ————	
Consular Invoice Fees			+ ————	
Certificate Fees			+ ————	
Other Costs:			+ ————	
Export Price ___ FREE CARRIER	————		————	
or ___ FREE ON BOARD	————		————	
or _____	————		————	
Freight Costs & Surcharges to	————		+ ————	
Transport Insurance Costs @ 110% of CIP/CIF			+ ————	
Other Costs:			+ ————	
Export Price ___ CARRIAGE INS PAID	————		————	
or ___ COST INS FREIGHT	————		————	
or _____	————		————	
Import Duties and Taxes			+ ————	
Custom House Broker Fees			+ ————	
Foreign Inland Freight Costs			+ ————	
Foreign Banking Fees			+ ————	
Other Costs:			+ ————	
Import Price DELIVERED DUTY PAID	————		————	
Distributor Mark Up @ ____ % of DDP			+ ————	
Import Price to End User				

Competitors	Unit Price	Currency	Exchange Rate	USDollars	Terms

DECISION: At what Import Price do I want a unit of product to sell to the end user? $ ————

Rationale:

DECISION: What will be my Market Entry Export Price and Terms for a unit of product?

Price: $ ————   Terms:

Rationale:

Completed by	Date	
Market Entry Export Price		Page 2

For example, in countries with ad valorem tariffs, you may want to ship a product unassembled in order to lower the customs value and assemble the product in the foreign market.

Since your competitors' prices are a major determinant of your export price, collect their price lists for each channel in which you will be selling your product. Ask potential customers for price lists (and yes, even your competitors, for historical price lists). Assuming that your competitors' price lists are not in U.S. dollars, you will have to convert them into U.S. dollars for comparison purposes. Look on the financial page of a major newspaper for the current exchange rate or ask your international banker.

If your final calculation of the import price is higher than your competitors' prices, you may be in the wrong foreign market, unless you can either differentiate your product from your competitors' products or reduce some of your costs. On the other hand, you may find that your calculated import price is significantly lower than your competitors' prices. In this case, you may want to increase your market entry export price to establish a price that provides a larger profit margin than your U.S. price.

During the Trial Run, export prices will be quoted in U.S. dollars. Although the changing value of the U.S. dollar will influence your buyers' costs and thus your price over time, during the Trial Run you do not want to complicate your life by having to deal with fluctuating foreign exchange rates.

Build the Foreign Buyer Database

In Step 3 of the Trial Run you will implement your action steps and use your foreign contact databases to reach and qualify potential end users, retailers, agents, and distributors and to track your results. Your job will be a lot easier and your efforts more productive if you design and build a computer database to maintain and manage your lists.

Your foreign buyer database should include all potential end users, retailers, agents, distributors, and other types of customers. It should also include company contact information; original source of the listing; products in which the customer is interested including quantity and use; background and qualifying information; a record of purchases including dates, products, and amounts; and a narrative record of contacts (see

Figure 2). This database becomes the core element of your Trial Run database.

The foreign buyer database will include worldwide contacts although the focus will be on contacts in your target market country.

Build your database with the names from previous inquiries. Ask your state EPO, trade association, and other exporters with complementary products for contacts. Ask current buyers for the names of potential customers in foreign markets.

One of the most convenient sources of Trial Run contacts is the federal government. The USDOC District Office will use its *Agent/ Distributor Service (ADS)* to identify a key list of five or six high-potential clients in your target country market, qualify the contacts, and determine that they have a positive interest in your product. (Note: The ADS service requires copies of your promotional materials in order to initiate their search. Therefore, you may want to delay finalizing this request until you have prepared the materials discussed in the next section.) The USDOC's *Export Contact List Service* (see Figure 3) and the USDA Foreign Agriculture Service's *Foreign Buyer Lists* are good sources of contacts. The Agency for International Development's *AID Importer Lists* can also be used to locate foreign contacts, and the agency's *AID Consultant Registry Information System* is a source of contacts for service organizations. Other potential lists include private sources of lists and contacts such as *Interdata* importer mailing lists and *International Directory of Importers.*

Trade show exhibitor and attendee lists are sources of contacts. Information on trade show lists and their costs can be obtained by writing to the show managers in the show directories such as *Exhibitions 'Round the World, International Trade Fairs and Conferences Directory,* and *International Tradeshow Directory.* Purchasing lists from trade publications can also be good sources of contacts. Many of these lists can be selected by product code/keyword, country, and type of contact (e.g., end user, agent, or distributor), to tailor a list that targets the specific types of customers of interest to you.

Libraries and telephone companies have the telephone directories and Yellow Pages for major foreign cities from which you can identify potential end users and representatives. You can also use library copies of the various export manuals to identify target country importer associations, trade associations, U.S. and foreign chambers of commerce, and other groups that may produce lists or directories that will help you target potential contacts. If your target country is in Europe, the *Export Guide to Europe* is a good source of contacts. The *Kompass* country

Figure 2. Foreign buyer database.

```
FOREIGN BUYER RECORD                              [Screen 1]

 ID:              _____              Source:_____
 CO-NAME:       _____
 ALPHA-NAME:    _____
 ADDRESS1:      _____
 ADDRESS2:      _____
 CITY:          _____  STATE:_____  CODE:_____
 COUNTRY:       _____  CTRY-CODE:_____  REGION:_____
 TEL:           _____  FAX:_____  TLX:_____
 FACILITY:      ___ ___ ___ ___ ___
 CHIEF-EXEC:    _____  CE-SAL:_____
 CE-TITLE:      _____  ENGLISH:___ ___
 PUR-AGENT:     _____  PA-SAL:_____
 PA-TITLE:      _____  ENGLISH:___ ___
 CONTACT:       _____  C-SAL:_____
 C-TITLE:       _____  ENGLISH:___ ___
 FOUNDED:       ___  #EMPL:____  OWNERSHIP:_____  Size:_____
 PARENT:        PID:  _____
 SUBSIDIARY:SID:      _____
 BUSINESS:      ___ ___ ___ ___ ___  SALES:_____
 ACTIVITY:      _____
 STATUS:        _____ CREATED:_____UPDATED:_____  BY:_____
```

```
FOREIGN BUYER RECORD                              [Screen 2]

 ID:_____
 INTEREST:  CODE    PRODUCT              QTY       WHEN
            _____   _____       _____     _____
            _____   _____       _____     _____
            _____   _____       _____     _____
 PURCHASES:CODE    PRODUCT       AMOUNT  QTY       DATE
            _____   _____    _____  _____     _____
            _____   _____    _____  _____     _____
            _____   _____    _____  _____     _____
 COMMENTS:  DATE    NOTE
            _____   _____
            _____   _____
            _____   _____
 CODES:     _____  _____  _____  _____  _____  _____
 TERRITORY: _____
 POSITION:  _____
 CHANNELS:  _____
 SEGMENTS:  _____
 CUSTOMERS: _____
 BANK:      _____
 PAY-TERMS: _____
```

Figure 3.   Sample from USDOC *Export Contact List Service.*

Commercial Information Management System
Trade/Export Mailing List

`===============================================`

Compserv Ltd.	R. H. Brown
1245 Carl Street	President
Ottawa, Ontario K1S 2E9	Phone: (613) 566-1472
	Year Established: 1970
Canada	No. of Employees: 27
	Relative Size: Small
	Information Date: 1/10/91
	Telex #:
	Cable Addr:

SIC-Code	Description
3573	Electronic computing equipment
	Int Agent; Leasing; Public'N; Int User
3662	Radio & TV communications equipment
	Agent; Distrib; Exporter; Importer; Int Agent

---

directories are good sources of contacts. Your international banker's trade promotion service may also be used to generate contacts.

Directories of directories such as *Trade Directories of the World* and *International Directories in Print* are valuable resources and may lead you to very targeted lists of potential buyers and distributors of your product.

By continually scanning trade journal and business publication stories and advertisements, as well as the trade lead sources such as the *Electronic Bulletin Board, AgExport's Trade Leads, AID Procurement Information* bulletins, *World Trade Center Network,* and the *Journal of Commerce* trade lead announcements, you will find updated sources of contacts to add to the Foreign Buyer database.

CASE EXAMPLE: Amerex Corporation manufactures portable fire extinguishers and sells its product in over fifty export markets. To build its foreign buyer lists, Amerex makes contacts using a variety of means including advertising. However, getting someone in a foreign market to photocopy the Yellow Pages section for fire extinguishers provides the Company with a valuable prospect list as well as market research information. It's a small thing, but it's valuable information for building the buyer list.

You should note that terms describing contacts vary greatly around the world and this can complicate your search for specific types of contacts. In some countries, distributors, for example, are referred to as agents. In addition, there are frequently multiple layers in the distribution network in a market and the terms used to describe these layers differ from country to country. For example, an importer is frequently the top layer in a country's distribution network.

Sign Up for EPO Promotional Events

Export promotion organizations sponsor many no-cost and low-cost promotional events that are designed to introduce you to potential foreign customers. In your initial meetings with the EPOs, you were introduced to some of these services. Now is the time to review specific opportunities with your USDOC District Office, state EPO, World Trade Center, trade association, and other EPOs. If there are events that are of interest and you have time to plan and prepare for them, consider signing up for the events now. The types of promotional events in which you will be most interested during the Trial Run are described below.

▲ *Foreign catalog/video shows.* The USDOC sponsors several such shows each year and, depending on the product and country focus of the shows, they can provide low-cost access to foreign markets. You will provide product literature and/or the video. The USDOC organizes the shows, recruits the foreign participants, introduces your company to the foreign buyers, and provides you with the contacts that expressed interest in your product. State EPOs frequently attend foreign trade shows and provide a similar service for companies at these shows.

▲ *Buying mission visits.* Foreign buyers frequently visit the United

States as individuals or groups looking for products to purchase or represent in their home markets. The USDA, USDOC, state EPOs, world trade centers, and trade associations work with these visitors to arrange one-on-one appointments with U.S. companies.

▲ *Foreign trade shows, matchmaker delegations, and trade missions.* EPOs regularly organize and lead delegations of U.S. companies to foreign markets and assist them in meeting foreign customers. These events are relatively expensive and beyond the basic Trial Run budget, but if your budget can afford the trip or if the EPO provides a subsidy, then a show or mission is a possibility. Because of the time it takes to properly plan and prepare for a foreign event (six to twelve months), foreign promotional events are usually not practical until the later stages of the Trial Run or during Phase II of the Fast-Track Exporting process.

▲ *Special target industry promotions.* EPOs that target high-potential export industries or product lines for special promotional efforts can be of significant benefit to you in entering foreign markets. If you have identified EPOs that sponsor such promotional services, contact them and request to be included.

CASE EXAMPLE: Goguen Industries, manufacturer of electronic components, sells its products to all types of customers ranging from sophisticated computer manufacturers to appliance makers. For many years the export opportunities bulletin of New York State's International Division had been coming across the president's desk. But, in 1988 the president decided to call the agency. A year later Goguen received the Governor's Award for Achievement in Export. How did it do it? That first call to the agency resulted in a $750 investment to participate in a foreign catalog show being sponsored by New York State in Spain. Success at the Spanish show led to participation in a state-sponsored trade show in the United Kingdom, where Goguen met a distributor in the next booth. That distributor now generates 50 percent of the company's export sales.

Develop the Promotional Methods and Materials

Promotional methods that you will consider using during the Trial Run include advertising, direct mail campaigns, and follow-up telephone and/ or fax campaigns. The use of these promotional methods will provide you with the initial worldwide and target market promotion you need to achieve your Trial Run objectives within the budget you have established.

Internationalizing the Company's Materials

All of the materials you use for your export promotional campaign should be internationalized.

The first step in internationalizing your letterhead, envelopes, business cards, and other materials is to add USA to your address, include your fax and telex numbers, and make sure your regular telephone number is listed (an 800 number is of no value to a foreign buyer). In addition, it is advisable to add your bank reference to your letterhead. The above changes will make it easier for your potential foreign customers to contact you.

The second step in internationalizing your materials is to selectively rewrite your sales letters and literature to adapt the materials to foreign markets. For example, all measurements and quantities should be converted to the metric system, since the metric system is the predominant standard for all but three nations in the world (the United States, Liberia, and Myanmar). Materials should be rewritten to present your story in simple, clear English using short, basic words and sentences. Remove slang words and cultural references that will not be understood by foreign readers. Unless technical words are likely to be understood, use generic words and pictures to describe your product. Review your materials for any objectionable content based on religion, culture, or politics. For the materials that will be developed for your target market, use the information in the *Culturegrams* and other publications to individualize your appeal to the culture and other characteristics of that market. Since it is unlikely that your Trial Run budget will support the rewrite of all of your materials, you will need to prioritize the internationalizing of the materials or start internationalizing your materials as they are reprinted or revised. There are a number of inexpensive measures you can take in order to tailor your literature during the Trial Run. For example, you may want to consider preparing an insert for your product brochure that would include metric conversions, if applicable. Pictures can communicate your message, and may explain a new concept, better than a translation of your text. This would be an inexpensive way to clarify terminology and present a committed image to the potential buyer.

The final step in the internationalizing of your materials is to translate key pieces into the language of your target market if you believe that English will limit the effectiveness of your promotion campaign. Initially you will not need to invest in having all of your product literature translated. You might start out with the translation of a brief sales letter and, if your budget allows, add translations of your business cards, a bounce-back card, and summary product literature. When having materials translated, anticipate that the process will involve two steps: First, a translation by a U.S.-based person qualified and experienced in the language; and second, a review by a native of the target country who understands your product. Unfortunately, translations never seem to be totally correct no matter how much care you take to recruit a qualified translator. The review of the translation in the target market will improve a good U.S.-based translation and keep you from sending out a poor translation that may damage your image and impede your Trial Run. To find local translation services, consult the listings in the *International Trade State and Local Resources Directory,* contact your state EPO or nearest world trade center, or look in the Yellow Pages of nearby metropolitan areas. For assistance in locating foreign-based persons to review your translated materials, ask for referrals from your state EPO, nearest world trade center, national trade association, and companies in your industry that are active in the market.

- -

CASE EXAMPLE: Wahl Clipper Corporation has a policy that all product literature will be translated by its distributor in the specific market. Their rationale is that the distributor knows the product and the best way to translate the company's message. In France the company's distributor prevented a marketing disaster by changing the name of the Groomsman product line. The home office learned that in French groomer means "man who cleans out the barn''—not exactly the image Wahl had in mind for their product.

- -

A translation service should be screened before you engage them to do your work. Ask for references who have used their services for the language and country you are targeting. Does the translator have native fluency in the language and keep current with changes in the language (and English if not an English-speaking native)? Is the translator expert in or has he/she worked in your product area? Will the translation be edited? Will the translation be camera-ready (for example, will the letter be typed for use on your letterhead, will the brochure text be typeset)? If additional materials are to be translated later, will the later translations be consistent with the current work?

Developing the First-Contact Materials

It takes time to develop promotional materials that will be effective in export markets. During this step you will prepare the materials that you will use to implement Step 3 of the Trial Run.

Advertising Materials. For the Trial Run we recommend that you prepare a small advertisement for insertion in *Commercial News USA*, the USDOC's worldwide promotional publication, and possibly *Showcase USA*. *Buyer Alert* is a USDA publication that can be used to advertise agricultural products. These are very cost-effective publications in relation to the anticipated worldwide response rate. Contact the publications, obtain their specifications, and prepare your advertising copy in English. You may use your current stock advertising text, but review it to make sure that it is internationalized. Also, consider that these advertisements will be addressing a worldwide audience as well as your target-country audience and that their objective will be to attract inquiries from potential agents and distributors, or end users and retailers, from around the world.

If you currently advertise in publications that are published in the United States and distributed abroad, review your advertising copy to internationalize it and to increase its appeal to foreign customers. A number of these U.S. publications are also distributed at foreign trade fairs.

During the Trial Run it may be too costly to consider advertising in your target market, but if this is an option, you may want to prepare an advertisement specifically for this market and identify appropriate target market publications using *Ulrich's International Periodicals Directory* and the recommendations of your national trade association and other companies in your industry.

Direct-Mail Materials. Focus the Trial Run direct mail materials at the foreign buyer database contacts you have collected in your target market. You will need to prepare a cover sales letter, a summary piece of product literature, and possibly a bounce-back card and/or price list.

▲ *Cover sales letter.* The cover letter is used to introduce your company and your objective, which is to solicit inquiries from potential representatives or end users. The letter establishes the credibility of your company and the fact that you are a reliable supplier of quality products to recognized customers. Provide your banking reference, the year your company was organized, size, and other basic facts about your company. Ask for the response you want (e.g., return of the bounce-back card or the order). Your response rate will be higher if you make it easy for the contact to respond, if your materials have communicated the benefits of your product or service in such a way as to convince the contact that your company can meet his/her needs, if you point out the competitive advantages and sale potential in the representative's market, and if you include some appealing offer, such as a free catalog or a special deal. Invite the contact to visit your company. Your letter should be personally typed and signed with few exceptions (a printed copy of a letter translated into Japanese characters is acceptable).

▲ *Product literature.* Your literature will probably be an existing piece that describes the product you are planning to export. Since this is an initial mailing and the mailing cost may be a factor, the literature can be a summary piece. It may be necessary to attach a label to your current literature or insert a supplemental sheet if additional information, such as metric dimensions and specific uses, will be necessary for the foreign customer to understand your product.

▲ *Bounce-back card.* The card is used to stimulate a response from a potential customer and to provide you with critical information that can be used to screen and qualify the customers. If you use a bounce-back card in your domestic marketing campaign, it may need modifications for use with foreign contacts (e.g., country in the customer's address, *USA* in your return address, or *prepaid postage will not apply*). If you do not currently use such a card, prepare a card or sheet requesting the items of information that you need to screen and evaluate potential customers. The items will normally include:

—Company information
—Contact information and authority to buy/decide
—Bank reference
—Type of entity such as sales agent, distributor, importer, end user, government, manufacturer
—Product need
—When product needed
—Frequency of need
—Quantity needed
—Geographic areas represented
—Your return address, including *USA* and your fax number

The specific questions on your bounce-back card will depend on your product, selected distribution channels, minimum order, and so forth. Coordinate the information on the bounce-back card with your foreign buyer database so you can enter it into the database.

A price list should be included only if you have established a firm market entry price and the sales letter you are sending asks for an immediate order. In most cases you will not provide a price list until you have received a serious inquiry from a potential customer and have identified the customer's position in the distribution network.

A consideration in preparing your promotional materials is weight, since postage is a major cost in large-scale, foreign direct mail campaigns. Limiting the amount of materials included in the mailings and using lightweight but quality paper will reduce your mailing costs.

EPO Promotional Event Materials. If you have signed up for promotional events sponsored by EPOs, materials will have to be prepared for these events. The first-contact materials and inquiry-response materials (see below) will be sufficient in most cases. However, it may be necessary to develop some supplemental materials specific to the event. For example, if you have signed up for a USDOC-sponsored video show you will need to either internationalize your current video or prepare a new video presentation. In most cases, the EPO sponsoring the event will provide you with guidance and direct assistance in preparing for the event.

Developing the Inquiry-Response Materials

Materials developed to respond to the inquiries that the above advertising and direct mail materials generate should allow you to provide an immediate response and to demonstrate your sincere interest in the potential customer's business. Don't wait until you start receiving inquiries in Step 3 of the Trial Run to figure out what your responses will be.

Analyzing the Inquiries. Anticipate a wide range of inquiry types, from those that cannot be understood because they are written in a foreign language to those that are making firm orders for your product. Your response materials must address this range of potential inquiries and consist of several sets of response materials rather than a single set.

The inquiries can be analyzed in two ways in order to determine your level of interest in responding: The type of contact (e.g., agent, distributor, end user, retailer, other), and the sales potential of the inquiry (e.g., can't determine, poor, good, excellent). Put these two sets of analysis factors in a matrix to identify the level of interest you have in each group of responses (e.g., no interest, interested, highly interested). The Inquiry and Response Matrix Worksheet (Worksheet 14) can be used to identify the types of inquiries you will receive and your level of interest in each type.

The next step is to define the response materials needed for each type of response. Again two factors, the types of inquiries and your levels of interest in each, can be used to create a matrix. For each cell in the matrix, list the response materials you will prepare. Worksheet 14 can also be used to prepare these lists. While it is beneficial to develop more than a single response to inquiries, efficiency dictates that you limit your sets of response materials to a reasonable number. For example, for all inquiries in which you have no interest, you may respond with a brief thank-you letter and piece of product literature. For "interested" inquiries, a set of response materials might include an individually typed and signed form letter and a kit of materials for each type of inquiry. And for "high interest" inquiries, you might immediately send a fax saying that a response is in the mail, prepare an individualized letter with a kit of appropriate information, and express mail the response

WORKSHEET 14. Inquiry and Response Matrix

INQUIRY & RESPONSE MATRIX	*FASTRACK*
	Success Through Fast-Track Exporting

Purpose: To categorize foreign inquiries and to plan the response that will be given to each category of inquiry. Directions: For each type of contact and at each level of sales potential, indicate the level of interest you have in the inquiry with 0 equal to no interest, 1 equal to some interest, and 2 equal to high interest. Within each cell, indicate the response materials that will be sent to this category of inquiry.

Company Name/Division _____

Product _____ Target Market _____

Sales Potential	Type of Contact / Level of Interest / Response Materials				
	Agent (A)	Distributor (D)	End User (E)	Retailer (R)	Other (O)
Can't Determine	Interest: 0 1 2 Response:	Interest: 0 1 2 Response:	Interest: 0 1 2 Response:	Interest: 0 1 2 Response:	Interest: 0 1 2 Response:
Poor	Interest: 0 1 2 Response:	Interest: 0 1 2 Response:	Interest: 0 1 2 Response:	Interest: 0 1 2 Response:	Interest: 0 1 2 Response:
Good	Interest: 0 1 2 Response:	Interest: 0 1 2 Response:	Interest: 0 1 2 Response:	Interest: 0 1 2 Response:	Interest: 0 1 2 Response:
Excellent	Interest: 0 1 2 Response:	Interest: 0 1 2 Response:	Interest: 0 1 2 Response:	Interest: 0 1 2 Response:	Interest: 0 1 2 Response:

Notes:

Completed by	Date

090

within twenty-four hours. If you decide to use a bounce-back card as one of your promotional pieces, you will have to include this card in your responses to inquiries from the advertisement and other sources that did not initially receive the card.

The Response Materials. Your response to the potential customer is extremely important. It is critical that you present information in a way that will continue to stimulate interest. You need to be concerned with both the type of information presented and the way in which it is presented.

Response materials that need to be developed are a sales follow-up letter, detailed product literature, background materials on your company, price quotations, and an agent/distributor kit if you are seeking representation in the market.

▲ *Follow-up sales letter.* Based on the response matrix above, you will probably need several letters for the various types of inquiries and your interest levels. This will allow you to individualize and personalize your response. In preparing your letters, assume that the potential customer has opportunities to deal with a number of sellers and is interested in learning how your product will enhance his/her business and profits.

▲ *Detailed product literature.* If the inquirer has already received the direct-mail promotional materials, you may want to respond with a detailed piece of product literature. Depending on your level of interest in the potential customer, this could be anything from a specifications sheet to a catalog.

▲ *Company background information.* Foreign customers are usually much more interested in your company than you might expect. Therefore, include a brief, one-page summary of your company's history and current position in the industry that is written so as to appeal to a foreign reader.

▲ *Quotations.* Export price quotations will have to be prepared in order to respond to inquiries from potential end users and representatives. In international sales your quotation sets forth not only the price of your product but numerous conditions of sale which are not included in a domestic quotation. In addition, in most countries your quotation will become a shorthand sales contract, if the buyer accepts your quotation without alterations, against which your company will be obliged to perform. For these reasons, it is important that you carefully develop your quotation materials so that they include the full terms and conditions for an export sale.

The number of quotations you need to prepare depends on such factors as to whom you intend to sell, whether there are multiple layers in the distribution network, whether you intend to use different shipping terms in your quotations, and whether you want to prepare different quotations for your worldwide and target markets. For example, if you intend to sell to end users and to a single layer in a distribution network, you will need at least two export price quotations. If you also intend to quote FCA or FOB for your worldwide markets and CIP or CIF for your target country market, you will need two additional quotations.

The types of sample quotations, either price lists and/or pro forma invoices, you need to prepare will be determined largely by the characteristics of your product and the needs of your potential customers. For example, if the price of your product is constant, a price list would be useful to a potential customer. However, if the price changes frequently and is usually established through negotiation, a pro forma invoice may be used to finalize the quotation. Frequently, potential customers will need a pro forma invoice to obtain a letter of credit or the foreign exchange required to complete the purchase.

Once you have determined the number and types of export price quotations you will need, prepare the price lists and/or sample pro forma invoices starting with Worksheet 13 prepared earlier in this Step.

If you are preparing one or more export price lists, take into account the adjustments that will have to be made in the price depending on the type of customer to which this price list is directed, discounts for various quantities, and other factors that you normally incorporate into your price lists. Then state your terms: minimum order, payment terms, shipping terms, and effective dates.

If you expect to need pro forma invoices, prepare sample pro forma invoices using your minimum order quantities. A pro forma invoice is prepared on an internationalized version of your commercial invoice, but there are significant differences in the pro forma invoice. For example, on the pro forma invoice you will indicate the following:

- ▲ That the invoice is a pro forma
- ▲ The country of origin of the product
- ▲ Payment terms, for example:

Irrevocable letter of credit in U.S. dollars with beneficiary [*your company's name*] advised by [*your bank and address*] and payable at 30 days' sight by [*your customer's bank*].

- ▲ Ports of export and import and carrier
- ▲ That terms are governed by *Incoterms 1990*
- ▲ Measures and weights in U.S. and metric terms
- ▲ Weight, dimensions, and cubic measure by unit and total order packed for export
- ▲ Product description in conformity with the HS/Schedule B product descriptions and in sufficient detail to allow for easy classification by customs officials
- ▲ Whether the product is new or used
- ▲ Total selling price of product ex works your premises
- ▲ Shipping and related export costs including crating, freight forwarder fees, consular and other fees, bank charges, inland freight and handling, air/ocean freight, and insurance
- ▲ Total invoice amount and shipping terms such as FCA, FOB, CIP, or CIF
- ▲ Estimated shipping date
- ▲ Price valid-through date
- ▲ Certifications such as the Export Administration Regulations destination control statement and your certification that the pro forma invoice is true and correct
- ▲ Your signature and title

Determine the specific U.S. and foreign government requirements for an invoice by consulting one of the export manuals listed in Appendix B and/or your international freight forwarder.

After preparing your price lists and/or sample pro forma invoices, provide copies to your freight forwarder and international banker for their review and comments. Their review will help you finalize price quotation materials that will clearly and accurately communicate your offer to potential foreign buyers.

Agent/Distributor Kit. A special kit should be prepared for response to selected inquiries from potential sales agents and distributors. In addition to the materials mentioned above, the contents of your kit might include:

▲ Product specifications, catalog, and sales aides
▲ Product and process background information
▲ Product samples
▲ Company annual report and other information on your operations, ownership, management, and market position
▲ Information questionnaire
▲ Proposed understandings or representation agreement

The Agent/Distributor Profile (Worksheet 15) can be used to request the information that you will need to properly screen and qualify potential agents and/or distributors. The requested information includes data on the principals, company contacts, company background, the company's interest in representing your company, company facilities in the market, companies and product lines presented, position in the distributorship network, and references.

For the proposed understanding or agreement, you will provide representatives in which you are interested with information on your expectations and commitments. This will require the preparation of two items: (1) A brief statement of proposed understandings for use in starting negotiations with potential representatives and (2) a draft of an agent and/or distributorship agreement that can be used in later negotiations and adjusted to the specific requirements of the laws and practices of your target or any other market.

In preparing your initial statement of proposed understandings, depending on whether the person is an agent or distributor, the following key points might be covered: minimum order and payment terms, commission/discount, territory, position on exclusive representation, training to be provided, advertising and other types of support, and how leads or direct sales into the territory will be handled. You may want to state that these understandings are intended to form the basis of a future agreement, thereby clearly stating that they are *not* an agreement. Or you may want to use these understandings during a trial period and indicate that they will apply only to the first shipment for sales up to a certain amount or until a specified date.

Before drafting your proposed representation agreement, consult the *Commercial Agency* publication and/or the *Guide to International Distributorship Agreements.* These guides will assist you in drafting and negotiating agreements with sales agents and distributors by defining the

(text continues on page 108)

WORKSHEET 15. Agent/Distributor Profile

AGENT / DISTRIBUTOR PROFILE   *FASTRACK*
                                                Success Through Fast-Track Exporting

Thank you for your interest in representing our product. This questionnaire will help our company learn more about your company. The information in this form will be maintained in confidence. Please return the form to:

Company Name _____
  Address _____
  City/Postal Code/State/Country _____
  Telephone _____ Fax _____ Telex _____

Facility Is: ___Headquarters ___Office ___Manufacturing Site ___Warehouse ___Research Center ___Service Center ___Product Showroom

Principal Officers/Owners:
  Name _____ Title _____ Phone _____
  Name _____ Title _____ Phone _____
  Name _____ Title _____ Phone _____

Company Contacts:
  Chief Executive _____ Title _____ English: __Speak __Write
  Sales Manager _____ Title _____ English: __Speak __Write
  Service Manager _____ Title _____ English: __Speak __Write
  Other _____ Title _____ English: __Speak __Write

Company Background:
  Year Founded _____ Number of Employees _____ Type Ownership: __Corporation __Partnership __Proprietorship __Government
  Parent Company _____
  Subsidiary Names _____
  Business Activity: __Commission Agent __Distributor __Wholesaler __Trading Company __Purchasing Agent __Retailer
    __Broker __Manufacturer/Producer __Other (Specify):
  Describe Business Activity _____
  _____
  List Primary Products Represented _____
  _____
  Annual Sales in US Dollars: $ _____ Range: __<$500,000 __<$5 million __<$50 million __>$50 million

Company Interests:
  Why do you want to represent our company? _____
  _____
  In which of our products are you interested? _____
  _____
  What quantities and when needed? _____
  _____
  In which territory are you interested in representing our product? _____
  _____
  Why do you think our product will sell in your market territory? _____
  _____
  What support would you expect from our company? _____
  _____

Agent / Distributor Profile   Page 1

Company Facilities in Market Area:

___Branch Offices ___Manufacturing Sites ___Warehouses ___Research Centers ___Service Centers ___Product Showrooms

Location of Branch Offices and Number of Representatives _____

Location of Warehouses _____

Location of Service Centers and Number of Service People _____

Companies and Product Lines Currently Represented. Include U.S. companies you represent:

| Company Name | Country | Product Lines/Brand Names | Type Representative | | Since | Annual |
			Agent	Dist.	Year	Sales
			Yes	Yes		US$
			Yes	Yes		US$
			Yes	Yes		US$
			Yes	Yes		US$
			Yes	Yes		US$
			Yes	Yes		US$
			Yes	Yes		US$
			Yes	Yes		US$

Do Any of the Above Product Lines Compete With Our Products? ___Yes ___No If yes, which products? _____

Are Any of the Above Product Lines Complementary With Our Products? ___Yes ___No If yes, which products? _____

Distribution Network:

In what territories does your company provide distribution? _____

What is your position in the distribution network? _____

What distribution channels do you use? _____

What customer segments do you serve? _____

Number of Customers _____ Payment terms normally offered to customers _____

What trade shows do you attend related to our product line? _____

Why do you believe you will be successful selling our product? _____

References:

Bank _____ Address _____

Business _____ Address _____

Contact _____ Title _____ Fax _____

Business _____ Address _____

Contact _____ Title _____ Fax _____

In the initial trial period, will you accept:

Nonexclusive agreement: __Yes __No   Payment by Letter of Credit: __Yes __No   Sales performance objectives: __Yes __No

Please attach the following: __ Annual Report __ Financial Information __ Company History __ Copy of Your Company's Letterhead __ Business Card __ Background Information on Key Personnel

Thank you for completing this profile and helping our Company learn more about your Company.

Completed by _____ Title _____

Telephone _____ Fax _____ Date _____

Agent / Distributor Profile

Page 2

090

elements of international representation agreements, pointing out the most important questions you will face and the most likely answers, and highlighting the risks you will face.

Then consult your international attorney for help in drafting your representation agreements. Foreign practices and laws regarding sales agents and distributors and the obligations that will be placed upon you and your representative differ greatly from U.S. law. You simply cannot ignore these legal differences without risking significant financial implications or being prevented from selling in the market in the future. Furthermore, avoiding written agreements will not relieve you of these obligations and may, in many cases, increase your risks because you will be totally unaware of their existence until it is too late. One of the risks you will face is the cost of terminating (even within the terms of an agreement) an agent or distributor relationship since the laws of many countries make termination either extremely difficult or expensive. If this is the case in your target market, it is better that you know it now rather than a year from now. Your international attorney can alert you to such risks and frequently advise you on ways to get around them or at least minimize the risk. For example, in a country where termination is difficult, you may not want to grant the representative the exclusive right to represent your product.

In drafting a representation agreement, keep the following in mind:

▲ *Legal environment.* Your agreement must be within the bounds of the export market's laws regarding employment, registration, antitrust, intellectual property rights, termination and indemnification, competition after termination, and taxes. Your agreement must also take into account U.S. laws that regulate your activities abroad such as the Export Administration Act and Foreign Corrupt Practices Act.

▲ *Business environment.* The way things are done in the export market needs to be taken into account. These conventions, right down to the meanings that are given to words, may be very different from your experiences and must be considered in drafting your agreement.

▲ *Agreement elements.* Your agreement will include the expiration date, products represented, territory represented, exclusivity (i.e., product, territory, customer), representative's obligations (e.g., government approvals, minimum order, payment, performance objectives, promotion, sub-representatives, inventory, competitive lines, reporting, use of trademark), your obligations (e.g., training and delivery), direct sales and leads, commission/discount, termination, post-termination (e.g., stock and after-sales service), and resolution of disputes.

Reviewing Related Materials

Prior to implementing Step 3, review other materials that are related to your export promotion effort to determine if changes are needed in order to accommodate export sales. For example, if your sales acknowledgment form has the terms of sale printed on it, these terms may need to be altered to reflect specific terms that are unique to an export sale.

Review any videos that you use in your domestic sales promotional efforts to see if adjustments need to be made for use in export markets. You may need to develop new video presentations in order to effectively introduce your company and product to foreign customers.

Update the Export Readiness Action Plan

The Export Readiness Action Plan outlines detailed tasks needed to prepare your organization and product for export, and during Step 2 you have addressed those tasks. Review and update your action plan to ensure that all tasks have either been completed or are in the process of being completed.

Step 2 has taken you a long way down the export fast track, and your export team is at the starting block. Your organization's export readiness has increased and you've brought on board the international expertise of several EPOs, determined your channels of distribution, established your market entry prices and terms, and built your foreign buyer database. Your promotion campaign has been planned and all your preparations have been completed.

Step 3:

Enter the Trial Market

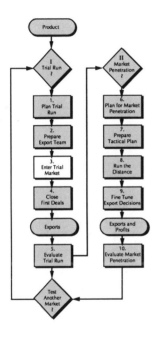

You're ready to go! Implement your promotional campaigns. Participate in EPO promotional events. And start responding to inquiries from your target market and from around the world.

Step 1's planning and Step 2's preparation activities have prepared your export team for this day, and you will soon be progressing to Step 4 and closing your first export deals.

Implement the Promotional Campaign

Submit your new internationalized advertising copy to *Commercial News USA*, *Showcase USA*, *Buyer Alert*, and the other U.S. and target-market publications in which you have decided to advertise. If you've decided to internationalize your current advertisements, submit those changes. Your Trial Run advertising campaign may be very minimal in terms of resource commitment, but it will introduce your product to worldwide markets and generate inquiries that will get you into export markets.

Initiating your direct-contact campaign should be as easy as hitting the GO key on your word processor. In Step 2 you built your foreign contact database and prepared your initial contact sales letter, summary product literature, and bounce-back card. Now, use mail-merge to generate individualized mailings to your potential foreign customers. Send your initial contact materials by airmail. If the number of pieces being mailed is large and mailing costs are a factor, check out the special mailing services of the U.S. Post Office's International Surface Airlift (ISAL) Program and similar services of private airmail consolidator and remailer organizations for lower airmail rates.

Getting a response from your foreign contacts may take a long time and a lot of follow-up by you. For example, it may take as long as a month for your letter to be delivered in some countries. There are countries in which the mail is frequently lost by the postal service. In other countries a foreign contact with an interest in your product may take several months to get around to answering your letter.

Therefore, you should follow up your initial mailing with a second mailing to those foreign contacts that have not responded within thirty days. For contacts that have been identified as high-potential prospects, a telephone call or fax might be a cost-effective and efficient means of generating the responses you want.

Participate in EPO Promotional Events

If you signed up for EPO promotional events—catalog/video shows, buying mission visits, foreign trade shows, matchmaker delegations, trade missions, and other special promotion programs—participate in these events and generate inquiries and contacts. Use the items you developed for the direct-contact promotional campaign as well as supplemental materials appropriate for the specific event.

Respond to Inquiries and Leads

Inquiries will be generated by your promotional activities, and leads will be disseminated to you by various EPOs with whom you have had contact. You are now prepared to screen and make timely responses to the potential foreign customers.

Use Worksheet 14 (Step 2) to start the screening process. If, for example, you receive an inquiry from an agent who appears to have no sales potential and you coded that cell in the matrix for a "0" or not interested response, place that response in a pile marked "0A." In the same manner, if you receive an inquiry from an agent who appears to have excellent sales potential and you coded that cell in the matrix for a "2" or high interest response, place that response in a pile marked "2A." By sorting your inquiries consistent with the Inquiry and Response Matrix, it will be easy to select the proper response materials to be sent to the foreign contact.

Compare your coded inquiries and leads to the response materials you specified on the Inquiry and Response Matrix, and select the appropriate response materials from the letters and other items you prepared in Step 2. Because of the planning and preparation prior to the implementation of your promotion campaign, you are in a position to provide timely and responsive replies to your potential foreign customers.

When it is necessary to respond with pricing information, use the price lists you prepared in Step 2 or prepare an individualized pro forma invoice. For example, if you anticipated making sales only to first-level distributors and prepared your price lists accordingly, you'll have to prepare a special quotation for a retailer. Otherwise, you will be forgoing the opportunity to take a larger profit margin on the sale. The Customer Export Quotation Worksheet (see Worksheet 16) will help you transform the market entry export price, established in Step 2, into a formal price quotation or pro forma invoice for a specific customer. Worksheet 16 also serves to document the basis for your quotation and records pertinent information on the buyer, the product and its export limitations, payment terms, shipping weights and dimensions, units ordered, shipping terms, transportation mode, and all the elements that are required to determine the total amount being quoted. Maintain the worksheet in the customer's file.

Maintain the Database

Maintaining and continuing to build the foreign buyer database is an ongoing process, and the pieces of information collected during the Trial Run will eventually create a more complete picture of potential customers in the target and other markets.

You can also use the database to track the results of your promotional efforts whether they be through advertising, direct mail promotion, or other methods. For example, you can use the responses to your promotions to assess the most productive sources of contacts. This information will be valuable if you proceed to Phase II in the target market or initiate Trial Runs in other target markets.

WORKSHEET 16. Customer Export Quotation

CUSTOMER EXPORT QUOTATION

FASTRACK ℠
Success Through Fast-Track Exporting

Purpose: To assist in preparing and documenting a price quotation or pro forma invoice for a specific customer. Directions: Refer to the Market Entry Export Price & Terms worksheet for unit cost information. Retain this worksheet in your customer's record.

Prepared For _____
Address _____
City/Code/State/Country _____

| Fax | Tlx | Their Reference | Our Reference | Date |

Product _____ HS/Schedule B Code _____
   New or Used _____ Country of Origin _____
   Import Permit # Required: __Yes __No   Number _____ Expires _____
   US Export License Limitations _____

Product Unit _____
   Shipping Basis: __Weight or __Measure? __US Tons or __Metric Tons? __Lb or __Kg? __Foot or __Meter?
   Unit: Net Weight _____ Gross Weight _____ Dimensions _____ Cubic Measure _____

Order Export Crated _____ Total # Units _____
   Points of Origin _____ Delivery _____ Destination _____
   Total Net Weight _____ Total Gross Weight _____
   Total Dimensions _____ Total Cubic Measure _____
   Explain Crating, Etc. _____

Transportation Mode: __Ocean __Rail __Air __Intermodal __Truck Delivery Time Constraints _____
   Freight Rate _____ Based on: __FCL __LCL __BBLK __Deck __Under Deck __Ventilation __Refrigeration
   Rate Minimum _____ Date to be Shipped _____ Shipped Via _____
   Container Dimensions _____ Container Cubic Measure _____

Payment Terms: __Cash in Advance __LC __DP __DA __30 days __60 days __90 days _____days __Open Account __Other:
   Explanation: _____
   Currency _____ Assumed Exchange Rate _____ Price Valid Through _____

Shipping Incoterms 1990:   FCA   FOB   CIP   CIF   Other: Explanation

Pricing Factors	Named Place	Notes on Costs	Amount	Comments
Unit Export Price EX WORKS	_____		_____	
Adjustment in Financing Fees		+/- _____		
Adjustment in Risk Insurance		+/- _____		
Adjustment in Banking Fee		+/- _____		
Adjustment in Other Costs:		+/- _____		
Unit Adjusted Export Price EX WORKS	_____		_____	
Distributors's Discount @ _____% of EXW		- _____		
Unit Distributor's Export EX WORKS	_____			
Export Price EX WORKS	_____	# Units Ordered X_____	= _____	

Customer Export Quotation   Page 1

Copyright Export Resource Associates, Inc., 1990

Worksheet 16 (*continued*)

Pricing Factors	Named Place	Notes on Costs	Amount	Comments
Export Crating/ Marking Costs			+ _____	
Freight Forwarder Fees			+ _____	_____
Loading			+ _____	
Cartage			+ _____	
Inland Freight by _____ to	_____		+ _____	_____
Unloadng Costs at	_____		+ _____	
Terminal Costs			+ _____	
Demurrage Costs			+ _____	
Special Ship Loading Costs			+ _____	
Consular Invoice Fees			+ _____	
Certificate Fees			+ _____	
Other Costs:			+ _____	
Export Price __FREE CARRIER	_____		_____	
or __FREE ON BOARD	_____		_____	
or _____	_____		_____	
Freight Costs & Surcharges to	_____		+ _____	_____
Transport Insurance Costs @ 110% of CIP/CIF		Type _____ Base _____	+ _____	_____
Other Costs:			+ _____	
Export Price __CARRIAGE INS PAID	_____		_____	
or __ COST INS FREIGHT	_____		_____	
or _____	_____		_____	
Import Duties and Taxes			+ _____	
Custom House Broker Fees			+ _____	
Foreign Inland Freight Costs			+ _____	
Foreign Banking Fees			+ _____	
Other Costs:			+ _____	
Import Price DELIVERED DUTY PAID				

Statement of Price and Terms:

Notes:

Completed by	Title
Customer Export Quotation	Page 2

090

Step 4:

Close the First Deals

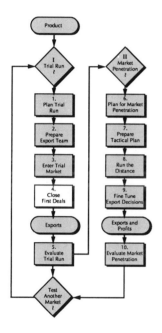

Closing your first Trial Run export deals is about to become a reality. The finish line is within sight.

The knowledge and expertise of every member of your export team will be called upon during Step 4 in order to achieve a smooth and successful export operation. Your investment in training and preparing the team members during Step 2 will pay off as you close the export deals. The contacts you established in Step 3 are now narrowed down to the high-potential contacts with whom you will consider doing business.

It's now time to assess these contacts and identify your best prospect, negotiate and finalize the representation agreements and sales, get the product produced and shipped, and collect from your new foreign customers.

Assess the Contacts

Qualifying Representatives

The follow-up information you receive from potential agents and distributors will provide you with a highly interested pool of contacts in the worldwide and target markets. Use this information to assess each representative's qualifications and ability to represent you in their market.

Conduct a second screening of prospective representatives using the Agent/Distributor Profile Worksheets and supplemental information returned by the representatives. The primary purpose of the second screening is to qualify the representatives whose experiences and expertise in the market match with your objectives and to identify a group of best-prospect candidates. A secondary purpose is to learn more about the export market—the sales potential for your product, the distribution channels and layers in the network, and the customer segments. Thus, the Agent/Distributor Profile Worksheet is also a market intelligence tool that will increase your understanding of the market.

The profiles allow you to screen out representatives who fall outside your general area of interest. Reviewing the profiles will also raise additional questions about the individual representatives as well as the market itself, which must be clarified before you can finalize the matching process. For example, it may be difficult to determine whether a prospect is an agent, distributor, or one of the various permutations of these types of representatives and where the representative is positioned in the layers of the distribution network. Obtaining the answers to these questions may require follow-up contact with the prospects or a call to your USDOC District Office, state EPO, or trade association.

CASE EXAMPLE: Wahl Clipper Corporation, the electric hair clippers manufacturer, makes a critical distinction between importers and distributors. Importers sell all kinds of products to all types of people. Wahl looks for distributors who sell directly to their customers—and specifically, who sell its kind of product into its market segments. This frequently requires more than one distributor in a market because the company sells into several market segments. Then Wahl builds a strong, long-term relationship with that distributor and indirectly with the distributor's customer.

When you have narrowed the prospects down to a group of best-prospect candidates, use the Agent/Distributor Evaluation Worksheet (see Worksheet 17) to evaluate your best-prospect candidates. What are the representative's strengths and weaknesses; what percentage of its total business would your product line represent; does the representative's handing of its current product lines demonstrate that it would be successful with your product; does the representative have the capacity to market, distribute, finance, and provide after-service for your product? Answering these questions will help you determine if the services of the prospective agent or distributor match your company's objectives and needs in the export market.

Approach the most promising sales agents and distributors and ask them to provide additional information on how they propose to market and distribute your product in their market. Ask for a preliminary outline of a marketing plan for your product with projected sales volumes. Also ask them to address the specific issues or concerns you have. For example: Will the representative provide for the translation of your materials? If repair parts are needed on site, will the representative maintain such parts in its inventory? If the representative's sales force or territory is too small to support your long-term objectives in the market, will the representative provide for the needed expansion?

If importers in a particular export market are required to register, find out if the representative is currently registered.

The above screenings and evaluations of prospective representatives narrow your list of candidates down to a select few.

CASE EXAMPLE: Goguen Industries has established firm criteria for evaluating potential representatives. The representative must sell a complementary product line into the same industry segment, have at least ten employees, have good trade and bank references, and be checked out by the commercial officer in the U.S. embassy or consulate. Goguen believes in a well-structured contract based on good legal counsel and an accurate translation. However, in order to skirt the legal issue of representatives becoming employees and the resulting costs of termination, the company likes to start the relationship off with a handshake and a trial period. This gives both parties a chance to get to know each other and make an educated decision about a long-term representation agreement.

WORKSHEET 17. Agent/Distributor Evaluation

AGENT / DISTRIBUTOR EVALUATION	***FASTRACK***
	Success Through Fast-Track Exporting

Purpose: To evaluate best-prospect agent/distributor candidates. Directions: Refer to information provided on the Agent / Distributor Profile worksheet.

Company Name _____
Address _____
City/Postal Code/State/Country _____
Telephone _____ Fax _____ Telex _____
Contact _____ Title _____

Products Seeking to Represent _____
Quantities / How Frequently / When Needed _____
Territories _____
Information received from and reputation with third parties:
___Companies Represented _____
___Bank Reference _____
___Business References _____
___Customer References _____
___Credit Checks _____
Representative's Business
Primary Business Activity _____
Strengths _____
Weaknesses _____
Match with our export objectives in market? _____
Percent of representative's business our product would represent? _____
Does the representative's handling of its current product lines:
Demonstrate ability to sell all current lines? __Yes __No _____
Pose a conflict of interest with our product   __Yes __No _____
Does the representative have the capacity to:
Effectively market our product? __Yes __No _____
Sell to key territories? __Yes __No _____
Properly position itself in the distribution network? __Yes __No _____
Use the best distribution channels? __Yes __No _____
Sell to the key customer segments? __Yes __No _____
Offer competitive payment terms to the customers? __Yes __No _____
Translate our product literature? __Yes __No _____
Maintain adequate inventories? __Yes __No _____
Provide effective after-sale service? __Yes __No _____
Is the representative's financial position strong? __Yes __No _____
How adequate is the proposed marketing plan for our product in the market? __Very Adequate __Adequate __Inadequate __None
Projected Sales _____
Does the representative speak English? __Well __Little __None   Write English? __Well __Little __None
Will the representative be a good fit with our company? __Yes __No __Maybe
Does the representative understand our business and product? __Well __Little __None
Issues That Have Been Resolved:

__Trial period	__**Payment term**	__**Marketing plan**	__Warranty/claims	__Leads/direct sales
__Products represented	__Sales performance obj.	__Mktg/sales aids	__Trademarks/etc.	__Registration/approvals
__Territory	__Minimum purchases	__Training	__Competitive lines	__Other:
__Duration of agreement	__Comm./discount/price	__After-sale service	__Reports	
__Exclusive representation	__Inventory level	__Quality control	__Termination/indemnities	

Comments:

Completed by   Date

090

Checking References

Check the references of prospective customers with whom you want to do business whether they be end users, retailers, or representatives. Two of the most convenient sources for obtaining reference checks are your international banker and the USDOC District Office. However, your most reliable source of references will probably be other exporters in your industry.

Your international banker will need the name and address of the potential customer's bank so that it can telex the customer's bank with a request for a reference. The customer's bank may respond with certain information—such as the number of years the customer has been with the bank, the customer's line of credit or some indication of the size of transactions in which the customer typically engages, and a summary statement of the bank's satisfaction with the customer—but not with detailed financial information. In addition to reference checks with the customer's foreign bank, your international banker may also have access to other sources of information not readily available to you, (e.g., Export-Import Bank of the United States).

The USDOC District Office can provide you with information on foreign customers through the *World Traders Data Reports* service. These background reports provide a thorough assessment of the potential customer's reputation in the market and a recommendation on whether the party would be a good trade partner and on what basis. The reports include information on key officers, number of employees, product lines, sales volume, bank and trade references, reputation, and other current information that may be available. The turnaround time on these reports can take up to ninety days if the company is not in the USDOC's database.

If your prospective customer is currently doing business with U.S. suppliers, these firms are going to be your most important source of information. The U.S. supplier can provide you with valuable information on the customer's paying habits and, in the case of potential representatives, how effective they have been in promoting the supplier's products. This word-of-mouth checking will provide you with some of your best information on potential representatives.

CASE EXAMPLE: Anitec Image, Inc., manufactures graphic arts silver-sensitized film and paper for a global market. When the company looks for a distributor, word-of-mouth is its most important research tool for locating the right organization. This means talking to people in the industry, reading local newspapers and trade publications from the market, and an on-site visit. The criteria the company looks for in a distributor include integrity, market knowledge, reputation, ability to maintain an inventory, and a stable financial position.

There are numerous sources for detailed credit checks. Dun & Bradstreet is a U.S. source for reports on customers in many countries. The publication, *Guide to Agencies Providing Foreign Credit Information,* lists foreign sources of credit information.

Visiting Best Prospects

A visit to further assess the credentials and operations of your best-prospect customers, especially agents or distributors in your target market, is highly desirable. But foreign visits will drive up the cost of your Trial Run and, if they are to be fruitful, will require a great deal of advance planning and preparation.

There is no argument that there are benefits to be gained from a visit with a potential customer. Your impressions of a potential distributor's operations, for example, will undoubtedly be very different after a visit than before—the staff, equipment, and facilities could be much more impressive than the distributor was able to convey through written communication, or they may not be there at all! The potential distributor's position in the layers of the distribution network and the customers to which it sells may be totally different than you had understood before the visit. A visit will increase your knowledge of the market. A visit will allow you to determine if you can work with the prospective distributor, lay the foundation for your mutual venture, and develop a feeling of comfort and confidence in the relationship.

You will have to weigh the costs and potential benefits of a visit to your target market and determine when to schedule such visits. Now? When you finalize the first representation agreement or sale? When you start on-site training? After sales achieve a significant level? When you can coordinate customer visits with a trade show?

If you decide to visit the target market during the Trial Run, the initial planning should begin well in advance of the departure date and you should have clearly defined objectives and an itinerary. Proper advance planning will not only maximize the effectiveness of your visit but also greatly minimize the costs. Planning factors to be considered include the length of the trip, timing, surrounding countries that should be visited, the type of information to be collected, individuals or organizations with whom to schedule meetings, passport and visa applications to be processed, travel and hotel arrangements to be made, appropriate business cards, and appropriate gifts for key individuals.

Allocate sufficient time to prepare for your visit to the Trial Run market. If you will be making a presentation, be sure to clarify your audiovisual needs prior to departing, since it may be difficult to locate the equipment you'll require. Learn something about the business practices of the target market before you leave home. Each country, of course, has its own business customs. However, there are a few universal customs that you will want to follow. Two publications, *Going International* and *Do's and Taboos Around the World* as well as publications in your export library such as *Culturegrams* will help you prepare yourself. Travel books can also be helpful, and they are usually updated annually.

Determine whether you will need a temporary export license from the USDOC Bureau of Export Administration and whether an ATA Carnet, which is a special customs document designed to simplify customs procedures for taking commercial samples or professional equipment abroad, can be used. The publication *Export Licensing Checklist* describes the process for obtaining a temporary export license. Information on the ATA Carnet can be obtained from your freight forwarder or from the United States Council for International Business (see Appendix A for contact information).

Identifying Your Preferred Partners

When you reach the point where you are ready to select your partner or partners in the target country and worldwide markets, clarify specifically the desired profile of your preferred partner. Then compare your best-prospect customers to the desired profile and select the partner with whom you want to initiate negotiations.

Your partners may include end users, retailers, sales agents, and/or distributors depending on the channels of distribution you select in each market.

If you are selecting an agent or distributor, use the Agent/Distributor Assessment Worksheet (see Worksheet 18) to establish your criteria, define your desired profile, and summarize the evaluation of each of your best prospect's qualifications. The comparison criteria should include the following:

- ▲ Market objectives
- ▲ Company size and characteristics
- ▲ Interest in your product
- ▲ Facilities
- ▲ Companies represented
- ▲ Product lines
- ▲ Distribution network and channels
- ▲ Customers
- ▲ Reputation
- ▲ Match with your organization and modes of operation
- ▲ Ability to sell your line and existing lines
- ▲ Ability to introduce and market your product
- ▲ Ability to stock inventory and provide after-sale service
- ▲ Financial stability

During the course of your contact with prospective representatives you identified their positions on issues that will be important elements of the eventual representation agreement you will negotiate. In Step 2 you prepared an agent/distributor kit that included either your proposed statement of understanding or a draft representation agreement. Assess the degree to which your positions on the agreement match those of the potential representatives. The extent of your agreement on these important matters will be a factor in your assessment.

Your summary assessment has now brought you to a preferred set of partners—end users, retailers, sales agents, representatives—for the target market as well as for other worldwide markets. It's now time to finalize your Trial Run representation and sales agreements.

WORKSHEET 18. Agent/Distributor Assessment

AGENT / DISTRIBUTOR ASSESSMENT	═══*FASTRACK*.
	Success Through Fast-Track Exporting

Purpose: To define the profile of your preferred representative and to compare your best-prospect candidates. Directions: Check the assessment criteria to be used and add other important criteria. Enter the profile of your preferred representative. Enter the name of your best-prospect candidates. Rate each candidate against the preferred profile in the Score column using a 0-10 scale with 0 for a no information and 10 for a high rating. Compute the Representative Index Rating.

Company Name/Division _____

Target Market _____ Seeking: ☐ Agent ☐ Distributor

Assessment Criteria	Preferred Representative Profile	Score	Score	Score	Score	Score
__Our market objectives						
__English capabilities						
__Years in business						
__Primary business activity						
__Sales volume/growth						
__Product to be represented						
__Order quantities/frequency						
__Commission/discount/price						
__Territories						
__Facility locations/types						
__Sales/service/etc. personnel						
__References US companies						
__References customers						
__References credit						
__Competitive product lines						
__Complementary product lines						
__Distribution network position						
__Distribution channels used						
__Key customer segments sold to						
__Ability to sell current lines						
__Ability to market our product						
__Strong financial position						
__Proposed mkt plan/sales proj.						
__Trial period/duration						
__Exclusive						
__Payment/other terms						
__Inventory levels						
__After-sales service						
__Warranty/claims						
__Trademark/patents/etc.						
__Termination/indemnities						
__Other:						
Total Score						
Number of Criteria Scored						
Summary Representative Index Rating = (Score) / (# Criteria)						

Note: Critical criteria may be given double weight by (a) multiplying the criterion's score by two and (b) increasing the Number of Criteria Scored by one for each criterion given double weight.

DECISION: Which agent/distributor is the preferred partner for this market? _____
Rationale:

Completed by _____ Date _____

090

Finalize Representation Agreements

In those export markets where you made the decision to use a representative channel of distribution, negotiate and finalize the representation agreements with your preferred agents or distributors.

Go back to your international attorney and review your draft representation agreement based on your increased knowledge of the specific markets, the requests of your preferred partners, and the laws and customs of the particular markets. Reread the *Commercial Agency* and *Guide to International Distributorship Agreement* publications. Then, prepare individual agreements for each representative. These agreements should be consistent with your Trial Run objective in each market.

Make sure that the Trial Run representation agreements do not lock your company into an arrangement that will be difficult or costly to change at a later date. For example, you may find that the preferred representative is ineffective in introducing your product into the market or that the representative channel of distribution is not your most effective channel if you decide to proceed to Market Penetration at a later point. Therefore, draft an agreement that will accommodate a trial period (for example, nonexclusive representation, payment by letter of credit, and sales performance objectives) during which the initial relationship will be tested. That will provide you with the long-term flexibility to alter or terminate the relationship in favor of a more effective Market Penetration channel of distribution.

The primary issues to be negotiated with the representative include:

- ▲ Products to be represented
- ▲ Territory
- ▲ Duration of agreement
- ▲ Exclusive representation
- ▲ Payment terms
- ▲ Sales performance objectives
- ▲ Minimum purchases
- ▲ Discounts/commissions and prices
- ▲ Inventory levels
- ▲ Marketing plans
- ▲ Marketing, advertising, sales support and aids
- ▲ Training
- ▲ After-sales service

   ▲ Quality control
   ▲ Warranties and claims
   ▲ Trademarks, patents, copyrights, and trade secrets
   ▲ Competitive lines
   ▲ Reports
   ▲ Termination and indemnities
   ▲ Leads from and direct sales into the territory

Other issues that might need to be negotiated include: government approvals; licenses; export control laws; *force majeure*; translations; location clauses; passover payments; new or old products; orders for discontinued products and parts thereof; insurance; repair manuals and parts; renewal clauses; registration fees; trade shows and demonstrations; loaned equipment and stock; assignability; choice of law; arbitration; disclosure or reporting of infringements; notification of changes in law affecting agreements; and modification of agreements by authorities.

The objective is to negotiate an agreement with each representative that ensures both parties long-term profitability in the market, fosters a cooperative and supportive relationship, minimizes the potential for misunderstandings, and provides a method for addressing differences that may arise in the future. For example, you need to assure the representative a large enough territory to make the sales effort profitable while small enough to ensure an aggressive selling effort. You will also need to assure the representative that it will be able to recoup the time and expense involved in establishing your product in the market.

Your representatives' successes are your successes, so negotiate and finalize agreements with which your representative, your attorney, and you feel comfortable.

Sell, Produce, Ship, and Collect

Whether you are dealing with end users, retailers, sales agents, or distributors in worldwide or the target markets, the Trial Run fast track leads you to the export sale. You must now finalize the export sale, produce and ship the product, and collect from the foreign customer.

Your export team has been planning for this day. Every member has been kept updated on the developments that led up to the receipt of these export sales, has pinpointed potential problems and solutions along the way, and is now ready to move into action.

Your international freight forwarder and international banker have been selected and are ready to help. You have maintained contact with your EPOs and know when to call on them for assistance.

Your export library is set up and includes *A Basic Guide to Exporting*, *Incoterms 1990*, and *Overseas Business Reports* ready for your use. In addition, you should consider ordering the *Unz & Co. Export Management Control System* (a set of standard forms for exporters) and either ordering or finding access to one of the export manuals listed in Appendix B.

Finalizing the Sale

On the basis of your price list or pro forma invoice and any subsequent negotiations, your foreign customer and sales department (in coordination with your export team) have finalized the sale—quantity, payment terms, shipping/trade terms, transportation mode, price, and other specifics of your sale. Assume that the sale includes the following agreements:

▲ *Order.* One container load of product
▲ *Payment terms.*

> An irrevocable letter of credit in U.S. dollars with beneficiary as [*your company's name*] advised by [*your bank's name and address*] and payable at thirty days' sight by [*your customer's bank*].

▲ *Shipping/trade terms.*

> CIP to [*destination point in customer's county*].

▲ *Shipping mode.* Multimodal

Now, let's go through a typical sale and address some of the specific questions you might face.

▲ *How does the letter of credit really work?* The payment terms, a 30-day letter of credit, will involve the following flow of activities. Your customer (the applicant) instructs its bank (the issuing bank) to issue a letter of credit in favor of you (the beneficiary). The customer's bank asks your bank (the advising bank) to transmit the letter of credit to you. Then you ship the product and present the letter of credit, required documentation, and 30-day after-sight draft (a demand for payment addressed to the customer's bank and signed by you) to your bank (the advising and negotiating bank). Your bank checks the documents against the letter of credit and sends the documents and draft to the customer's bank. The customer's bank reviews the documents, accepts the draft, and notifies your bank of the acceptance of the draft and the maturity date of the accepted draft (thirty days from the date the customer's bank sights the draft). Your bank advises you of the acceptance by the customer's bank and the maturity date of the draft. In the meantime, the customer's bank releases the documents to the customer who uses the documents to clear the goods through customs and obtain delivery of the shipment. At the maturity date and upon receipt of the funds from the customer's bank, your bank credits your account for the amount of the draft.

▲ *How does a CIP container shipment work?* The shipment of one container using CIP (Carriage and Insurance Paid To) anticipates the use of multimodal transportation—in this case we will assume rail to the coast and transfer to a ship. CIP means that you will contract for and pay the transportation and cargo insurance to an agreed point at the named place of destination (e.g., the port in your customer's country). Thus, you will pay and invoice your customer for the total selling price of the product ex works plus the shipping, insurance, and related costs. You will obtain the U.S. export license and clear the shipment through U.S. Customs, and your customer will be responsible for clearing the shipment for import. When you deliver the loaded container to the first carrier (the rail carrier), your customer has *accepted* the shipment and bears all risks of loss and damage from that time forward. Thus your cost and risk terminate at different points—cost at the named destination in the customer's country and risk at the delivery to the first carrier in the United States.

▲ *What paperwork starts the process?* The sales department will typically receive a *purchase order* from the customer and respond with an internationalized *order acknowledgement* or *sales confirmation* form and instructions to assist the customer in completing the application for the letter of credit. A point of caution, however: There is a potential hazard with the forms since the customer's purchase order and your responding form may have contradictory sales terms and conditions. If this is the case you will have to decide either to negotiate the differences with the customer or to accept the risks created by the differing terms.

Your international banker will receive the *letter of credit* from your customer's bank and send you the letter of credit and a notification letter advising you that a letter of credit has been issued in your favor. The letter of credit is a major hazard zone, and it must be carefully reviewed by your international banker, freight forwarder, and selected members of the export team. Determine that the letter of credit is consistent with your sales agreement and that you can comply with all provisions of the document down to dotting the *i*'s and crossing the *t*'s. Logic does not apply when your customer's bank is looking for discrepancies; the bank pays on correct documents rather than the underlying transaction; if the documents are not 100 percent correct, the customer's bank does not have to pay under the letter of credit. For example, your street name may be misspelled on the letter of credit; this can prevent you from collecting; therefore, a solution must be discussed with your international banker at the time you receive the letter of credit. You may not be able to meet the shipping date on the letter of credit, in which case you will have to request that the customer initiate an amendment to the letter of credit. The amount on the letter of credit may not include all the shipping charges that will appear on your commercial invoice, thus requiring your customer to initiate an amendment to the letter of credit. For detailed information on letters of credit and the relationship between your customer, your customer's bank, your bank, and you, refer to the publication *Guide to Documentary Credit Operations.* The guide describes letter of credit transactions and contains the "Uniform Customs and Practices for Documentary Credits," the universal standard for letters of credit throughout the world.

In your initial visit to your USDOC District Office, you determined whether a validated export license was required to export your product from the United States and, if so, to which countries. If such a license is required for the country to which you are shipping, the *Application for Export License* must now be completed by your staff or freight forwarder and submitted to the USDOC Bureau of Export Administration. Consult your copy of the *Export Administration Regulations* for the procedures for processing your application, and contact your USDOC District Office or the Bureau of Export Administration's Export Counseling Division if you need assistance. The validated license is granted on a case-by-case basis for a single transaction of either one or multiple shipments. The Bureau of Export Administration has an Export License Application and Information Network (ELAIN) for electronic submission of applications.

Electronic submission reduces the time it takes to obtain an export license. However, your first validated export license will probably be submitted on hard copy and a minimum of thirty days should be allowed to obtain approval. You should note that the validated export license is one of the hazard zones in exporting, so learn the rules and comply with them. The federal government is making great strides in reducing the controls on the export of U.S. products and, while this is reducing your exposure to the hazards of export licensing, they are still there.

CASE EXAMPLE: Cambridge Products, Inc., produces patented livestock feed additives and a mold inhibiting product. When Cambridge started exporting, the company had very little international experience. Throughout the initial export stage, Cambridge relied heavily on the USDOC District Office and the company's banker to help them through the transactions. Every time a new order came in the company used the USDOC. The banker helped get the company through the registration approvals in the foreign market and the shipping and closing process.

Producing and Shipping the Product

Production of the order can begin (if the product is not in stock) when you know that you can fulfill all your obligations under the terms of the sale and letter of credit. Throughout the following process, you will want to refer to one of the export manuals (see Appendix B) for specific guidance and/or rely on your freight forwarder for direction on what documents are required and how they are to be prepared.

Your freight forwarder will now book your shipment with the carrier and make arrangements for special export packing, containers, cartage, and other services you will need.

Once the product has been produced and is ready to go, pack the product in the container for shipment. If any preshipment inspection is required under the terms of your sale, arrange the inspections with the specified independent parties and obtain the *certificates of inspection.*

Your export team will prepare the internationalized commercial invoice, packing slip, and shipper's letter of instructions to the freight forwarder.

▲ *The commercial invoice.* This must contain all the details of the agreement and meet all the specifications of the letter of credit. For example, the description of the product must be exactly as stated in the letter of credit. The invoice must contain the appropriate destination control statement as required by the *Export Administration Regulations* and other needed certifications as required by your letter of credit. The country of import may require specific information that must be included in the invoice, and these requirements will be noted in the export manual or provided to you by your freight forwarder. Since your customer will in most cases use a commercial invoice to clear the shipment through customs, the description of the product must be detailed enough to allow customs officials to classify the product for tariff purposes. The invoice may also be used to establish the value upon which the duty will be paid; thus, the total selling price must be clear and shipping and related costs must be broken out separately.

▲ *The packing slip.* This will be required only if there is more than one container or packaged unit included in the shipment. The packing slip indicates the items included in each container or package and the markings on each. This document must be consistent with the letter of credit and commercial invoice in every respect.

▲ *The shipper's letter of instructions.* This letter authorizes the freight forwarder to act as your forwarding agent and specifies the terms and conditions of the sale and other detailed information the forwarder needs in order to proceed with the shipping and related arrangements and paperwork.

You will now notify your freight forwarder that the container is packed and that it and the following documents are ready: the letter of credit, commercial invoice, packing slip, shipper's letter of instructions, and certificates of inspection. From this point on, your international freight forwarder will take the lead in getting your paperwork completed and shipment delivered to your customer.

Customs invoices, consular invoices, and certificates of origin will be prepared by your freight forwarder if required. The *customs invoice* is a special form required by some countries (e.g., Canada) that contains your declaration as to the value of the products shipped. The *consular invoice* is a special form required by some countries on which the consulate of the customer's government certifies as to value of the shipment, port of shipment, destination of shipment, and place of origin of the merchandise. Many countries require a *certificate of origin*, a document that certifies the product (or a major portion of the product) was produced in the United States, that is signed by you, a local chamber of commerce, and/or the consulate of the customer's country.

If special packing and marking are required, your freight forwarder will take care of these matters. Your freight forwarder will also arrange the required cargo insurance for the shipment.

The Shipper's Export Declaration, the transportation document, certificate of insurance, and other required documents will now be prepared by your freight forwarder.

▲ The *Shipper's Export Declaration (SED)*. The SED is a USDOC form filed by your company (the exporter of record) for all shipments (except those to Canada) in excess of $2,500 FOB U.S. port (or $500 if shipped under a validated export license or if shipped by U.S. mail). Your freight forwarder will complete this form and provide it to the carrier who will in turn file it with U.S. Customs at the port of export. The information contained on the SED includes the country of ultimate destination, the HS/Schedule B numbers for each item being exported, the FOB U.S. port value of the shipment, and either the validated export license number or the general export license symbol. If your shipment requires a validated export license, you cannot complete the SED until your license application has been approved and the license number received. If a validated export license is not required, you must enter a general export license symbol, of which there are about twenty options depending on the product category and country of destination. For example, the general export license symbol *G-DEST*, the lowest common denominator license, covers the shipment of products for which a validated export license is never required. Other general export license symbols are used when a validated export license is required for one or more countries, but not the country to which you are shipping. In order to determine your general export license symbol, ask for assistance from your USDOC District Office or the Bureau of Export Administration's Export Counseling Division or refer to the *Export Administration Regulations.*

▲ *The transportation document.* This is a receipt for the product and a contract of carriage to a designated point and party. The document must be consistent with the letter of credit. In this case the appropriate transportation document is a combined transport bill of lading (as opposed to a marine bill of lading or an air waybill) since you are using multimodal shipping and delivering your container to the carrier at a rail yard rather than at the dock. The transportation document is important because it shows whether the product has been delivered to the carrier on time and whether the shipment is clean (without visible damage). The document may be negotiable, meaning that it conveys title to the shipment, or nonnegotiable. Because you are using a letter of credit, your document will be negotiable and must be endorsed by you when presented to your bank with the letter of credit and other documents. The transportation document must have the same destination control statement that appears on the commercial invoice.

▲ *The certificate of insurance.* This certificate is evidence that you have insured the shipment against loss or damage. The insurance must comply with the specific coverage indicated in the letter of credit and be in an amount equal to 110 percent of the CIP value. Your freight forwarder has an open cargo policy under which you can be insured. Normally, you will obtain all-risk (but this does not include war, strikes, and other specific circumstances), door-to-door coverage.

Once the freight forwarder has delivered your container to the first carrier, your shipment is on its way. Your freight forwarder prepares, assembles, and forwards the required documents to your customer, your bank, and you. Your customer will be notified that the product has been shipped and provided with the required arrival information. At this point, you will receive an invoice from your freight forwarder covering all the shipping and related charges as well as the freight forwarder's fees.

Collecting on the Sale

Your freight forwarder has presented your bank with the letter of credit, the 30-day after-sight draft, and all the documents required in order to comply with the provisions of the letter of credit (e.g., certificates of inspection, commercial invoice, packing slip, combined transport bill of lading, and insurance certificate).

Now your bank (the advising/negotiating bank under the letter of credit) checks the draft and documents against the letter of credit to determine if there are any discrepancies. Was your shipment delivered to the carrier in time? Was your letter of credit presented prior to the expiration date of the letter of credit? Are the various documents consistent with each other? Does the description of goods on the invoice differ from the description on the letter of credit? Are the amounts on the commercial invoice and draft the same?

If your bank finds discrepancies on the documents, you have three options:

1. Correct the discrepancies.
2. Request your bank to contact the customer's bank to ask the customer to waive the discrepancies.
3. Have your bank send the documents to the customer's bank on a collection basis.

If your bank finds the documents in order or if it receives a waiver of documents from the customer's bank, the draft and documents are sent to the customer's bank (the issuing bank)—assuming that option 3 was not used.

The customer's bank checks the documents against the letter of credit for discrepancies. If none are found, it accepts the draft and notifies your bank of its acceptance of the draft.

Thus, thirty days after your customer's bank has verified the documentation and accepted the draft, your bank will receive the funds from your customer's bank. Then your bank credits your account for the amount of the sale.

You've now completed a Trial Run export sale! You've crossed the Trial Run finish line and you're on the road to becoming a successful Fast-Track Exporter.

Your Unique Situation

The typical shipping and collection situation probably doesn't fit your specific situation. If you have a supportive international banker and freight forwarder, work with them to develop the shipping collection process that will be best for your company. If you don't have or need such support, we have given you the primary EPO and written resources that you can use to do it yourself. Other companies in your locale with export experience can be called upon to tutor you through your first shipments.

If, for example, your shipment is of relatively low value and small, you may use open account payment terms and ship by mail or air courier. For information on mail and air courier shipping, these publications will be of help: *Exports By Mail, International Mail Manual, Express Mail International Service Guide, Federal Express Worldwide Service Guide,* and similar publications available from other international air courier services.

Track the Results

Your first Trial Run sale will lead to other export sales in your target country and worldwide markets. These sales need to be tracked and documented in the foreign buyer database you established in Step 2 in order to complete the final step in the Trial Run—the evaluation of the Trial Run.

You have put a lot of effort into your Trial Run, so make sure that you keep track of the results you will need for your evaluation step.

Step 5:

Evaluate the Trial Run

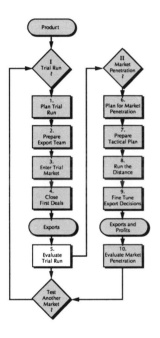

Your final step on the Trial Run is to determine just how successful you have been in expanding your markets through export. Evaluation is an essential step in Fast-Track Exporting because it is one of the tools you use to become a more effective and more profitable exporter.

It's now time to evaluate your Trial Run results.

Review the goal and objectives you established in your Trial Run Plan in Step 1. These goals and objectives define what you wanted to achieve in the Trial Run and what constituted a successful Trial Run. What was your Trial Run goal? What were your Trial Run objectives for the worldwide market? What were your Trial Run objectives for your target country market? Enter your goals and objectives on the Trial Run Evaluation Worksheet (see Worksheet 19).

Compare the results you have achieved in sales and other areas with your Trial Run goals and objectives. Assess how effective you were in selecting your most exportable product and target country market. How satisfied were you with the training provided to your export team, your promotion materials, and your channels of distribution? Did your EPOs and ESOs meet your expectations? Record your evaluation and the changes you will recommend to improve your next Trial Run at a new target country market on the worksheet.

If you have entered into representation agreement, how satisfied are

WORKSHEET 19.   Trial Run Evaluation

TRIAL RUN EVALUATION	**FASTRACK** ™ *Success Through Fast-Track Exporting*

Purpose: To determine how successful you have been during the Trial Run.

Company Name/Division _____

Period Being Evaluated

Trial Run export goal (Worksheet 9):

Was this goal appropriate?   Yes   No   Somewhat.   Why?

To what degree did you achieve the Trial Run objectives (Worksheet 9):   % Achieved

1. Worldwide Objectives:

_____   _____

_____   _____

_____   _____

_____   _____

Were these objectives appropriate?   Yes   No   Somewhat.   Why?

2. Target Country Objectives:

_____   _____

_____   _____

_____   _____

_____   _____

Were these objectives appropriate?   Yes   No   Somewhat.   Why?

How effective was your product selection process?   __Effective __OK __Needs to be Reviewed
Recommended Changes:

How effective was your target market selection process?   __Effective __OK __Needs to be Reviewed
Recommended Changes:

How effective was your training for the Export Team?   __Effective __OK __Needs to be Reviewed
Recommended Changes:

How effective were your promotional, response, and other materials?   __Effective __OK __Need to be Reviewed
Recommended Changes:

How effective were your channels of distribution?   __Effective __OK __Need to be Reviewed
Recommended Changes:

Did the EPO services you used meet your expectations?   __Yes __Somewhat __Need to be Reviewed
Recommended Changes:

Did the ESO services you used meet your expectations?   __Yes __Somewhat __Need to be Reviewed
Recommended Changes:

How satisfied are your agents/distributors with their sales?   __Satisfied __OK __Need to be Reviewed
Recommended Changes:

How satisfied are the end-users with your product and service?   __Satisfied __OK __Need to be Reviewed
Recommended Changes:

DECISION: How satisfied are you with the success of the Trial Run?   __Very Satisfied __Satisfied __OK __Not Satisfied
Rationale:

Completed by   Date

Copyright Export Resource Associates, Inc., 1990   090 your agents or distributors with their sales, your product, and the support you are providing? If sales have been made to end users or retailers, how satisfied are they?

The evaluation of your Trial Run is the final step in Phase I of the Fast-Track Exporting process. You are now ready to make two critical decisions.

Decide the Next Steps

You must now decide what steps you will take to continue your progress in Fast-Track Exporting. You have two decisions to make:

1. *Continue to expand your markets through export.* If you decide to continue expanding your markets, go back to the top of the Phase I process and start your next Trial Run. Target another high-potential export market and initiate the process over again. The evaluation of the current Trial Run will allow you to improve the effectiveness of your next Trial Run and reduce the time it takes you to test new high-potential markets.

2. *Proceed to the market penetration phase.* If you decide to move on to Phase II in your current Trial Run market and implement the Market Penetration Fast-Track Exporting process, you will proceed to Market Penetration Steps 6 through 10 presented in the next section.

Phase II

Market Penetration

Maximize the Market's Potential Through Market Penetration

Phase II of the Fast-Track Exporting process provides a comprehensive framework for penetrating the Trial Run market. During this phase, you will put your company on an advanced five-step fast track to maximize its potential in a confirmed high-potential market.

Phase I took a very prescriptive, "vertical" approach to getting you on the fast track in the Trial Run market. It provided specific actions to ensure that you had the right information at the right time to make the best decisions while utilizing minimal resources. You are now making the transition to Market Penetration. Phase II will take you to a more sophisticated, "horizontal" level of international trade activity by providing a decision-making framework within which you apply your increasing knowledge of the market and your skill and expertise as an international marketer.

When the evaluation of the Trial Run market demonstrates that the market has significant potential, you proceed to systematically develop a long-range strategic and tactical plan and take the actions necessary to penetrate the market.

Steps 6 and 7 of the Fast-Track Exporting process will take you through the following planning process:

- ▲ Developing the framework for planning Market Penetration
- ▲ Formalizing assumptions on which to base the plan
- ▲ Describing target market factors impacting the plan
- ▲ Making decisions on internal considerations
- ▲ Holding a management strategic session
- ▲ Developing your company's strategic export plan
- ▲ Developing the tactical plan

Steps 8 through 10 will take you through the remaining Market Penetration process.

These steps cover:

- ▲ Running the distance
- ▲ Fine-tuning the export decisions

▲ Evaluating market penetration
▲ Staying out front in the long-distance run

The Market Penetration Commitment

The Market Penetration process requires a greater commitment to a specific target market based on the results of the Trial Run. The previous combination reactive and proactive effort in the target market becomes a sophisticated, well-planned and -implemented long-range market penetration program.

Reaffirming your commitment at this time is important because you will need to allocate additional resources—both human and financial—to this expanded effort. You and others in your organization must be prepared to travel abroad and to allocate sufficient resources to achieve the objectives of each trip. Products may need to be adapted to be more readily accepted by the market. Promotional and communications expenses will be significantly higher due to greater involvement in the market.

Successful market penetration requires an examination of your organization in terms of its readiness to undertake the expanded export activity. Decisions will need to be made and actions taken to help ensure your success. This may entail a restructuring of the export function, assuming additional export responsibilities internally, and/or providing additional training to personnel. The management group must also be prepared to devote more time to strategic planning in order to maximize your company's effectiveness in the target market.

If the results of your Trial Run were positive and you are ready and willing to make the necessary commitment, then you are in a good position to continue on the fast-track and reap the benefits of market penetration.

The starting point for this process is to review the various market entry options available to your company. In Phase I, the option was limited to either direct or indirect exporting. During Phase II, you will want to explore other options ranging from continuing to export from your U.S. facility to establishing a wholly-owned manufacturing subsidiary in the target market. Factors that will influence your decision include costs associated with the entry method, level of competition, degree of control desired, amount of risk associated with the country, legal considerations, the nature of the product or service being sold, and long-term market potential.

Reviewing Market Entry Options

Market penetration requires that you be receptive to considering both exporting and nonexporting market entry methods. Exporting market entry methods can include an expansion of your export activity from the United States, the establishment of a foreign branch or sales office in the target market, or the formation of an international strategic alliance. Nonexporting market entry methods include a wide range of penetration approaches such as licensing, franchising, joint ventures, wholly-owned subsidiaries, or other forms of manufacturing in the target market. Each of these options is discussed below:

Foreign Sales Office

In this case, the manufacturing of the product is handled by your domestic production facility and marketing is the responsibility of the foreign sales office. The main reason you may decide in favor of this option is because you want to have more control over the marketing of your product. The foreign sales office may, at least in the preliminary stages, continue to sell to the distribution network that you established during Phase I. The advantage of establishing a sales office is that your company has a presence in the market and there is greater opportunity for feedback related to the current market situation as well as projected trends, competition, and other information that will be useful for both strategic and tactical planning.

As a second phase in the development of your foreign sales office, you may decide to eliminate your distributor(s) and assume responsibility for the distribution function. Using this approach, you will eliminate at least one layer of distribution channel members, but the functions previously performed by outsiders must still be provided. For example, warehousing and delivery can be handled by your foreign sales office or contracted to an outside party.

While the decision to establish a foreign sales office clearly places additional demands and responsibilities on your company, it also provides additional benefits. You can anticipate greater sales to your target market and an increase in market share. Efficiencies created through greater control should result in a reduction of distribution costs as a percentage of sales. Also, greater involvement in the market should lead to more effective decision making regarding product and pricing strategies.

CASE EXAMPLE: Bondhus Corporation established sales offices in Canada and Japan because of insufficient volume from distributors in place. By 1979, the company had acquired experience in international markets and felt that given the proximity and ease of communication with Canada, volume should have been much higher. After a direct presence was established, sales began to increase significantly. In Japan, Bondhus products were competitive and sales were good, but it was clear that there was still untapped potential. The company learned through its customers that its distributor had poor business relationships with the customers and that they did not like to deal with him. Instead of taking a chance on another bad distributor in this major market, Bondhus decided in 1986 to open a sales subsidiary in Japan.

CASE EXAMPLE: Anitec Image establishes subsidiary sales companies in countries where it has achieved a 10 to 15 percent market share. The sales subsidiaries warehouse products to more rapidly supply the market. They are also responsible for training and customer relations as well as for facilitating global management. The sales subsidiaries are staffed by nationals recruited out of the industry who are brought in on a regular basis to the technical training facilities in Binghamton, New York for product training and technical updates. Expatriates are used for some top management positions.

The decision to establish a foreign sales office should be made only after careful evaluation of the target country. What are the fixed costs that would be incurred in relation to additional sales projected? Expenses such as rent and personnel costs will vary widely from country to country.

If you find that your target market is a relatively high cost country, this option will be less attractive. Stability of the country and its currency would also impact this decision as would your ability to comply with standard business practices.

International Strategic Alliance

In order to avoid many of the obstacles typically associated with exporting, you may want to consider establishing a strategic alliance with a foreign manufacturer of a complementary product. One approach is to enter into a marketing agreement whereby the manufacturer in your target country sells your product through its distribution network. Advantages include access to a well-established distribution network, a trained sales force, and a servicing vehicle if required. Your chances of achieving immediate sales are excellent.

On the flip side, that manufacturer may be interested in developing a joint marketing agreement whereby your sales organization would market its product. You would be adding a new product or product line without incurring product development costs. The end result of a joint marketing agreement could be an immediate increase in domestic profits as well as rapid penetration of the foreign market.

You should put the agreement in writing, and you must address the same issues as in your distribution agreements. For example, under what brand name will your product be sold? Where will packaging and labeling take place? How will servicing be handled? What geographic area will be covered? And how will pricing be established? The agreement should also protect your patent and intellectual property rights and include non-compete and nonmanufacture clauses. Your international attorney will be able to guide you in constructing an agreement.

When evaluating potential strategic alliance partners, carefully examine their sales and distribution capabilities, reputation in the market, and financial stability.

- -

CASE EXAMPLE: LecTec Corporation goes beyond traditional marketing by establishing alliances. When the company president met the director of Siemens' medical division at World Med, an international medical trade show in Minnesota, he took the opportunity to propose a strategic alliance that centered on the use of LecTec's disposable medical products with compatible Siemens' equipment. Under the resulting agreement, LecTec's products are now sold under private label in almost every country.

- -

Licensing

Under a licensing agreement, you give a manufacturer in your target country permission to produce the product for a specific period of time and under certain predetermined terms and conditions. You can also license the use of intellectual property rights such as patents, trademarks, and production processes know-how to a foreign licensee. In return, the licensee will manufacture and market the products produced under this agreement and you will be compensated through royalties based on sales and possibly other fees.

The advantage of this market entry method is that your product can be produced in the target market without any capital outlay from your company. It may also be a solution to trade barriers that you faced during the Trial Run. In addition, you immediately have an organization that is knowledgeable about the market and the distribution channels in that market—that is, if you select the best licensee.

- -

CASE EXAMPLE: Murdock, Inc., the manufacturer of custom aircraft parts and hot press machines, found it necessary to select a market penetration entry method based on careful consideration of each target market. In most markets, Murdock uses a direct sales approach. However, in France, where much of the industry is state-owned and business attitudes can sometimes be very nationalistic, Murdock has operated very successfully through a licensee. The French company that holds the license is a manufacturer of specialized equipment in a similar industry segment and a natural fit. Murdock also has a successful licensee in the United Kingdom for similar reasons.

- -

CASE EXAMPLE: Cambridge Products, Ltd., found it necessary to enter into a licensing agreement for successful market penetration in certain markets. For example, the Australian government has limitations on the amount of product that can be imported and in order to meet customers' needs, it is necessary to manufacture the product in that country.

Another advantage is that the licensee may have technologies or other capabilities that can be useful to you in the U.S. market. Should this be the case, you may be in a favorable position to purchase the technology or arrange for a licensing agreement whereby you also become a licensee. The variations on this approach are far-reaching. You or the licensee may develop technologies that can be incorporated into the licensing agreement as these opportunities arise.

A major drawback to licensing is that you are perhaps training a future competitor. You are teaching the licensee how to produce your product with your know-how or you are allowing the licensee to produce according to your patented processes. Ideally, you will develop a strong preference for your brand name in that market so that if your licensee chooses to produce a competitive product in the future, it does not automatically mean the loss of your customer base.

CASE EXAMPLE: Little Giant Pump Company has rejected the idea of licensing. Because the company has been successful in selling through national distributors in each market, a licensing arrangement has not been needed. "We want to keep our products proprietary," says the senior vice president. "We don't want to take the risk of having the licensee go into business for himself with a copy of our product."

A second drawback to licensing is that the percentages for royalties and other fees paid to you may be minimal. Even though you will not be investing capital, you will be investing time in the training of the licensee and forfeiting your company's rights to sell in that market during the time of the agreement. You must weigh the value of that contribution against the projected earnings through royalties.

In order to maximize the financial return to your company, you should conduct a careful and thorough screening of potential licensees. Since your earnings are based on a percentage of sales and your investment is measured in terms of management and training time, you want to select a licensee that is able to produce a quality product and market it in an aggressive fashion. You want a licensee that is interested in establishing a productive relationship with you and possesses the type of reputation in the market that you want associated with your product.

Your agreement should cover many of the same issues that you addressed with your distributor during the Trial Run. What is the length of the agreement? What geographic region is covered by the agreement? What sales performance is expected based on your assessment of market potential? In addition, you should include quality standards that the licensee must adhere to throughout the production process. It is critical to determine whether or not the licensee's existing quality assurance system is sufficient to meet the required standards.

You will want to take every step possible to help ensure that your company will have a certain degree of control over the licensee no matter how perfect the selection appears. Ideally, you can provide some necessary and unique components to the product from your U.S. facility. This will enable you to have control in two ways. First, the product cannot be produced without your input, and second, you will have more information on the total number of units being produced by the licensee.

Another action you should take to protect your long-term interests is to file the registration for your product in the name of your company and not in the name of your licensee, even though the licensee will volunteer to simplify the process for you by handling this detail. This action will give you flexibility to renew the existing agreement, select a new licensee, or make a decision to establish your own production facility in the market at some later point without having to negotiate ownership rights to your product name or trademark.

Good advice at this point would be to seek legal counsel from your international attorney. A relatively minor expenditure up front to develop an attractive licensing agreement for both parties is much less painful than a long, tedious, and costly legal battle to undo an inadequate and poorly designed agreement.

Franchising

Franchising, a form of licensing, provides another opportunity for your company to sell rights—trademarks, brand names, patents, or know-how—to a foreign franchisee. Franchising is used extensively in the service industry by fast food, hotel, convenience store, training, business services, and other sectors where trademark or brand name recognition automatically creates demand because of the highly successful marketing efforts of the franchisor.

The franchisee in the target market is allowed use of the specified right for a certain period of time at an agreed upon rate of compensation to the franchisor. In addition, the franchisor usually provides management and/or training services or sells a related product to the franchisee in order to achieve the goal of creating recognition, acceptance and a uniform product offering.

Franchising is a particularly desirable strategy for companies who have already saturated the domestic market with their products and services. For small or medium-size companies, franchising provides capital that can be used to strengthen the position in the U.S. market. For the potential franchisee, it is an opportunity to own a business with a well-established brand name and proven operating procedures. These factors tend to greatly reduce the risk of failure associated with start-up businesses.

In order to develop a successful franchising strategy, it is necessary to fully understand the target country market and determine appropriate geographic regions to be handled by a single franchisee. It is also important to be certain that the population base is adequate to support the sales volume necessary for the franchise operation to succeed. Per capita income, for example, is often a key factor in determining the viability of this approach.

In some cases, it may be appropriate to establish a master franchisee in the target country and allow that organization to sub-license in order to adequately cover the market. This approach has the advantage of minimizing the number of franchisees you will need to deal with; however, you will be less aware of problems that may arise within the network. It is safe to say that image problems in one location will impact the reputation of other locations as well. Another option would be to establish each franchise on an individual basis so that all relationships are with you, the U.S. franchisor. The franchisee may feel that there are greater benefits to this approach because the service provided to them may be of higher quality.

A good source of additional information on franchising is *Survey of Foreign Laws and Regulations Affecting International Franchising.*

Joint Venture

In some respects, a joint venture is similar to licensing in that you are involved in an arrangement with a foreign producer to manufacture your product. However, in the case of the joint venture, you usually have a capital investment and are part of the management team. In other words, you are a partner in the venture. Your decision to enter into a joint venture is likely to evolve because of a positive export experience during the Trial Run.

CASE EXAMPLE: Murdock, Inc., built its initial success in Japan using direct sales, despite strong support of national industries. Japan became the company's major export market at 50 percent of export sales. In September 1989, Murdock decided to further improve its position in Japan by entering into a joint venture with a medium-size Japanese steel company. The Japanese company had developed a new type of lightweight stainless steel that could be formed by using Murdock's technology, and they saw the joint venture as a chance to develop a market for the new product through Murdock's existing connections in the industry. Murdock saw a way to expand its market and overcome many of the nationalism, language, and cultural barriers that were present in Japan. The new joint venture company is marketing primarily in Japan to the automotive, aircraft, and other industries. Murdock is enthusiastic about the joint venture and the prospect for ongoing success.

Your contribution to the joint venture could be in the form of capital, equipment/machinery, know-how, materials, or some combination of the above. The exact combination depends on the existing capabilities of your joint venture partner and the availability of necessary resources and equipment in that market. The level of financial investment will depend on the amount you are able to negotiate with your joint venture partner and, in some cases, the percentage ownership that is allowed by the government in the target country.

CASE EXAMPLE: In the case of Murdock, Inc., they supplied the equipment, technical know-how, and some capital. Employees of the joint venture came from Japan for a three-week training program at Murdock's facilities in California. They will come back for refresher courses as necessary. And in the meantime, employees of Murdock have visited Japan to train and troubleshoot. The joint venture partner in Japan brings the new product, the majority of the start-up capital, and its Japanese identity to the venture. A third party to the venture, Murdock's initial representative in Japan, also has equity in the joint venture and continues to be responsible for the marketing function. With highly developed marketing channels and a good reputation, the representative company opens valuable doors for the new joint venture.

Normally, your financial rewards are greater with the joint venture approach versus licensing as a market penetration method. Instead of a small percentage royalty based on sales, you will be receiving a share of the returns based on the level of your investment. You also have a greater degree of control over the direction and growth of the venture because you participate in the management.

The joint venture approach to market penetration carries with it a number of risks. Your financial risks are greater than with a licensing arrangement because you are making a more substantial investment in the operation, assuming more liability in connection with the operation, and entering into a partnership type of arrangement. Therefore, you must carefully assess both the market and the potential joint venture partner against the projected return on your investment and your ability to achieve the desired degree of market penetration through this vehicle.

While there are hazards associated with manufacturing in a foreign market, some of these risks may be minimized through the joint venture arrangement because foreign governments are generally very supportive of this approach and are less likely to impose regulations and restrictions that would adversely affect the operation. The reason for this support is that you will be aiding in the development of the country, or at least an industry sector, by transferring technology and/or management skills as well as creating employment. A number of governments of countries in Southeast Asia provide incentives to encourage the formation of joint ventures. Governments of East European countries also tend to look favorably on joint ventures because in addition to the technology transfer that is involved, there is also the possibility of generating hard currency by exporting some or all of the production from the joint venture.

As in licensing, there may be some component to the product or some material that you sell to the joint venture. It is critical to iron out policies related to the pricing of any materials that you sell to the joint venture. You can use these pricing policies as a tool to influence where profits are generated which will, in turn, affect tax treatment. Also, you can use pricing of components or materials sold to the joint venture by your U.S. operation as a means of transferring funds out of the joint venture country. This is particularly relevant in countries where there are severe restrictions on repatriation of profits.

Other issues to resolve at the outset include policy decisions regarding if and when profits will be disbursed to each party. Either you or your joint venture partner may be in favor of reinvesting profits to accelerate growth while the other party may prefer to disburse profits on a regular basis. You should also jointly establish policies related to other areas where disagreements are most likely to arise. In order to put your company in an advantageous position, you must decide in advance how the joint venture fits into your overall global strategy and then establish goals, objectives, and policies for the joint venture that are consistent with your company's overall direction.

Foreign Manufacturing Subsidiary

The entry method requiring the greatest level of commitment to your target market is to establish a wholly-owned foreign manufacturing subsidiary. This means that you as the parent company are in control of the organization. It is your company.

This market entry method may evolve from a joint venture relationship in cases where your joint venture partner chooses to get out of the business, or a situation may arise where you are able to buy out your licensee. You may also discover opportunities to buy an existing production facility, thereby simplifying some of the complexities that would otherwise be involved in building a manufacturing facility. For example, you would avoid the headaches of the design and construction process and dealing with contractors in the target market. In addition, you would most likely retain some of the management, staff, and production workers associated with the existing facility. This would reduce the length of your learning curve by tapping existing expertise.

If you decide to pursue the acquisition option, it may be difficult to locate a facility that meets your criteria. Much of your success in locating an adequate facility will depend on the type and level of technology required for your production process. What you need may simply not be available in your target market and you may need to build a facility to your own specifications.

Whether you are interested in establishing a wholly-owned subsidiary by purchasing an existing facility or constructing a facility to suit your needs, you should research government regulations in your target country regarding wholly-owned subsidiaries. A number of governments have strict regulations regarding ownership by foreign entities, while others provide incentives to encourage this approach.

- -

CASE EXAMPLE: Bondhus Corporation established a manufacturing facility in Barbados in 1986. As a benefit for investing in the country, the company pays no income tax for its first ten years of operation. It also is able to ship duty-free to the European Community, Japan, Canada, and the United States. Labor costs are also low. While the company president devoted about half of his time to the facility during the first four years of operation, he is now confident that local management will be effective.

- -

In assessing this market entry method, you must determine whether or not the advantages of complete control, the potential for greater return on investment, and elimination of potential conflicts between you and a foreign partner outweigh the problems and complexities involved in establishing the subsidiary such as capital outlay, providing the management team or expertise, and developing the marketing channels.

Foreign Contract Manufacturing or Assembly

Other variations of producing in the target country include contract manufacturing or assembly by a foreign manufacturer. Contract manufacturing, whereby the producer in your target market is under contract to manufacture your product, is a solution to production but normally does not include responsibility for marketing. You must make additional provisions for this function. This might be accomplished through utilizing an agent or distributor or establishing your own sales subsidiary in the target market.

The main advantage of contract manufacturing is the relative ease with which you can enter into or withdraw from the agreement. If you find it necessary to manufacture abroad, for cost or other reasons, and you have concerns about the risk factors, contract manufacturing provides a safer Market Penetration approach than investing capital in a wholly-owned subsidiary. As with the licensing option, you may want to export only a necessary component from your U.S. facility to prevent the contract manufacturer from easily acquiring knowledge of the complete production process. This also provides additional sales opportunities for your domestic operation.

The other possibility is to have your product assembled in the target market. This would mean that all or most of the production of parts would take place in your domestic operation and would be exported to the target market for assembly and distribution. This approach may enable you to reduce transportation costs because the product will probably be less bulky in an unassembled state. In addition, tariffs are usually lower on unassembled products because it creates employment opportunities in the foreign market. Distribution may or may not be included as the responsibility of the assembly operation, depending on that organization's capabilities and distribution networks in place, if any.

If you decide to pursue the assembly option, you must consider whether or not you will contract with an existing facility, enter into a licensing agreement for the assembly, or establish your own assembly operation. Again, your final decision will depend on the degree of risk you are willing to assume and the amount of control you wish to retain over the operation. Another factor in your decision should be the market potential. If your assessment based on the Trial Run indicates that the market is stable and a high growth rate is expected, you may want to maintain a greater degree of control over the assembly operation.

An important factor to keep in mind is that any time you transfer the manufacturing responsibility to another entity, you must consider how to best implement and monitor quality control procedures. Quality control is a great concern because it impacts on your company's image in the market and may result in product liability issues that emerge as a consequence of poor quality. In cases where quality control appears to be a problem, you may want to put one of your people on site to monitor quality or hire a qualified individual from the local market to oversee quality assurance.

Selecting the Market Penetration Method

Your final decision on the best Market Penetration strategy for your company must be based on a careful assessment of the current market situation, future projections, and your company's own internal strengths and weaknesses as well as your strategic direction. As mentioned earlier, no one Market Penetration strategy is suitable for each and every market that you decide to penetrate. Each market must be evaluated based on the risks and opportunities specific to that market. The best way to help ensure success in the market is to have a thorough understanding of your product, your company, and the target market characteristics. Each of these issues is presented in greater detail later in Phase II.

The option you select also depends on a number of factors including tariff and nontariff barriers to exports, transportation costs, availability of labor and other resources, the degree of control you want to maintain over the operation, your ability to adapt to the local requirements from your U.S. location, the preference that a foreign government might have for buying locally produced products, issues of taxation, and other factors.

The issue of taxation requires special attention. It is important to explore the impact of international taxation on your overall operation. You should address this issue with an accounting firm that is knowledgeable about taxation on income earned through an overseas operation and transferred to your domestic operation. The U.S. regulations require that you be assessed the U.S. tax rate on that income. You are, however, allowed to deduct the taxes that you pay to the foreign government so as to avoid double taxation.

You will want to implement a strategy whereby you can delay payment and/or reduce the amount of taxes due on earnings from your foreign sales operation. Minimizing taxation is not simply a matter of understanding the U.S. regulations on repatriated earnings but also being able to develop a strategy to reduce your tax rate in high tax countries. Your international tax accountant will be able to provide you with the best options for establishing your entity in the target market.

Many countries use tax reduction, deferral, or forgiveness as a means of attracting investment into their regions. This possibility should also be explored as you determine your Market Penetration method in the target country. You may find a number of other incentives that make it desirable for you to establish a presence in the market.

As in most cases, the more you invest in terms of capital and time and the greater risk you are willing to assume, the greater will be the opportunity for long-term financial reward. Thus, it is important to have a long-term strategy to help ensure that you make the best decisions at each step in your global expansion.

Step 6:

Plan for Market Penetration

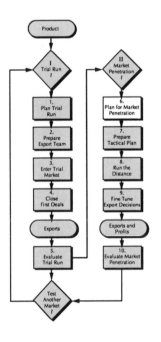

To successfully penetrate the market in a timely and organized manner, it is critical to go through a strategic planning process to ensure that no opportunities go unexplored and no problems go unresolved. This process will enable you to maximize your return on time and resources committed to Market Penetration.

During Phase I of the Fast-Track Exporting process, the amount of time and resources spent on planning was minimal. The information accumulated and the decisions made in the Trial Run will now serve as the basis for launching your planning process for Market Penetration.

Develop the Framework for Planning

Your first task in the Market Penetration process is to build the foundation for planning. This will help to ensure that management, members of your export team, and others responsible for successfully implementing the plan have a clear picture of the rationale for Market Penetration and the high degree of commitment by top management. The planning foundation should be developed by preparing a brief executive summary of the direction your company is headed in exporting and how it evolved to this point. This would include a brief overview of the product(s) selected for export and why; the target market priorities and why; the market entry method and rationale; and the Trial Run export objectives and how they were achieved.

You should also summarize your reasons for deciding to expand your level of export activity through Market Penetration. Review existing policy statements and adjust where necessary to institutionalize management's commitment to the expanded export initiatives. Finally, reflect on the type of corporate identity you are attempting to achieve or maintain. By defining this at the outset of your Market Penetration planning, it will help you and others to make consistent decisions throughout the planning process—all of them leading to the same image for your company.

Initially, the executive summary should be provided to the management team for review and discussion. Then each manager should create a forum to discuss the information with employees in their work units. The purpose of this approach is twofold. First, the people within your organization that are or will be involved in the export program need to know the role and importance of exporting within the organization and what has transpired to date. Second, those not directly involved in the export process need to be brought into the fold in order to truly internationalize the organization.

Review Your Assumptions

The next task is to review the assumptions that you stated at the beginning of your Trial Run phase. A number of these may shift from the assumption category to fact or be eliminated as an incorrect assumption. Now add new assumptions to your list based on the experience you gained during the Trial Run. As stated earlier, it is extremely important to state your assumptions in writing because many of your decisions and those of your management team will be based on educated assumptions rather than fact. You will want to maintain documentation on the circumstances that lead to certain decisions.

Assumption statements should cover a number of topics. A major area to consider is your company and its readiness to penetrate the market. A review of your assumption statements completed during Phase I will be a helpful starting point. Your assumptions should include broad statements about the company and its ability to sustain an intensive, long-term export effort in the target market and to continue pursuing additional Trial Run opportunities in a new market. You should also state more specific assumptions such as how management will fit additional or expanded responsibilities into their schedules, how resources will be reallocated to meet the requirements of the Market Penetration program, and how staff will be prepared to ensure effectiveness at fulfilling new or added responsibilities. Taking time at this point to define your assumptions regarding these internal issues will help you to progress through the planning process more quickly.

A second set of assumptions should relate to the economy both domestically and internationally. What factors have changed since you developed your initial assumptions? It is important to keep in mind that often times the most accurate assumptions made about a foreign economy are based on a clear understanding of what is happening in the domestic economy and why. The same normally holds true for assumptions you make about your industry. Being aware of developments in your industry here at home will help you to interpret developments in your industry abroad.

By establishing assumptions about the economy and the industry in your Market Penetration country, you should be able to make some assumptions about the market potential for your product in the target market and, to a lesser extent, in the international market as a whole. These assumptions will help you to make more specific sales projections and to allocate production capacity later in the process. In addition, you will eventually want to prioritize your export markets and market potential will, of course, be one of the factors you will consider in making this determination.

In addition to the above areas, any general or specific assumptions you can make about your target market will, indeed, be helpful when you begin the development of your strategic plan.

CASE EXAMPLE: Bondhus Corporation of Monticello, Minnesota, believes that much of its planning effectiveness is due to the importance placed on establishing and clearly stating assumptions. Assumptions helped Bondhus define its planning environment, and this led to the setting of better goals and objectives for the company.

Describe the Target Market

Now that you have developed your framework for planning and established a number of assumptions, you can begin to focus more specifically on the targeted penetration market. In undertaking this third task, it will be necessary for you to draw on both assumption and fact. You should begin this task by providing an overall view of your product in relation to the market. What were the main conclusions from the Trial Run phase? How has the product fared against the competition? What are its strengths and weaknesses? How is your product positioned in terms of price and quality? How has the product been used in the target country and what market segments comprised the primary users? What market segments would you classify as secondary? Did your product serve as a substitute for another product that was either more expensive or in short supply? Were you surprised at any new uses that the buyers discovered for your product?

Reviewing the Market Segments

You should also begin to refine your understanding of your market segments and the channels through which they buy. Begin by listing the various segments to which you sell (e.g., industrial, government, or original equipment manufacturer). Under each segment, to the extent possible, indicate the categories of customers within each segment, continuing the process until your channel reaches the end user/buyer (for example industrial distributor to service center to manufacturer).

It will be useful to become more familiar with the characteristics of your buyer categories. How much do you now know about the buyer or potential buyer of your product? Is it possible, at this time, to develop a profile of the most likely buyer throughout the channel in each of the market segments to which you sell? The profile should address who buys, how they buy, when they buy, where they buy, how often they buy, who influences the decision to buy, and the traditional channels of distribution through which they buy. Depending on your product, you may have to obtain additional information for the profiles.

The Market Segments and Channels Worksheet (see Worksheet 20) will assist you in the process of recording your market segmentation and buyer profile information. Now go back to the beginning of this exercise and assign percentages to each segment.

Initially, some of your percentages will be based on assumptions; however, this will become a very useful management decision-making tool once you establish an accurate picture of the segments and channels.

By developing these profiles and understanding the behaviors and motivations of the buyers in your target market, you will be in a good position to develop both the strategic and tactical plans for successful market penetration. Likewise, should you not have a clear understanding of your primary and secondary market segments, it will be difficult to effectively allocate resources to marketing efforts that will optimize sales.

To a certain extent, the buyer profiles will be based on the assumptions you made earlier and the knowledge you gained during the Trial Run. However, you can rely on your agent, distributor, or other representative(s) to provide useful information for this purpose. In addition, information obtained from inquiries you have received over the past several years from buyers located in your target market, the region, or from foreign inquiries in general will be useful. The EPO and/or ESO networks that you established earlier will also prove to be a valuable source of information as you attempt to more specifically describe your customer segments.

It is clear to see the benefit of developing these customer profiles if you are handling the marketing function through your own organization; but you may not, at first glance, understand the reason for going through this exercise if you are using agents, distributors, or other importers in the target country to assume responsibility for marketing your product. The answer is this. You know more about your product and how to effectively market it than any outside organization could know. In order to increase Market Penetration, you must assist and support your representative in the target country. The best way to do this is to be knowledgeable about each market segment that is to be addressed.

In analyzing demand for your product in greater detail, you will want to refine your information on total market size for your product categoty and the past and projected growth rate. Assess market share

WORKSHEET 20. Market Segments and Channels

MARKET SEGMENTS AND CHANNELS

$\overline{\overline{FASTRACK}}$
Success Through Fast-Track Exporting

Purpose: To prioritize the high-potential market segments and to identify the channel members through which each market segment buys.
Directions: Enter the market segment categories to be reached in the first column. List the Level 1 channel members to whom you sell followed by the Level 2 channel members to whom they sell, etc. until you reach the end users in that segment. Estimate the percent of sales for each segment. For greater clarity, convert the segments and channels into a pie graph starting with your company at the center and radiating out to end users in the outer ring.

Company Name/Division _____

Product _____   Country _____

Market Segment Category	%	Members of Channels by Level			
		Channel Level 1	Channel Level 2	Channel Level 3	End Users

Comments:

Completed by _____   Date _____

Copyright Export Resource Associates, Inc., 1990

090

from domestic production and from competitive products imported from the United States and elsewhere.

Reviewing the Market Environment

Finally, a thorough review of the environment is in order. Categories for which data should be obtained include demographic, economic, political, infrastructure, social, business, legal, U.S. export hurdles, target country import hurdles, distribution factors, and competition. Again, start with what you learned about the environment during the Trial Run and then continually add to your knowledge so you are able to take advantage of opportunities and avoid pitfalls.

One of the most useful research tools for gaining a thorough understanding of the market is the *Comparison Shopping Service* through your USDOC District Office. The research will be done by the U.S. Embassy/Consulate personnel in your targeted country or they will contract with a research organization. Even though you are already selling in the market, this report will be an invaluable means of developing a more complete picture of the market for your product and confirming or invalidating earlier assumptions. The service is available for over fifty countries, and the report will be custom-tailored to your firm.

The U.S. Embassy staff will conduct on-the-spot surveys to determine key marketing facts about your product and competition, including sales potential, comparable products, distribution channels, going price, competitive factors, and qualified purchasers. To aid in this process, you will need to provide complete sets of catalogs and brochures that show product specifications, applications, and prices in detail. Also, if you are represented in the market by an agent or distributor, provide the name and address and advise the Embassy if they may contact the individual during the course of conducting the survey. The time frame needed to complete the report is about forty-five days.

- -

CASE EXAMPLE: LecTec Corporation uses the USDOC Minneapolis District Office to optimize its resources. For example, it used the Comparison Shopping Service to study the cardiac electrode market in Germany, the United Kingdom, and South Korea (LecTec produces a product used in conjunction with electrodes). This research report provided answers to many of LecTec's questions about the market and identified potential distributors and end users. The company was provided with enough information to aggressively pursue those markets. The quality and comprehensiveness of the service were outstanding, according to the company's chairman.

You may also wish to contract with someone in the target country to conduct market research. Names of consulting firms can be obtained through U.S. chambers of commerce abroad and the commercial or agricultural attache in the U.S. Embassy in the target country. Refer to the *World Chamber of Commerce Directory* and the *Key Officers of Foreign Service Posts* for the names of resource contacts. You might also wish to utilize the research services of one of the large public accounting, law, or public relations firms with offices or affiliate relationships worldwide. This approach would enable you to work with a local firm and eliminate or at least reduce communication problems. These organizations most likely offer other international trade services as well.

In selecting an organization to conduct your research, you should be sure that the person assigned responsibility for the project has had previous experience in the target country. You will want someone who is knowledgeable about what data is available and the limitations of the data. For example, how is public information typically gathered in your target country and for what purpose? How frequently does the government in your target country update information and, again, for what purpose?

To minimize costs, research for existing data that will help to answer your questions. However, depending on the sophistication of your target country, the necessary data may not be compiled. If this is the case, your researcher will need to be fluent in the language and have a thorough understanding of the culture to conduct the necessary research and convey accurate results.

To supplement your research efforts, you should meet with the USDOC International Economic Policy Office (Country Desk) and USDOC Trade Development Office (Industry Desk) in Washington, D.C. Contact information for these units can be found in the *USDOC Telephone Directory.* This visit is advisable even though you may have spoken to individuals in these offices by telephone earlier. You should also visit the Embassy of your target country. Use the *Foreign Consulate Offices in the U.S.* publication to identify appropriate contacts. Even though their primary role is not to assist U.S. exporters, they will have country and industry information that will be useful in your planning.

If you are marketing your product in Japan, you can utilize the services of the Japanese External Trade Organization (JETRO). One of JETRO's functions is to assist U.S. exporters interested in developing or expanding exports to Japan. This organization has offices in New York, Chicago, Los Angeles, San Francisco, and Houston. The organization sponsors international trade promotion events, offers seminars on doing business in Japan, and provides information on trade opportunities in Japan.

Some companies will be able to receive financial assistance from the federal government to conduct research, provided their target market is classified as a developing country. The U.S. Trade and Development Program (TDP) has a program aimed at the U.S. private sector, offering 50-50 cost sharing to a company that conducts its own feasibility study of specific export and/or investment projects. Contact information can be found in Appendix A.

Review Internal Considerations and Decisions

At this point, you know where you are headed and why and you have a reasonably good understanding of your target market based on the Trial Run and additional research. Your next charge is to take a close look at your own organization. It is time to determine what decisions and/or changes must be made in order to maximize the success of Market Penetration.

Reassessing Readiness to Export

The best approach is to begin by reassessing your readiness to export. Using the same format that you used in Phase I, the Export Readiness Assessment and Action Plan Worksheet (see Worksheet 8), will allow you to see how your organization has grown in terms of its ability to deal effectively with export transactions. You can quickly determine both your strengths and weaknesses as they relate to the expanded export program. Your final score will undoubtedly be much higher than the first time you went through the process. Regular reassessments will enable you to continue making decisions that will constantly improve the effectiveness of your organization because you can focus on improving weaknesses and capitalizing on strengths.

Increasing the Expertise of the Export Team

One of the main considerations to explore is the level of expertise of your export team. On the plus side, you know that their export skills are better than when you made your first Trial Run decision. Through that process the export team gained experience in export transactions, documentation requirements, and a basic understanding of export procedures. Your initial experience was so successful that you decided to expand your effort in the Trial Run market. However, now you are talking about a little more than export skills. The export team must be able to respond to the new demands that will be placed on your organization as you become more aggressive in export markets. They must develop a wide range of more sophisticated international business skills, including knowledge of the culture and business practices. Language skill, at this point, would be very helpful in developing and maintaining strong relationships in your target country.

You should reassess the export-related tasks and responsibilities and repeat the process of inventorying knowledge and skills among existing personnel. This exercise will assist you in determining the type of additional training needed, who should be included in the training, and what additional staff, if any, must be hired. It will also be useful as you adjust or redesign position descriptions to reflect the new or expanded responsibilities.

- -

CASE EXAMPLE: Anitec's personnel and management style reflects its commitment to exporting. At the headquarters in Binghamton, New York, personnel with international experience are preferred. But if the right blend of technical and international expertise cannot be found, Anitec trains the people it has on staff to meet the demands of exporting. Management's style is hands-on, gaining understanding of the company's markets and unique situations that exist from country to country by traveling extensively. This allows them to respond more quickly and effectively when problems arise.

Educational programs that you explore at this point will be of two types: (1) those providing broad country market information and (2) those related to a specific aspect of exporting. Every department in your organization will have a need for more advanced training. Top management should participate in executive global round tables or briefings. This will enable the management team to more accurately develop a three- to five-year strategic plan, be aware of new opportunities, and monitor critical issues and concerns. Programs of this nature are organized on a country or regional basis and are held in the United States or abroad. In some cases, they focus on a specific industry outlook within the region. Business International Corporation, the American Management Association, and the World Trade Center Association are excellent sources of executive development (see Appendix A).

A second type of education deals more with specific elements of the export process. Useful programs might include topics such as preparing for a foreign trade show, export documentation and traffic, the international business plan, competitive analysis, understanding and maximizing tax incentive strategies for exporters, preparing for a foreign visit, and other topics that address the more complex issues of an expanded export program. The above organizations as well as local, state, and federal export promotion organizations, colleges and universities, and private sector training firms offer a wide range of international training programs.

Again, it is important to commit to international business education at all levels of the organization and for all departments. To supplement your education program, you will want to expand your international library to include more publications that focus on current events such as *International Trade Reporter: Current Reports.*

CASE EXAMPLE: Bondhus Corporation is committed to the training and development of all its employees. Each person develops his or her own program, with the company contributing the equivalent of up to 15 percent of that person's salary for training. While no specific international courses are required, managers make suggestions if certain skill areas need strengthening.

Looking at the Need for an Export Department

You will need to decide if an export department will be required to meet the needs of both the export program and the organization's goals and objectives. As the demands of the Market Penetration program increase, there is a tendency for staff who have both domestic and export job responsibilities to give a lower priority to the export tasks because they are more time-consuming. Consequently, the export program will begin to stall. An export department devoted exclusively to pursuing foreign markets is one way of ensuring that Market Penetration is a priority for those assigned the responsibility. If an export department is to be created, you will need to decide which individuals will become part of the new unit and if it will be necessary to hire additional management or staff. Creation of an export department will not preclude the need for a companywide export team.

CASE EXAMPLE: Naremco, the parent company of Cambridge Products, Ltd., started getting inquiries for their livestock feed additives and mold inhibiting product over twenty years ago. In 1974 it decided to approach exporting in a more structured way and established an international division within the company. After several years it was decided to establish a subsidiary company to handle exports. In 1980, Cambridge Products, Ltd., was formed to run Naremco's international operations. Today, Cambridge Products accounts for about 15 percent of Naremco's sales and has customers in Australia, Asia, Central and South America, Canada, the Caribbean, the Middle East, and Europe.

Modifying the Product for the Market

Based on your decision to penetrate the market, will you have greater chances of success if you modify or adapt the product in some way? This could include adaptation of the physical product, the packaging/ labeling, or the service to be provided as part of the product. The product may generate sales without any modification; however, at this point, the goal is to penetrate the market, so you must be willing to consider changes that will help to ensure the desired level of sales.

Some of the major factors that influence the necessity to adapt your product include the technical skills of the user; labor costs in the target market and the impact your product might have on those costs; educational level necessary to understand or use your product; level of income necessary to purchase and maintain your product; degree of maintenance required and availability of servicing; climatic conditions affecting the product; voluntary or mandatory standards compliance; governmental regulations affecting purchase or usage; buyer preferences impacting demand for your product in its current form; competitive or substitute goods available and acceptable to the buyer; method of shipment and its ability to meet required delivery schedules while remaining price competitive; and cultural factors impacting the acceptance of your product as it currently exists. Of course, the degree of impact of any of these factors will depend on the type of product you are exporting into that market. For example, culture is a much more significant factor if you are marketing a consumer nondurable versus a product intended for the industrial market.

One of the most important considerations in finalizing an adaptation decision is the cost of modifying the product. This cost must be weighed against the profits that would be realized through a higher volume of exports to the target market. It will be helpful at this point if you review the assumptions you made about your market potential and the overall view of your product in relation to the market.

As exporting becomes a more significant percentage of your overall company sales, you should ensure that new products be designed for a global market. Research and development should consider product characteristics as they relate to international markets at the developmental stage. For example, meeting the standards of high potential export markets at the drawing board stage will be a lot less costly than allocating resources to do this under a product adaptation strategy. Developing a product that requires minimal after-sale servicing will alleviate many of the complexities of successfully developing export markets for your product. Designing a package that will be acceptable in several markets will save time and money later.

CASE EXAMPLE: Wahl Clipper Corporation believes that in order to be competitive in a global marketplace, particularly with consumer goods, it is necessary to design and/or adapt the product to meet customer expectations. Wahl's success in the export market is largely due to the fact that the company has been willing to adapt to various electrical voltages and cycles, translate the information contained on the package and the instructions, and price in local currency to the extent possible.

Satisfying the Customer

Customer satisfaction is a critical aspect of successful Market Penetration and can sometimes be difficult to monitor. The more you rely on outside marketing assistance and the less feedback you demand from your representatives, the less likely you can be responsive to the needs or demands of the market. Clearly, the only way to meet the needs of the customer is to understand those needs and be in a position to monitor changes in the needs. This reinforces the need for learning more about your market segments.

Customer satisfaction goes hand-in-hand with customer service. Service is as important in your export markets as in the domestic market and you should have policies and procedures in place that clearly address this issue. If you are exporting to distributors who are in turn making the product available to the end user, you must work to ensure that you provide the required level of service to your distributor and that quality service is assured throughout the channel. After all, the service provided by channel members is going to affect your sales, profits, and reputation.

Providing quality service and ensuring customer satisfaction will require that you and your export team have a clear understanding of the culture, local customs, and business practices in order to establish and maintain good customer relations. Regular communication will foster the development of relationships that will be critical to your success.

CASE EXAMPLE: Benfield Electric International, Ltd. (BEI) has found success by operating according to the philosophy that customer satisfaction comes first. And offering great service is sometimes problematic for BEI; it must meet its customers' critical delivery requirements while relying on the performance of the manufacturers with which it works. BEI works to create customer satisfaction in a number of ways. Above all, the company strives to provide fast and timely delivery. The quality of the final delivery is ensured through careful packaging. BEI uses heavy duty materials, photographs the material and export markings for documentation, and provides detailed packing lists so that the customers can manage the incoming product. "It is important to use whatever methods are necessary in packaging to avoid a dissatisfied customer who has lost time and money due to poor quality packaging," says BEI's president. He further states that inadequate service, even on occasion, would probably cost BEI the relationship. And that is the second major component of BEI's service philosophy for building long-term relationships. Cultural sensitivity and personal interaction are the cornerstones of these relationships. BEI found that the real difficulties of exporting arise out of human nature, nationalism, mistrust, poor communication, and misunderstanding of local customs. To overcome these difficulties and create the long-lasting relationships, "we use common sense and good judgment. We treat people the way we wish to be treated,'' says BEI's president.

Financing Market Expansion

Begin thinking about what level of financial resources will be committed to this expanded export activity. For this stage of export, it will be necessary to do the following:

- ▲ Travel to the market to meet with buyers and gain a better perspective on the market itself.
- ▲ Participate in trade shows either as a way of identifying distributors/buyers or as a cooperative effort with your existing distributor.
- ▲ Internationalize your company by translating brochures or at least the product descriptions and a cover letter.
- ▲ Identify training opportunities for management, staff, and production personnel.
- ▲ Obtain data or conduct limited market research.

Based on the needs of your company and your product, you will have to prioritize the activities to be undertaken and commit appropriate levels of financial resources to ensure successful implementation.

Your actual budget will be prepared at a later point when you develop your export sales forecast and other planning documents. Ideally, you will develop a one-year budget and then prepare budget estimates for three to five years into the future.

Adjusting Policies and Procedures

Another internal consideration is the development of policies and procedures related to export. Policy statements provide a focal point for management and other personnel to understand the course of action the company will take. Procedures that are carefully developed will minimize the time required to perform specific export functions.

Now you are ready to begin the process of developing your company's strategic export plan. You have a clear picture of where your company is going and why, you have established a frame of reference by stating your assumptions, and you have completed an analysis of your target market and internal factors that will affect export plans and decisions. You are now ready for the final preparatory task to be completed before actually developing your company's strategic export plan. You should now plan a strategic focus session for your management team.

Hold a Strategic Focus Session

Prior to formulating the strategic plan, management should spend a few days, preferably away from the office, participating in a strategy session to develop a consensus on many of the issues related to export and to develop the foundation for a strategic export plan that can be supported by the entire group. This approach helps to ensure comprehensive planning because it encourages input from each of the functional areas of the organization—marketing, sales, finance, research and development, transportation, credit, shipping, production, inventory, personnel, and administration. The most productive approach to this type of session is to have each manager prepare information addressing the strategies, issues, and opportunities related to his or her respective department, which will be presented and discussed during the session.

Rethinking the Issues

This is also the time to discuss issues such as alternatives to your current export distribution method or market entry strategy, export pricing policies, and other highly strategic decisions that must be reviewed in light of your expanded export goals. If you are currently selling through an agent or if you have established a distribution agreement, you should ask yourself if that approach will be adequate to achieve your long term export goals. The decision regarding the best way to penetrate the foreign market will depend primarily on three factors: (1) the nature of your product, (2) the level of resources you are able to commit, and (3) the degree of control you want to maintain over the export activity.

Defining the Session Objectives

The objectives of the strategic planning session should be clearly defined and announced well in advance. The time commitment on the part of management will be substantial, so it is important that advance preparation be sufficient to ensure the achievement of the objectives. The following objectives will guide you in planning:

1. *Review the company's Export Readiness Assessment and Action Plan as revised in the previous section.* The purpose of this review is to ensure that all managers have a common understanding of how the organization has progressed since its initial export activity. It will enable the management team to examine the strengths and weaknesses, as well as problems and opportunities. This, in turn, will serve to guide the strategic planning process.

2. *Participate in briefings regarding your industry in a global market.* Ideally, you would invite a guru from your industry to lead a round-table discussion as a kick off to the overall strategic planning session. The type of person you invite will depend on financial resources available for this purpose. Possible speakers range from a local economist to an appropriate representative from your industry association, to a nationally or internationally recognized expert in your industry. You could also consider contracting with an international research firm with industry expertise and have them conduct a customized research study for presentation at the strategic session.

Some of the questions to be explored during this session include: What are the trends and projections for your industry internationally? What global economic indicators are tied to your industry? How can you best anticipate changes and their impact and then develop strategies to capitalize on opportunities?

Getting input such as this from outside your organization will be extremely useful as a means of stimulating new ideas, generating enthusiasm and interest among management, and providing opportunities to network with experts in the industry. It will also serve as a deterrent to developing tunnel vision or the tendency to fail to examine the situation from every angle.

3. *Include international trade as part of the company's mission statement.* You may already have a mission statement; and if so, you should review it to ensure that it is broad enough to encompass your commitment to an expanded international effort. There will be less chance of misdirected activity if both the management team and the staff have a clear understanding of the company's scope—the who, what and how of your business. They can then take ownership of this vision and feel a greater

sense of accomplishment as goals come to fruition. There is no substitute for employees taking a personal interest in the destiny of the company.

The mission statement should clearly and concisely state the purpose of your company's existence. Each company must develop its own mission statement based on the purpose it wishes to serve and then goals, objectives, and strategies are developed within the context of the mission.

4. *Establish goals for the export program and formulate the basis for a strategic export plan.* A significant effort should be made to establish realistic goals, because the strategic plan will be based on a long-range approach to achieving those goals. Your company's goals should be established within the context of the level of resources that are being committed to the export effort. This, then, implies that there is a limit to the number of goals that can be successfully pursued.

Based on the goals that are established, the remainder of the session will be devoted to developing a consensus on the general direction of the strategic export plan. The end result should be twofold. First, management should agree on a conceptual framework that will enable the company to identify and respond to opportunities in the global market. Second, there should be further definition regarding the responsibility of each member of the management team as it relates to the requirements of the expanded export program.

It is not advisable during the session to attempt to finalize the strategic export plan. Instead, an individual or team should be appointed to prepare a draft of the strategic plan based on the consensus reached at the session regarding mission and goals.

5. *Determine how the strategic export plan will be integrated into the company's overall plan.* You have formally acknowledged export as a critical element to the company's success. During the Trial Run, export activity may have been thought of as isolated from the domestic business. At this point, management should decide how to best integrate the export plan with the company's business and marketing plan to help ensure that both domestic and international strategies are consistent.

Develop the Strategic Export Plan

The strategic export plan should extend over a three- to five-year period. As you become more familiar with exporting and your target market, it will be easier to plan for this length of time. Your ability to do adequate long-range planning will be influenced by the type of product you produce and your industry. If your technology changes rapidly, it will be more difficult for you to plan far into the future than if your product has a relatively long life cycle.

CASE EXAMPLE: Anitec Image believes that the export market should never be treated as secondary or as an outlet for excess capacity. The export plan is part of the overall planning and budgeting process in which three-year goals, reviewed annually, are set for each market. Anitec calls this the rolling three-year forecast. This process helps Anitec deliver the same quality product and service worldwide.

The plan you develop should be dynamic and have the flexibility to be adjusted to reflect changes in the market, respond to problems, and take advantage of opportunities. At the same time, it must be solid enough to command the long-term commitment of time and resources. The strategic planning process is one of constant review, evaluation, and modification to move the organization toward its goals.

The plan itself is based on objectives and strategies. Specific objectives are established as an extension of the broad goals agreed upon during the strategic session. They are statements of the results that are necessary in order to successfully achieve the goals. Since most companies measure success in quantitative terms—dollars of profit, volume of sales, number of orders, percentage of total market, number of clients served, reduction in cost per order processed—it follows that objectives would be expressed in quantitative terms. The company is then able to measure the degree of success by comparing actual performance to established objectives.

Having established both goals and objectives, your next step is to develop long-range strategies that will move your company toward the achievement of the goals and objectives. This is a continuation of the process you began at the strategic planning session. Now you must take the strategic direction that was agreed upon and develop it into a more specific road map that charts the course you will follow. Your direction is not charted in stone, and as with any good road map, you have the option to make minor modifications in your route or to change direction completely depending on the circumstances that you encounter during the course of the trip. If you make a wrong turn, there are opportunities to rectify the situation and still reach your destination.

The strategic plan provides long-range direction for a number of factors including rate of growth; market share development; products to be marketed internationally; market segments to be targeted; image to be projected; distribution channel strategies; advertising, promotion, and other communications strategies; and pricing strategies.

In addition, production strategies should address existing plant capacity as it relates to longer range growth projections. If expansion is required, plans must be developed far in advance to arrange for the necessary capital expenditures and implementation timeframe to minimize interference with existing production. At the other extreme, you may be projecting excess capacity due to anticipated future developments in your industry. In this case, the strategic plan addresses the situation by developing alternative uses for the excess capacity. One example might be to develop a private label component to your manufacturing opportunities. Producing for OEM accounts in foreign markets might be another option.

Based on your goals, objectives, and strategies, it will be necessary to develop a projection of what it will take in terms of resources to successfully implement the plan. This includes time, manpower, and financial resources. The key at this point is to make a definite commitment that the strategic plan will be implemented, that it will be modified and adjusted when necessary, and that the total package of necessary resources will be available to those who are assigned the responsibility for successful implementation. Ongoing commitment is the single most important factor in determining the success of an export effort.

CASE EXAMPLE: Bondhus Corporation, a manufacturer of hex tools, believes that the real benefits of exporting are only realized by those companies who have a continued commitment from the top. Resources tend to shift as priorities shift; so unless exporting remains a top priority, it will be difficult to maintain the resource commitment. Planning is a major component of that commitment.

The strategic plan is management's tool for keeping the company on track in fulfilling its mission and achieving its goals and objectives. For this reason, it is necessary to have a system that enables management to easily review progress, evaluate results, and determine necessary modifications. You can now begin to understand the importance of establishing quantitative objectives, which are translated into projections and then later measured against actual results.

It should be stressed that the strategic plan is not a stagnant document with a beginning and ending date. It is a dynamic, continuous document that never becomes useless or outdated. With each planning cycle, you simply roll the plan out for another year or two. The first attempt to develop a strategic plan will be the most difficult and time consuming; from that point, it is a matter of refining and updating the information and establishing goals and objectives that reflect the expanding opportunities available to the organization.

Step 7:

Prepare the Tactical Plan

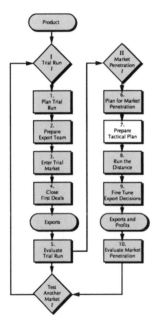

In this step, your company prepares a plan outlining the specific actions it will take to implement the strategic plan. Usually tactical plans cover a period of from twelve to eighteen months. For market penetration planning, it is best to formulate a one-year tactical plan with specific actions that will address each of the objectives developed in the strategic planning process. In addition, you should project for an additional six months because of the lead time necessary for many international events. You will, in effect, have an eighteen-month rolling plan that will help to ensure a smooth and continuous export operation.

Determine the Actions

The tactical plan outlines specific actions to be taken to implement the strategies. The following discussion addresses many of the factors you will need to consider.

Adapting the Product

Make any necessary product adaptation to better meet the needs of the target market. It may be necessary for you to develop a compromise position when you assess the requirements of the market in relation to resources, manufacturing capability, and your profit goals. The necessity for product alterations will be greater in cases where you have significant competition or when the product is not new to the market. In order to facilitate product adaptation decisions, you should establish policies to guide your decision-making process and provide a framework for evaluating each market.

Reviewing Your Packaging and Labeling

Packaging and labeling requirements will need to be reviewed. Results may range from minor modifications to totally recreating the packaging. Government regulations may have caused you to make some modifications during the Trial Run. Now you will want to more closely examine the packaging needs throughout the channel of distribution. How will the product be handled? What quantities will most likely be purchased by each level in the channel? What size and type of packaging will the end user prefer to purchase? What type of information must the label provide? Is the required information sufficient to stimulate sales or should additional information be included? What is the cost of the packaging in relation to the value of the product, or in relation to how much the end user is willing to pay for the product? How does your packaging fit into the overall promotion of your product? How might cultural differences impact packaging and labeling requirements? How will your packaging technology respond to the growing concerns for environmental protection?

Reviewing the Brand Name and Trademark

You will also need to consider the impact of your current brand name and trademark on product sales to your target market. Your brand is important internationally because it provides a means of differentiating your product from that of your competitors. In many cases, a strong brand name in the domestic market will enhance your sales abroad, so you may decide to market under the same brand in all countries. In other instances, it may be advisable to establish a separate brand name for each market using local terminology. Weigh the advantages and disadvantages of each approach in relation to your Market Penetration goals. For example, if your brand has a reputation for quality, that reputation may follow your product around the world. It is also easier to coordinate your promotional materials if you market under one brand.

On the other hand, the culture may not be accepting of a foreign brand, it may have an inappropriate meaning in the target country, or it may already be registered in that market. Thus there may be a need to establish brands on a market by market basis. If your company is small and your brand is not widely known, you may be in a good position to private label for an established distributor or a large retail chain. Your brand policies will depend on how your company can best achieve its objectives in each market.

Arranging for Service and Warranties

Service and warranties are also part of the product strategy and are often more difficult to offer to the foreign buyer. If post-sale servicing is a critical element for your product, you must ensure that appropriate arrangements are made as part of the distribution decision. You might also explore ways to minimize the level of after-sale servicing that will be required. For example, use components or materials that tend to be the most maintenance free. The end user will, for many types of products, be concerned with the warranty and the distributor's ability to stand behind the foreign manufacturer's warranty. If you choose not to extend a warranty on an exported product, you may find that this is illegal in some markets or your distributor feels it's necessary to provide a warranty in order to be competitive. Consider working out an arrangement with your distributor or some other organization to extend and/or service the warranty.

In order to facilitate the quality of service, you may want to consider providing training for your distributors or other representatives at your facility or at their location. Training would cover all aspects of repair, installation, and other servicing requirements. It is important to establish service policies that enable your company to develop and maintain an image of providing a high level of service. After all, it is the reputation of your brand name at stake.

- -

CASE EXAMPLE: Little Giant, a pump manufacturer, requires that its foreign distributors be able to provide high quality after-sale service. This approach differs from the service structure in the United States, where service depots are established and wholesalers are not required to have technical knowledge. Even though its warranty claim rate is extremely low for its industry (just one percent compared to 5 to 6 percent for many of its competitors), Little Giant expects a high degree of service commitment from international distributors. Little Giant managers visit with its foreign distributors at least once a year; the distributors are either brought to Oklahoma or the company managers go to the country. Little Giant finds that face-to-face meetings are essential to building the relationship, reviewing business, and dealing with any service or training needs the distributors may have.

CASE EXAMPLE: Wahl Clipper Corporation has a policy of not extending its warranty to foreign sales. However, Wahl's distributors frequently add their own warranty. One distributor even doubled Wahl's U.S. warranty period because of the confidence the distributor had in the company's products.

Implementing the Promotion Strategy

Your tactical plan should clearly identify the specific actions to be taken to implement the promotion strategy. For example, what type of advertising campaign will you implement in the target export market? Will personal selling be required, and if so, how will this be conducted? What sales promotions will be utilized in the market? Which trade shows will be targeted? How will additional publicity be achieved? How will the company coordinate a public relations program? Each of these issues must be addressed in very specific action steps to help ensure that sales, market share, and other objectives are met.

Advertising can be a highly effective method of communicating with organizations in your channel of distribution as well as with end users.

Depending on your product and the extent to which advertising must be used as a means of promotion, you may need to establish policies regarding responsibility for advertising. You may choose to maintain control over this function or you may decide that all or part of the responsibility should rest with your foreign representative.

You might provide an advertising allowance to your representative and depend on that organization to determine both the appropriate message and publications. Normally you can expect your representative to match your financial contribution. Your representative may also assist you in establishing an advertising budget and media plan for the target country.

In addition to advertising the specific product, you may also find it to your advantage to place corporate advertising in targeted publications. This helps to establish your company and your brand and will provide additional support to your foreign representative.

The type of media selected for your advertising campaign depends on the promotional objectives that were established as part of your strategic plan. It is a mistake to assume that the same type of media you use domestically will be available in your target country. For example, in a number of countries, government restrictions prevent use of television or radio for commercial purposes. You may also have difficulty obtaining information regarding circulation and reader demographics when you attempt to prioritize publications.

Finally, you may find it necessary to change the message contained in your advertising depending on the reasons that the product is purchased and/or the way the product is used. The extent to which you can use the same message in your target country that you do domestically depends on the type of product you are marketing. Consumer goods generally require a more tailored approach than do industrial goods.

During the Trial Run, you probably relied heavily on direct mail to reach potential buyers or representatives. As you move into Market Penetration, it may be advantageous to expand your direct mail activity to give greater exposure to your company, brand name, and product. If you have a representative in the market, you can refer potential buyers to that individual. You can obtain mailing lists through the services recommended in Phase I or others that you learned about through the Trial Run. Remember to let your representative know that you are planning a direct mail campaign. This will allow for advance preparation for the expected increase in requests and also eliminate the possibility that the representative will feel you are trying to circumvent its level in the channel of distribution.

Many products will be sold through the sales force of your foreign representative. This means that you will usually have no direct control over the selling effort. It will most certainly be in your best interest to provide any type of training that will help to ensure the effectiveness of the sales force. This may involve technical training so these people will be fully knowledgeable about the product, how it functions, relevant technology, use and applications, and any other technical data that will enable them to make an appropriate sales presentation. You may also find it necessary to provide sales training to help tailor the sales message regarding product benefits and its advantages over the competition. In addition, they should be aware of the sales projections and other marketing information that you have developed for that market. Many companies also offer a variety of incentives to the distributor's sales force to increase the degree of interest in promoting the product.

Sales promotions, point-of-purchase displays, and various other incentive programs are used in many foreign markets just as they are in the United States. However, it is critical to examine laws and practices on a country-by-country basis to prevent conducting inappropriate promotions. You should also depend on your foreign representative to provide guidance as to the appropriateness of this promotional approach. The representative is likely to favor give-aways but not product price reductions that will cut into profits. Be sure that you understand the laws and practices related to this area of promotion.

A major component of your promotional plan will probably be participation in international trade fairs. The purpose of your involvement will be twofold. First, it will provide an excellent opportunity to expose your product to potential buyers and/or distributors; and, second, it will allow you to learn about your competition first hand and obtain other valuable market data. Once you establish representation in the market, you may want to exhibit along with your representative. It is important to keep in mind that international trade fairs are attended by potential buyers from many countries. With this in mind, you must be prepared to provide information about your product in the most appropriate languages. For example, participation in a European trade fair may require translations into German and French, as well as the English version. Trade fair participation is discussed in detail at the beginning of Step 8.

Additional publicity regarding your company and your product can be achieved by regularly submitting news releases to appropriate industry or customer-oriented publications. The releases can relate to new product developments, company recognition or any other information that would have a positive impact on your company's image in the eyes of customers, distributors, the foreign government, and any other group that is important to your organization. Even though many of these will go unpublished, the cost is minimal and the results can be surprisingly positive.

A well-coordinated public relations program will be important to a successful Market Penetration strategy. You will want to be on top of developments in your target country that might impact your product, and be prepared to demonstrate that you are a responsible company. For example, as nations around the world become more concerned with environmental protection, you may establish and announce new corporate policies having a positive impact on this issue. If, for some reason, your product has created a problem for end users, you should provide an immediate response to minimize the long-term damage to future sales in that market. Good public relations will not solve every problem; however, having policies in place to deal with these types of issues will shorten your response time considerably. But remember, the key to effective public relations is being in touch with your target market.

The Schedule of Promotional Activities Worksheet (see Worksheet 21) provides a format for scheduling your promotional program. This should include the timing of activities such as direct mail promotions, follow-up calls or mailings, trips abroad, product news releases, trade show participation or attendance, development of new promotion materials, and other relevant activities. This schedule will help you to assign responsibilities among the export team and plan work schedules.

Planning for Distribution

If, during Phase I, you established a distributor in the target market and you plan to continue with that arrangement, you must determine whether or not the distributor needs additional support from your company. If so, you should jointly develop a plan for the actions to be taken and the level of support required to ensure success.

If the market potential is relatively great, you may feel that maintaining a closer relationship with the distributor network will help to ensure greater market share for your product. This may lead to a decision to provide additional support to that network by having a company person on site. Depending on your product, you may feel that while the distributor reaches the appropriate market segments, sales could be sub-

WORKSHEET 21. Schedule of Promotional Activities

SCHEDULE OF PROMOTIONAL ACTIVITIES															

FASTRACK
Success Through Fast-Track Exporting

Purpose: To organize and schedule the export promotion program.

Company Name/Division _____

Product		Country							Year						

Team Member Assigned	Promotional Activity	Month													

Notes:

Completed by		Date													

Copyright Export Resource Associates, Inc., 1990

090

stantially increased by having someone from your company who is more knowledgeable about the technical aspects of the product participate in the marketing activities. This would also be desirable if you are involved in an industry with rapidly changing technologies or product applications.

It may be unrealistic to expect that the distributor will be in a position to keep up with the advancements. If your long-range plan is to establish a foreign subsidiary in the market, you may view the in-country office as a natural evolution toward that goal. If you are exporting to several countries in the same area, you may choose to establish a regional office in addition to or instead of country offices.

You should review the agreement you established with your representative during the Trial Run. Based on the above discussion, is it necessary to modify the agreement? Or having gained considerable experience during the Trial Run, you may decide that your company's objectives would be better served by selecting a new representative.

In the event you decide to sever the relationship with an existing distributor and arrange for new representation, you can use your contacts in the market and the techniques described in Phase I to identify an appropriate representative.

Actions taken in regard to distribution should be based on the requirements to get your product into the hands of the buyers. In some markets, this might require utilizing multiple channels and a number of distributors to reach the various market segments. Your tactical plan should also address the need to provide motivation to all members of your distribution channel.

Reviewing Transportation Objectives

As you move into Market Penetration, you may be able to lower per unit transportation costs as a result of the additional volume you are shipping. During the Trial Run, you may have relied on consolidation services and are now shipping full container loads. If you have a bulk commodity, you may have filled only part of a vessel and are now in a position to utilize a charter service solely for your product or secure better rates from a shipping line. You may have initially relied on the services of a foreign freight forwarder for arranging for your transportation needs ranging from completing shipping documents to negotiating shipping rates. You may now want to consider assuming some of these functions in-house, or at least be actively involved in obtaining shipping information on a regular basis to ensure that your forwarder is providing you with the best options. Keep in mind that best does not always mean cheapest. Transportation costs and reliability can often mean the difference between success and failure in a foreign market. It is advisable to have in-house expertise if not full control of this function as you move into Market Penetration.

Reviewing Price and Terms

In establishing your market penetration price, consider the additional information that you obtained regarding your competitors' pricing, the appropriateness of your current price for each market segment, the impact of additional sales volume on price and profit objectives, and expectations of the various levels in the channel of distribution to which you sell. You should also review terms of sale and payment methods. You may have established a strong relationship with your representative or other buyers and find it possible to modify your terms and/or payment method to reflect the nature of the relationship. For example, you may have required a letter of credit during the Trial Run and now feel comfortable doing business on open account, reducing both the complexity and cost for your buyer. In addition, you may have decided that in order to increase your competitiveness in the market, you will need to offer extended payment terms.

Establish the Budgets and Forecasts

After identifying the tactical steps to be taken in order to successfully implement the strategic plan, you will need to prepare corresponding sales forecasts, expense budgets, and projected financial statements. Annual sales forecasts should be completed to correspond to your company's fiscal year beginning and ending dates. The forecast should be compiled on a monthly basis to assist other planning areas such as production, inventory control, shipping, and purchasing. These figures will also serve as a managerial tool to set sales goals for your foreign representative(s). The Annual Sales Forecast Worksheet (see Worksheet 22) is an example of how you can project and track monthly sales.

Project sales forecasts in both dollars and units based on the specific objectives you established earlier. By stating all of the assumptions used to prepare the forecast, you have a means for management to adjust

WORKSHEET 22. Annual Sales Forecast

| ANNUAL SALES FORECAST | | | | | $\equiv$**FASTRACK**
Success Through Fast-Track Exporting |

Purpose: To forecast annual export sales and compare planned to actual sales.

Company Name/Division _____

Product			Country		Year

Month	Amount		Units		Comments
	Planned	Actual	Planned	Actual	
Total					
Over (Under) Plan					

Notes:

Completed by			Date		

Copyright Export Resource Associates, Inc., 1990

090

the forecast to reflect change. Without assumption statements, it will be difficult to maintain any accountability for the final numbers. Assumptions will be based on an analysis of the past, current and projected market status, industry trends, competitor analysis, and other relevant factors.

The accuracy of income forecasts cannot be overstated. You will make many decisions based on anticipated income level. You may hire additional staff, expand production capacity, or approve a higher level of spending based on projected income. Some of these decisions will be difficult to undo without great expense—some are irreversible. Plans to increase overhead should be made only after careful assessment of export projections and the corresponding assumptions.

Also, keep in mind that you are working in a complex international environment with a lot of unknowns. Plan for setbacks so that your income stream will reflect the ups and downs likely to occur in your export sales.

You should then project sales for each market segment identified earlier as priority segments on the Sales by Market Segment Worksheet (see Worksheet 23). It is important to develop the projection based on market segments as this will assist you in allocating resources. In some cases, you may have separate distribution channels established for each market segment. In other cases, it may be a matter of allocating resources for more than one promotional program. You may have different pricing strategies or varying product modifications for each segment. In any event, you will want to know the percentage each segment contributes to total sales.

In preparing your export budget, be sure to include items such as product adaptations, contract services for translations, market research, foreign travel, trade show attendance or participation, foreign advertising, promotional materials, bank charges, and other expenses that are the result of the expanded export efforts. In addition, it may be advisable to join industry associations in your target country or you may decide to comply with voluntary standards in order to gain greater acceptance in the market. For example, Japan has a number of voluntary standards certifications, such as Japanese Industrial Standards and Japanese Agricultural Standards, that enhance the marketability of your product. You or your staff may want to attend international trade conferences to obtain information helpful to your strategic planning. It may be necessary to expand your export library to include more sophisticated trade information or to add on-line database services. Also, you will most certainly have

WORKSHEET 23.   Sales by Market Segment

SALES BY MARKET SEGMENT									FASTRACK
									Success Through Fast-Track Exporting

Purpose: To project annual export sales and compare planned to actual sales for each market segment. Note: Refer to Worksheets 20 and 22.

Company Name/Division _____

| Product | | | | Country | | | | Year |

Market Segment Category	Annual Amount				Annual Units				Comments
	Planned	%	Actual	%	Planned	%	Actual	%	
Total									
Over (Under) Plan									

Notes:

Completed by   Date

Copyright Export Resource Associates, Inc., 1990

increased communication costs due to your increased use of fax, telex, international express mail, and overseas telephone calls.

If you made a decision during your strategic planning to expand your production capacity or facility or make some other capital expenditure, you should include a portion of the capital budget in your annual tactical budget.

Expense budgets should also include assumptions that served as the basis for determining the required level of spending and how this allocation is going to achieve the desired export results. Be sure to develop adequate methods of controlling the budget. You will want to closely monitor expenditures related to the export program so that discrepancies can be identified and the budget modified.

Based on the information developed for your budget and sales forecasts along with other financial data, you should prepare projected financial statements.

Develop the Operational Plan

Another component of the tactical plan is the operational plan, which provides a timetable for implementing the tactical plan and assigns responsibility to members of the export team. Keep it very short, preferably using a checklist approach that identifies what action is required, who is responsible for implementation, and by what date the action item should be completed. This plan will provide a vehicle for accountability within the organization and help to ensure that all tasks in the tactical plan are implemented.

Step 8:

Run the Distance

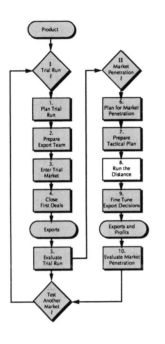

There is no substitute for visiting the market to get a better understanding of your product in relation to market needs, competition, and issues that have an impact on the marketing and sale of your product.

Visit the Market

Perhaps the best way to get an overall view of the market, your industry, and key players in that industry is to participate as an exhibitor in an international trade fair. This represents a relatively effective route to expanding export activity, particularly if the fair is carefully selected. In addition, it is a useful means of conducting both product and market research.

Exhibiting abroad will take the same degree of advance planning, market research, and preparation as required for your major domestic events—perhaps even more. The Trade Show Timetable and Checklist (see Worksheet 24) will assist you in preparing to exhibit at an international trade show and monitoring your show and show-related tasks.

The process starts from twelve to twenty-four months before the date of the show if you want to reap the maximum benefits from your participation. An early start will give you time to select the best show

(text continues on page 195)

WORKSHEET 24. Trade Show Timetable and Checklist

TRADE SHOW TIMETABLE & CHECKLIST	*FASTRACK*
	Success Through Fast-Track Exporting

Purpose: To plan and check your progress at every stage of the trade show process.

Trade Show _____

Open Date	Close Date	City / Country

Planned / Done	Task	Assigned To
	12 - 24 Months Before Show:	
___ ___	Establish initial objectives for exhibiting at a show.	_____
___ ___	**Identify major shows in foreign Trial Run or Market Penetration market that are** appropriate for your product and customer segments.	_____
___ ___	Contact EPOs for information on shows.	_____
___ ___	Contact U.S. exhibitors at shows for information on shows.	_____
___ ___	Contact foreign agents/distributors for information on shows.	_____
___ ___	Contact foreign customers for information on shows.	_____
___ ___	Attend shows as a visitor.	_____
___ ___	Determine best-prospect shows for your product and customer segments.	_____
___ ___	Obtain exhibitor information from the show organizers of each of the best-prospect shows.	_____
___ ___	Obtain exhibitor information from each of the U.S. or trade association pavilion organizers for each of the best-prospect shows.	_____
___ ___	Assess best-prospect shows.	_____
___ ___	Decide show at which you will exhibit.	_____
	9 - 12 Months Before Show:	
___ ___	Obtain current exhibitor information and registration forms from show organizers.	_____
___ ___	Obtain current exhibitor information and registration forms from U.S. or trade association pavilion organizers.	_____
___ ___	Decide whether to exhibit as part of a U.S. or trade association pavilion.	_____
___ ___	Submit show contract and deposit to show/pavilion organizer.	_____
___ ___	Submit hotel reservation and deposit.	_____
___ ___	Establish show and show-related objectives.	_____
___ ___	Prepare the show budget.	_____
___ ___	Prepare action plan for show, assign responsibilities, set deadlines.	_____
___ ___	Prepare action plan for show-related activities, assign responsibilities, set deadlines.	_____
	6 - 9 Months Before Show	
___ ___	Collect background materials on country, culture, customs, doing business, etc.	_____
___ ___	Start preparing exhibit layout.	_____
___ ___	Start preparing pre-show, show, and follow-up promotion materials and literature.	_____
___ ___	Start preparing materials and literature that will need to be translated.	_____
___ ___	Start preparing samples and gifts that will be given away.	_____
___ ___	Start preparing pre-show advertising and other promotional information.	_____
___ ___	Start preparing show-related activities.	_____
	3 - 6 Months Before Show:	
___ ___	Submit Agent/Distributor Service request to USDOC.	_____
___ ___	Collect mailing lists of potential agents/distributors and customers.	_____
___ ___	Finalize exhibit, equipment, and product for display.	_____
___ ___	Finalize pre-show promotion materials and literature.	_____
___ ___	Finalize show promotion materials and literature.	_____
___ ___	Finalize after-show follow-up materials and literature.	_____
___ ___	Finalize samples and gifts.	_____
___ ___	Finalize pre-show advertising and other promotional information.	_____
___ ___	Place pre-show advertising and other promotional information.	_____
___ ___	Apply for temporary export licenses if required.	_____
___ ___	Apply for ATA Carnet if required.	_____
___ ___	Apply for passports, visas, international drivers license, and other documents.	_____
___ ___	Finalize show-related activities.	_____

Trade Show Timetable & Checklist	Page 1

Copyright Export Resource Associates, Inc., 1990

Planned / Done	Task	Assigned To
	3 Months Before Show:	
____ ____	**Mail potential agents/distributors and customers pre-show materials and literature.**	_____
____ ____	Plan shipment and return of exhibit, equipment, product for display, show materials and literature, samples, gifts, and booth survival kit.	_____
____ ____	Plan pre-show interpreter.	_____
____ ____	Plan booth staffing by employees, agents/distributors, temporaries, and interpreter.	_____
____ ____	Plan after-show interpreter.	_____
____ ____	Obtain vaccinations and health certificates.	_____
____ ____	Plan booth services (e.g., electricians, lighting, furniture)	_____
____ ____	Have international attorney review sales and representation agreements.	_____
____ ____	Continue to finalize show-related activities.	_____
	2 Months Before Show:	
____ ____	Pre-arrange meetings with potential agents/distributors and customers.	_____
____ ____	Ship exhibit, equipment, product for display, show materials and literature, samples, gifts, and booth survival kit if by ocean freight.	_____
____ ____	Confirm pre-show interpreter.	_____
____ ____	Confirm booth staffing by employees, agents/distributors, temporaries, and interpreter.	_____
____ ____	Confirm after-show interpreter.	_____
____ ____	Orient employees staffing booth.	_____
____ ____	**Purchase airline tickets and make related travel arrangements.**	_____
____ ____	Confirm hotel reservations.	_____
____ ____	Continue to finalize show-related activities.	_____
	1 Month Before Show:	
____ ____	Confirm pre-arranged meetings with potential agents/distributors and customers.	_____
____ ____	Ship exhibit, equipment, product for display, show materials and literature, samples, gifts, and booth survival kit if by air freight.	_____
____ ____	Confirm arrival of exhibit, equipment, etc.	_____
____ ____	Confirm that passports, visas, and other required documents are in order.	_____
____ ____	Confirm that vaccinations and health certificates are in order.	_____
____ ____	Obtain some foreign currency and travelers checks.	_____
____ ____	Continue to finalize show-related activities.	_____
	At Show — Before Opening:	
____ ____	Last-minute check of all booth and other preparations.	_____
____ ____	Set up booth.	_____
____ ____	Meet with and orient booth staff to booth, pavilion, show, company, product, pricing and terms, etc.	_____
____ ____	Hold pre-arranged meetings.	_____
____ ____	Carry out show-related activities.	_____
	At Show:	
____ ____	Hold pre-arranged meetings.	_____
____ ____	Collect bounce-back cards.	_____
____ ____	Conduct business as planned.	_____
____ ____	Assess competition.	_____
____ ____	Prepare daily notes on contacts, developments, etc.	_____
____ ____	Brief booth staff each day.	_____
	At Show — After Closing:	
____ ____	Debrief booth staff.	_____
____ ____	Dismantle booth.	_____
____ ____	Ship exhibit, equipment, product, etc. home.	_____
____ ____	Hold pre-arranged meetings.	_____
____ ____	Follow up on business transacted at show.	_____
____ ____	Carry out show-related activities.	_____
	After Return From Show:	
____ ____	Brief sales staff on businsss transacted at show, show-related activities, and follow-up required.	_____
____ ____	Screen and qualify bounce-back cards.	_____
____ ____	Enter bounce-back information in Foreign Buyer Database.	_____
____ ____	Mail after-show follow-up materials and literature.	_____
____ ____	Follow-up on business transacted at show and at show-related activities.	_____
____ ____	Provide follow-up information to agent/distributor.	_____
____ ____	Prepare evaluation report on show and recommendations for future participation in show.	_____

Completed by	Date
Trade Show Timetable & Checklist	Page 2

for your product and customer segments. Since many of the most well-attended trade shows are completely sold out up to a year in advance, an early start will give you the best chance for participation. In the event you are unable to meet the deadline for participation as an exhibitor, you can nonetheless benefit by attending and learning more about your competitors, the buyers, new developments in the field, and other information that will be useful in the further development of your Market Penetration strategy.

The Trade Show Timetable and Checklist (Worksheet 24) identifies each task that must be completed, beginning with establishing objectives for exhibiting at a show through the completion and evaluation of the show, as well as recommendations for future participation in the show. This thorough approach will help to ensure that you do not omit some critical steps in the planning process or that you fail to be totally organized in order to fully reap the benefits of participation.

Foreign trade shows are frequently order-taking events, particularly in Europe. Attendees come to the show ready to buy on the spot or to negotiate representation agreements. Some companies claim they do most of their business in a country or region in their trade fair booth. In other countries such as Japan, shows are a means of introducing your company and your products. Therefore, you must determine what to expect from trade show attendees in your target market, what they will expect from you, and set your show objectives accordingly.

Examples of objectives might be that you are looking for on-the-spot sales or new customers, you want to introduce a new product or service, you want to find representatives, you want to gain exposure or study the market, you want to evaluate the competition, you want to train, support, and build sales for agents and/or distributors, or you want to gather information on market preferences.

Each objective should be stated so that it is specific and measurable (e.g., to close ten minimum-quantity sales within sixty days after the show). Objectives may also indicate the resources that you expect to allocate in order to achieve the objective. Given your initial statement of show objectives, seek out appropriate shows for your company in the target country. The following sources can be of help in identifying possible trade shows and in assessing their potential:

USDOC District Office
USDOC Commercial Attaches in the U.S. Embassy
State international trade office

National trade association
Previous U.S. exhibitors at show
Current/potential agents/distributors
Current/potential customers
Foreign Embassy or Consulate in the U.S.
Industry journals
Business America
Country Marketing Plan (USDOC District Office)
Exhibitions 'Round the World
Export Guide to Europe
International Tradeshow Directory

The USDOC sponsors the Overseas Trade Fair Certification Program which means that our government selects certain fairs based on their value to U.S. manufacturers and then makes an effort to attract foreign buyers. The events that are certified by the USDOC are announced in the back section of almost every issue of *Business America*, which you should have subscribed to during Phase I. Before certification, the USDOC must feel confident in the fair organizer's ability to produce a successful event and the organizer must have a track record of success.

The existence of a United States, state, or trade association pavilion at the show may be a factor in selecting your first trade show in the target market. The pavilions usually offer extra promotional services, better facilities, and pavilion services to assist you in planning and preparing for the show. In many cases, they also provide informational briefings, host social events during the show, and make introductions.

The recommendations of other U.S. exhibitors that have attended the show can help you assess it and they can offer concrete recommendations for increasing your success at the show. So, too, can customer or agent/distributor contacts, either current or potential.

If time and budget allow, it is always advisable to visit a show before you make your decision to attend. Talk with exhibitors and attendees, and then make your own assessment of the appropriateness of the show for your company. Rushing to exhibit at the wrong show is costly and can delay your success in the market, so take time to select the best show for your company and product.

Once you select the most appropriate trade show, there are a number of specific planning steps that must be taken. Obtain the exhibitor materials for registration and make your hotel reservations early to secure your first choice hotel. Determine the results you are expecting both during and after the fair, as well as the criteria by which you will evaluate the success of the show.

Establish a budget for participating in the trade fair that includes total costs associated with the exhibit, travel, and all related expenses. Factors such as exchange rate variances, import duties or import bonds, refreshments to be served in your booth, and special requirements of the booth itself are potential costs that do not have to be considered in budgeting for a domestic trade show. Keep accurate records of these expenses so you have a means of assessing cost/benefit and for developing trade show budgets in the future.

Decide who will staff your exhibit and make sure it is someone authorized to transact business on your behalf. If your product is highly technical, you should consider having one of your engineers available in your company's booth. If you have an overseas distributor who will be representing you at the show, you should still consider having someone from your company go to add prestige and assist the overseas distributor; and, at the same time, that person can evaluate and train your representative as well as gather competitive data.

Develop and implement a promotional program several weeks before the event. You will not want to take any chances that your prospective customers will not stop at your booth. You should utilize the *Export Contact List Service* available through your USDOC District Office to obtain the names and addresses of potential customers. Then prepare a brief letter inviting them to visit you at your booth and provide them with the booth number or location. You should also include information about your product, perhaps even a small product brochure. Mailing lists can also be obtained from trade organizations, publications, chambers of commerce, and other sources. You should also apply for a listing in the official fair catalog and explore the cost of placing an advertisement in the directory. Most exhibitors and attendees will keep the directory as a resource long after the exhibit is over.

Learn about foreign business practices before you leave home. An excellent and entertaining resource that provides an overview on this topic is the book or video series entitled *Going International* (see Appendix B).

Examine your product/company literature, catalogs, and other promotional material. You should consider preparing a brief description of the products on display in the appropriate language, as well as develop a conversion table based on the metric system if this is relevant to your product. In order to minimize expenses, you could prepare a translated version of your product and company information to be used in conjunction with your regular catalogs and brochures. Consult one of your EPOs or your *International Trade State and Local Resource Directory* for sources of translation assistance.

Select a freight forwarder to assist you in getting your booth furnishings and sample product or demonstration equipment to the trade show location. Most major trade shows designate an official forwarder and it may be most efficient to utilize that organization provided the price is right. You should seek advice from your forwarder regarding packing, marking, and documentation that will be required to ensure that everything is available when you need it.

Determine whether or not an ATA Carnet, which is a special customs document designed to simplify customs procedures for taking commercial samples or professional equipment abroad, can be used. If a Carnet is appropriate for the country and your product, you will be able to avoid extensive customs procedures; and since you will make arrangements in advance, your goods can clear customs accompanied or unaccompanied. This procedure allows you to save time, effort, and expense. Discuss this option with your freight forwarder or your USDOC District Office.

If you are planning to export products or equipment for demonstration purposes at a trade fair and your product falls into the validated license category, you must complete an application for a license covering a temporary export. This application will require all the documentation that is normally required to obtain a validated license; however, it does not require the usual supporting documentation issued by either the consignee or the country of ultimate destination. Instead, you must attach a statement attesting to the fact that the goods are for exhibition purposes and will be returned to the United States after their use abroad unless other arrangements have been authorized by the Bureau of Export Administration.

If you know prior to the original trade fair that the product will be exhibited at later trade fairs, you can list the other exhibition destinations on the original export license application and, if approved, no further authorization for demonstration will be required.

In the event that you plan to sell, re-export or otherwise dispose of your trade fair goods, you need prior authorization from Commerce's Bureau of Export Administration. Failure to obtain proper export licenses is a violation of the law and can result in penalties to individuals and companies. The Bureau of Export Administration has a Trade Fair Coordinator unit in its Export Counseling Division who will assist you in complying with this process. The contact information can be found in Appendix A.

Other considerations include checking on import duties, trade restrictions, and patent and trademark protection. In addition, you will want to have established credit and payment policies and have an understanding of credit risk insurance so that you are in a good position to negotiate with your potential customers.

You will want to make the most of this trade show opportunity by spending as much time as possible at the exhibition site, making sure your company's booth is always staffed, viewing other exhibits, and collecting and distributing business cards.

Also, be prepared to conduct business while you are in the target country. If you plan to have business meetings at your hotel, remember that the image of your company is affected by the level of hotel at which you stay. If your hotel is not adequate for your needs, you can sometimes make arrangements to use an office at the U.S. Embassy or one of the consulates. If you are involved in agriculture, the Foreign Agriculture Service may provide this service.

Reassess Existing Distribution Channels

If you selected a representative during Phase I, you will want to carefully evaluate performance and make a decision as to that organization's continued role with your company. Your initial selection of a representative may have been based on limited information about the individual and the market. During the Market Penetration phase, you will want to begin relying on your own contacts as they are developed. Additional contacts will be developed by undertaking such activities as attending or participating in foreign trade shows, implementing direct mail campaigns, and working with trade or industry associations. In other words, the selection you made earlier may no longer be appropriate in pursuing your longer-term objectives.

(text continues on page 200)

CASE EXAMPLE: Bondhus Corporation made a decision to appoint new representatives in most of its initial markets. The company used the services of several EPOs and its own recruiting effort to locate potential representatives and took care to select and appoint qualified and experienced representatives. However, the company did not visit the distributors before making the appointments. Upon later evaluation, the distributors they selected for the Trial Run were not given high marks for their ability to successfully assist Bondhus in the Market Penetration goal. In almost every instance, Bondhus later replaced its initial sales distributors in order to achieve its Market Penetration objectives. Now Bondhus's policy is to visit every new distributor before finalizing the appointment.

You will gain a great deal of information by traveling to your target market. However, do not overlook the benefits of inviting existing or potential distributors to visit you at your facilities. If they are planning to come to the United States for other reasons, you may offer to pay transportation from their U.S. location to your office. The advantage of this approach is that if the potential buyer commits time and money to meeting with you, they will feel more of a need to transact business. After all, they will be required to report on the accomplishments of their visit to the United States and will not want to go back empty handed.

CASE EXAMPLE: LecTec Corporation stays in touch with its local USDOC District Office to take advantage of visiting trade delegations. In fact, LecTec takes every opportunity to invite prospective customers to visit its facility and provide them with product samples. "We have people coming through almost every other week these days," says the director of international marketing. "It helps people get to know us better." LecTec believes that this kind of marketing activity can be more effective and more economical than visiting foreign markets.

The image of your product or service and the long-term success of your company in the target market depends on selecting appropriate representation. There are many types of agents and distributors and major differences in the manner in which companies operate within each category.

Select a representative who covers the geographic area that you want to have covered. In some cases, one representative can cover an entire country or region. In other cases, the country may have logical territories with each one requiring a representative. During the Trial Run you may have selected only one distributor for a country or a region. Now it is time to reassess that decision on the basis of your current knowledge of the market.

Also, the type of product you produce will influence the number of representatives you need in your target country. Your decision at this point needs to ensure that the representative will have a large enough territory to make the sales effort profitable while small enough to ensure an aggressive selling effort to penetrate the market.

In addition to your own assessment, you can rely on information from other companies that have been represented by the organization. This will shed light on factors such as reliability, business reputation, and overall success. Sources of information include the USDOC's *World Trader Data Report, Dun and Bradstreet International*, international divisions of major banks, and private credit reporting organizations. Perhaps you have already used these sources to aid in your decisions during the Trial Run. If you have not, you should make it a point to use one or more of them for future decisions.

When you get to the point of negotiating the details of the representation agreement, there are several issues that you should address if you are making a change in representation from the Trial Run. What will be the duration of the agreement? In most cases, the representative will want a long-term exclusive agreement because of the time and expense involved in establishing your product. You will want to commit to a nonexclusive shorter-term agreement to avoid being locked into an unacceptable arrangement. The representative will bargain for an automatic renewal clause and you will want to protect yourself by including language that will allow for easy termination. Your representative will most likely want you to provide support for various promotions or sales training. This is one request that you should strongly consider. Your representative's success is your success.

Other issues that must be clarified in the final agreement include the question of your representative also promoting products that compete with yours, who pays the customs, if any, levied against your product, and how discrepancies will be resolved.

You should expect your representative to provide valuable information that will be used for both your strategic and your tactical plan. This will include information about the market, the users, the sales potential, and other relevant data. Good representatives are normally willing to share information because they realize there is a big advantage to having your assistance in planning the marketing strategy. It is not inappropriate to have your representative submit an annual marketing plan indicating how it will promote the product, what opportunities and problems it anticipates, and what level of sales it intends to achieve.

CASE EXAMPLE: Bondhus Corporation works closely with its distributors to maximize sales. "We push them to work with us as a team," says the president. Instead of offering concessions and treating the importer as a customer, the company looks for ways to increase sales for both parties. It invites distributors to work with it on annual joint marketing plans, offering them a 10 percent bonus to be used for promoting Bondhus's products if they participate. "Distributors own and run their own businesses, but for us, it's almost like having our own sales office," notes the president. "And although we're demanding, we've never lost rapport with anyone."

Legal issues that should be addressed in the agreement include laws that would impact the agreement, the specifics of protection of intellectual property rights, how disputes are resolved, and noncompete clauses in the event of termination. Use an international attorney to help you develop the agreement.

Once you work the wrinkles out of your agreement, you can begin to work hand-in-hand with your representative(s) to jointly develop an effective Market Penetration program. Joint activities might include the development of the tactical plan for the market, joint participation in trade shows, cooperative advertising or other promotions, joint primary research, and jointly establishing sales goals.

In order to establish and maintain a harmonious relationship with the representative, you should probably refer all sales inquiries or leads from that market to the representative. This will be a demonstration of support for your representative and encourage a mutual sharing of information. If you anticipate cases when this will not be done, negotiate in advance to minimize potential resentment.

Reevaluate Price and Terms

Through your research and as a result of what you learned during the Trial Run, you will have a good idea of how your product or service must be priced to achieve Market Penetration. You have also learned more about the specific costs involved in exporting your product and you know that it is not sufficient to mechanically add a markup to your overall costs. You should feel confident in your ability to view pricing as a marketing element to be varied in order to achieve the marketing objectives that have been established for your target country.

In finalizing the price with your representative or other buyers, remember that middlemen expect price discounts based on the level of service they provide. For example, if your representative takes title to the goods and stocks inventory, it will expect to be compensated for these services through greater discounts. Therefore, the level of service to be provided should be clearly understood prior to quoting a price to the representative.

You should establish a price/quantity list for each type of buyer and also terms of payment to correspond with your relationship with the buyer. Terms of payment options generally include cash in advance, open account, sight draft, time draft, date draft, delivery orders, consignment sales, factoring, and letter of credit. Your decision as to the appropriate terms at this time will depend on the level of risk involved, the size of the order, relationship with the buyer, and company policy. Keep in mind that terms of payment can be a significant negotiating tool and can greatly affect your competitiveness in the target market.

During the Market Penetration phase, you have specific objectives related to sales volume, market share, and positioning your product in relation to the competition. You will be able to use price as one means of achieving these objectives. For example, if your objective is to gain 40 percent of that market, you may want to establish a relatively low selling price and achieve profit goals based on volume. In another instance, you may find that your product is in the early stages of the product life cycle, making it relatively new and unique to the market. You may choose to establish a relatively high price initially and then reduce the selling price as competition enters the market. In any event, goals and objectives, production and export costs, competition, and external factors will all play a role in establishing and adjusting your export price.

Balance Risks and Opportunities

During the Market Penetration phase, you are making a greater commitment to your target market. You are willing to invest resources in adapting the product to better suit the market. You are expending time and money to visit the market in order to conduct research, learn more about the culture and business customs, work more closely with your representatives, and meet the appropriate individuals from government or industry. You may even have decided to establish your own company sales office in that market. In order to safeguard against unexpected problems, you should do a thorough assessment of the actual or potential risks in your target market. Your USDOC District Office and your international banker can provide valuable assistance in your effort to identify and assess risk.

    With the many events taking place today in the global political arena, the stability of many countries is of concern. Your assessment should help you to determine what impact political unrest, economic downturn, or other changes would have on your ability to conduct business as usual.

    As you increase your involvement and investment in the market, your sales can become adversely affected by poor communication and transportation facilities or capabilities within the target country. The potential problems that could arise due to your inability to communicate in a timely manner or to guarantee delivery on a timely basis should be assessed.

    During the Trial Run, you were probably quoting your selling price in U.S. dollars. As you become more established in a market, you may find that to be competitive and to better serve your customer, you will want to quote in the currency of your target market. While this approach might result in greater sales, you must also consider the potential financial risk to your organization by assessing the stability of the target country currency. If the currency has a history of instability, you should probably continue to quote in U.S. dollars or at least remain in a position to adjust your pricing on a regular basis. This means that you would not be able to distribute price lists but would quote prices based on the currency situation.

CASE STUDY: Mate Punch and Die Company offers premium products, so prices were set just below the market leader's prices and quoted in local currency in the major markets. The currency exchange risk was a calculated risk it was willing to take to gain market share. Not all individual markets have a separate price sheet. Mate made a decision to develop price lists in eight major currencies. In several cases, the prices are the same across different markets simply to reduce the total number of price lists that must be administered and managed.

Whether or not you have the cushion to quote in foreign currency and absorb any potential losses due to changes in the exchange rate will depend on the profit margin that you build into your pricing. This factor and your assessment of the currency's stability will help you to determine the appropriate pricing policy for minimizing this type of risk.

Another currency-related issue that you may have had to address during the Trial Run relates to the convertibility of the currency and the ease with which you are able to take hard currency out of the country. In some cases it may be earned by your company sales office located in the country and in other cases it might be payment for goods exported from the United States. This problem will be particularly relevant if you are marketing to countries with nonconvertible currencies.

In developing a Market Penetration strategy for these countries, you may need to find ways to work within the monetary limitations of your buyer. It may be necessary to consider countertrade as a means of receiving payment for your exports. For example, you may be willing to accept partial payment in U.S. dollars and part in raw materials to be used in your production process. Another option would be to accept payment in finished goods that could be sold to a third party. Still another possibility would be to have your product assembled in that market and accept part of the production as payment. This would enable you to use your existing channels of distribution to move the product and receive payment. In any event, these markets require creativity and patience.

Step 9:

Fine-Tune the Export Decisions

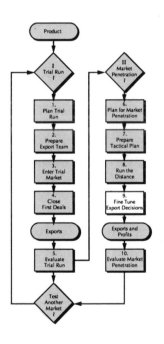

During the Trial Run, the concern was primarily to negotiate a price and receive payment. The goal was to make it safe and simple for you, the exporter. Now you want to improve your position in the market and fine-tune your export decisions. First and foremost, you want your customer to be successful and to achieve the desired profit margins from the sale of your product.

Increase Your Customer's Profits

There are a few measures you can take other than lowering your selling price to help ensure this result. First, consider the possibility of structuring better financial arrangements for your customer. One way this might be done is to accept letters of credit that extend beyond your existing terms—perhaps 60, 90, 120 days or longer. This will allow your representative more time to generate revenue on the sale of your product before payment is due. You can still collect on the letter of credit immediately by discounting it to your bank. This is true for other negotiable financial instruments as well. Your customer may be willing to pay all or part of the discount fee or agree to have you add it to the selling price up front.

You will want to explore ways to reduce your costs of exporting, which will enable you to pass the savings on to your customer with the goal of further Market Penetration. Is your comfort level with your customer and with the target country such that you can move away from a confirmed letter of credit as the required method of payment? This will save on confirmation fees charged by your bank. If you move away from letter of credit to documentary payment, your customer will not have to pay banking fees associated with opening a letter of credit for your account.

Shipping costs can be substantially reduced as your company evolves into a smooth export operation. By this point, you are not simply trying to get the goods to their destination, but you can actively negotiate with various shippers to get the best rates and delivery schedules, which will result in cost savings for your customer. It may also be desirable to bring more of the transportation planning and documentation function in-house to reduce the costs associated with the international freight for-warder.

If your product is conducive to bulk shipping, you may want to consider utilizing a Foreign Trade Zone (FTZ) in the target market and allow your importer to assemble or package the product at that point. Duties paid by your importer would be lower on bulk or unassembled products. Also, the lower duty rate would not be assessed until the goods were taken out of the Zone. This benefit would provide incentive for your importer to carry more inventory. Refer to appropriate country section in one of the export manuals for information on FTZs located in the target market.

Simplify the Export Process

In addition to minimizing costs that are passed on to your customer, you will also want to explore methods to simplify the export process. If you require a validated export license, you may want to consider applying for a special class of validated license. If you have ongoing sales to a pre-approved consignee, you may qualify for a distribution license. A project license is available in cases where a number of shipments are made over time to a project being undertaken abroad. Another special category of validated license is the service supply license, which is intended to expedite the servicing requirements for U.S. products sold abroad. These licenses will relieve some of the burden involved in exporting a product requiring a validated license, but they do require considerable effort on your part and possibly on the part of the importer to acquire and maintain.

Selling to the importer on open account will also tend to simplify the export process. This issue will surface rather quickly when you are exporting to Canada and increasingly to the European Community. The buyer is likely to feel that since you can easily obtain information regarding creditworthiness, you should apply the same payment terms as for your domestic sales. This decision should be made only after the importer has established financial credibility and country risk factors have been weighed. Your international banker can help you determine whether or not this is advisable.

Explore Export Financing Options

There are a number of agencies that offer financing programs to exporters. Many states and some major cities have established export finance authorities as part of their export promotion program. These programs usually provide pre-export loan guarantees for working capital needed to produce your export order. Some also provide the loan itself. Contact your state international trade program to determine the availability of this type of program in your state.

There are also approximately twenty U.S. government programs that provide financing to U.S. exporters. Some of the categories of assistance in addition to export financing include investment loans, guarantees on service contracts, and working capital funds for distributorships. The primary agencies are discussed briefly below.

▲ *Export-Import Bank of the United States.* One of the leading agencies providing financing assistance to U.S. exporters is the Export-Import Bank of the United States (Eximbank). Eximbank would be particularly useful if you required medium- and long-term financing for a large project and/ or the sale of equipment. It can also provide pre-export working capital loan and/or guarantee programs. Through the Foreign Credit Insurance

Association (FCIA), Eximbank also provides insurance to U.S. exporters, enabling them to extend credit terms to their overseas buyers.

Eximbank and FCIA jointly offer an export credit insurance program for short-term export sales, which is anything 180 days or less. The main advantage of this program is that it protects foreign sales receivables. By carefully utilizing the export credit insurance program, you are able to protect your receivables against political and commercial risk, be more competitive by offering more favorable payment terms to the buyer, and benefit by leveraging your accounts receivable. All of these are advantages in that they allow you to broaden your market penetration while, at the same time, minimize your risks.

With Eximbank guarantees and/or FCIA insurance, you will be able to borrow money against your foreign receivables, which are otherwise usually excluded from your bank's borrowing base.

In addition to the short-term Eximbank program, there are several other programs intended to support medium-term export sales of up to five years and long-term up to ten years. Initially you may want to contact your state export promotion organization or your international banker to discuss Eximbank's programs and ask for assistance in contacting and working with Eximbank. Some state export finance programs have negotiated an umbrella policy through Eximbank which allows them to offer Eximbank programs to exporters in their state. Your international banker can also assist you in accessing Eximbank programs.

▲ *Foreign Credit Insurance Association.* The Foreign Credit Insurance Association (FCIA) has been mentioned in conjunction with Eximbank. As indicated, the export credit insurance offered by FCIA provides a high degree of protection to you as an exporter. FCIA administers this program on behalf of its member private insurance companies and Eximbank. The private insurers cover the normal commercial credit risks such as insolvency or default. Eximbank, on the other hand, assumes all liability for political risks including war, revolution, or confiscation or other acts on the part of the foreign government that prevent or delay payment.

Through FCIA, it is possible to obtain a master policy designed to cover all of your sales to overseas buyers. This type of policy would insure against political risk and possibly commercial risk without the red tape associated with applying for coverage for each individual shipment.

FCIA has numerous other export insurance programs. Again, start by contacting your state export promotion organization or your international banker. They will be able to advise you on the appropriateness of FCIA's programs for your needs and help you to work with the agency. In addition, a small business advisory office is available to assist firms interested in using the programs and services. Contact information can be found in Appendix A.

▲ *U.S. Small Business Administration.* The U.S. Small Business Administration (SBA) is another source of financing assistance. Contact the field office in your region to obtain details of the various export financing programs. The SBA has programs that allow you to borrow funds to purchase equipment and materials needed to manufacture your products. There are also programs that help to finance costs associated with the Trial Run and Market Penetration such as consulting services, travel to your target market, trade show participation and related expenses, and market research.

The SBA also offers a loan guarantee program which assists you in obtaining short-term working capital from your bank. The main requirement is that you must have a definite export sales contract. The SBA has a number of other programs that may be helpful as you develop a clear understanding of your export financing needs.

▲ *Overseas Private Investment Corporation.* The Overseas Private Investment Corporation (OPIC) is another agency of the U.S. Government whose main purpose is to insure U.S. investors overseas. The agency provides insurance policies covering U.S. companies against political and commercial risk related to investments in developing countries and has direct financing available for qualifying projects.

Contact the OPIC office in Washington, D.C., your state export finance program, or your international banker to discuss OPIC's programs in more detail.

▲ *Commodity Credit Corporation.* The Foreign Agricultural Service, which is the international marketing arm of the U.S. Department of Agriculture, provides protection to U.S. exporters of agricultural products. The CCC Credit Guarantee Programs are available to the exporter or the exporter's bank and protect against nonpayment by the importer's bank. Contact your state Department of Agriculture or the U.S. Department of Agriculture listed in Appendix A.

▲ *Other sources of financing and investment.* In addition to the U.S. government agencies, there are a number of international development banks that provide financing for large public projects in developing countries. The U.S. contributes funds to these agencies to support the development of the infrastructure in these countries which, in turn, will contribute to economic development in those regions. For example, the World Bank provides funding for numerous projects in developing countries. The private sector from all contributing or member countries are entitled to bid on projects funded by the World Bank. The Agency for International Development (AID) and its subagencies also fund numerous projects in developing countries. However, this agency is funded entirely by the United States, and foreign governments that are recipients of the financial awards are required to purchase exclusively from U.S. suppliers.

A good listing of these and other financing programs is provided in *The World Is Your Market: An Export Guide for Small Business.*

The main point to be emphasized is that in today's competitive global marketplace, financing may well be the determining factor in successful Market Penetration. In many instances, it is no longer good enough to produce a high-quality competitively priced product. The importer may shop around for a seller who can offer financing terms. With proper guidance, it is very likely that you can gain a competitive advantage by utilizing these programs specifically designed to assist U.S. exporters.

Improve Your Margins

Improved transportation management will most likely have the effect of more efficient production and inventory planning. The bottom line will be cost savings by minimizing inventories due to better coordination between production, inventory control, shipping, and transportation.

Reexamining minimum order size may lead to cost savings. Market Penetration should mean that you are selling more units of product which, in turn, should result in lower per unit costs and better shipping rates based on quantity. Since you made the decision to penetrate the market, it is probably realistic to expect your importer to increase quantities ordered. Again, your decision is whether to strive for increased profit margins or pass the cost savings on to your importer with the goal of greater market penetration.

You may also be in a position to reduce costs and increase your profit margins by utilizing a Foreign Trade Zone (FTZ) in the United States. If you import materials or components used in the production of your export product, you may be able to import the materials into an FTZ. Should this be the case, you could import in larger quantities and probably receive price discounts, store the materials in the FTZ until needed for production, and pay the duty only as you remove units from the zone.

Taking this a step further, you could consider the possibility of manufacturing in the zone. In this case, you would avoid paying any duty on the products that were produced and exported. Duties are paid on the units for the domestic market only as they are removed from the zone.

Refer to one of the export manuals for a listing of FTZs in the United States. A representative from the zone will be able to assist you in determining the financial benefits to utilizing this facility.

Explore tax benefit incentives that can help to increase your profit margins. The Foreign Sales Corporation (FSC) is one such incentive provided by the U.S. government. By meeting FSC requirements, you can obtain a tax exemption on export profits. In order to minimize cost and complexity, a small FSC can be organized so that up to $5 million in export sales qualifies for FSC benefits. There is also the option of participating in a shared FSC to spread the operating costs over several companies. You may wish to obtain the Price Waterhouse publication entitled *Foreign Sales Corporation.* Ordering information can be found in Appendix B.

Many U.S. manufacturers rely on using imported materials or components in the production of their export products. If you fit into this category, you may be eligible for drawback and receive a refund of all or part of the duty you paid on the imported materials. Application for the drawback is made at the time your product is exported. During Phase I, you should have ordered a publication entitled *Discover Dollars In Drawback.* Review this information to determine your eligibility, the regulations, and the application procedures.

Go Direct to the Major Buyers

As you become more proficient at dealing with the international marketplace, you may want to consider exploring opportunities to participate in major public sector projects in developing countries. The U.S. Trade and Development Program (TDP) funds project planning to help U.S.

companies compete for and participate in these projects. The funding is provided to the foreign government, which, in turn, contracts with a U.S. firm to perform a feasibility study. U.S. AID, World Bank, and OPIC projects would also provide opportunities to sell direct to major buyers or serve as a subcontractor to a major project. These programs have been underutilized by U.S. exporters. Contact the various development agencies to obtain subscription information for their procurement bulletins.

Ensure a Smooth Export Operation

To help ensure smooth performance of export responsibilities, it is advisable to periodically conduct an interdepartmental export round-table involving individuals from sales, finance, credit, and shipping/transportation. The purpose of this exercise is to define the role of each division, determine shared goals and linkages, identify and solve problems, and document the flow of responsibilities. Conducting this session at the time additional export responsibilities are assumed in-house will prevent problems that might cause you to miss the boat later.

In addition, you should develop a vehicle within your organization to keep employees abreast of developments related to your international activity. This might be accomplished through a column in the company newsletter or through regular in-house memos.

Avoid Export Pitfalls

It is important to distinguish between risks and pitfalls. Most risks associated with exporting can be controlled either through appropriate insurance programs or through bilateral or multilateral agreements negotiated between the U.S. government and our trading partners. Pitfalls, on the other hand, are usually problems that can arise due to an oversight on your part as exporter. Some potential pitfalls are common to all companies and others may be more relevant to particular products, industries, or country markets. The following list is intended to heighten your awareness that pitfalls come in many sizes and shapes. Add to this list any pitfalls that you experienced earlier and want to avoid and potential pitfalls that might be common in the export of your product or specific to your target country market. This will be a handy reference for the individuals responsible for a smooth export operation within your company.

▲ *General liability.* Make sure your export shipments are insured either by you or by the importer. Should the vessel cause or sustain heavy damage, the shipping line may declare general liability. In this event, costs are divided among those who had merchandise on board. Your international freight forwarder can provide you with the specifics of this pitfall.

▲ *Termination of representation agreement.* Know the laws regarding agreement termination in your target country and establish an agreement that protects your organization. An international attorney can provide guidance to help avoid pitfalls associated with this aspect of exporting.

▲ *Shipping terms.* The United States is one of the few countries that does not require the use of Incoterms for purposes of stating shipping/ trade terms. Make sure you and the importer have the same understanding about the meaning of the terms used. If in doubt, talk with an international freight forwarder.

▲ *Adequacy of infrastructure.* Check to make sure that the port to which you are shipping has the facilities to unload your goods for release to the importer. This is particularly true for large items. The freight forwarder or the steamship line can provide this information.

▲ *Sales agreement.* Make sure that your sales terms are consistent on your formal quote sheet, pro forma, price list, or other forms used to finalize a sales agreement. When you receive a foreign purchase order, check stated terms, including fine print, before responding with an order acknowledgement. This calls for careful review by both your sales and finance departments.

▲ *Letter of credit compliance.* Immediately upon receiving the letter of credit, check and recheck the requirements to make sure you can comply. Also, verify that there are no discrepancies in relation to other documents. Your international banker or freight forwarder will also be willing to review the collection documents.

▲ *Antiboycott regulations.* The United States has an established policy of opposing restrictive trade practices or boycotts fostered or imposed by foreign countries against other countries friendly to the United States. These laws prohibit you from participating in foreign boycotts or taking actions to support such boycotts and is enforced by the U.S. Department of Commerce. For example, it is illegal for you to comply with the boycott against Israel imposed by the Arab countries. Discuss these regulations with your USDOC District Office.

▲ *Antidiversion.* To help ensure that U.S. exports go only to legally authorized destinations, the U.S. government requires a destination control statement on shipping documents. This notifies the carrier and all foreign parties that the U.S. material has been licensed for export only to certain destinations and may not be diverted contrary to U.S. law. Check with your USDOC District Office or international freight forwarder.

▲ *Fraudulent documents.* Some countries have an established reputation for transacting business with fraudulent letters of credit and other documents. When dealing with a questionable country, be sure to talk with your international banker before finalizing a sale or shipping the goods.

▲ *Nontariff barriers.* In addition to understanding the impact of tariffs on the competitiveness of your product, conduct sufficient research to learn about nontariff barriers. This will enable you to adjust your marketing strategies to minimize the impact of these barriers. The country desk officers at the USDOC International Economic Policy Office can help you get an understanding of these barriers (see Appendix A).

▲ *Antidumping regulations.* Dumping, or selling your products abroad below cost or at a price less than in the domestic market, may result in an additional duty imposed by the importer's country. The purpose is to prevent you from forcing local competitors out of the market by, in effect, canceling the price differential. The USDOC Trade Development Office industry officers can advise you of concerns related to your industry.

▲ *Kickbacks/bribes.* The United States requires that you conduct offshore business under the same ethics that are applicable in this country. The best protection is to avoid making any type of questionable payments or presenting gifts that could be interpreted as bribery. This can become a pitfall when an exporter simply wants to expedite the process. Know the laws of the United States and the laws of the foreign country and get legal advice should you have any doubts.

Step 10:

Evaluate Market Penetration

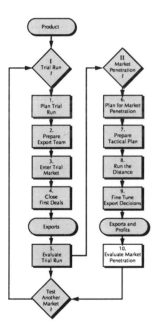

It is critical to evaluate actual results against projections on a regular basis. The foreign representative must be a part of this process and must provide information for this purpose. Projections versus actual results must be evaluated on a country basis as well as on a market segment basis.

You can refer to the Annual Sales Forecast (Worksheet 22) presented in Step 7. By regularly filling in the information on a monthly basis, you will be in a good position to compare actual sales to the level of sales projected when you developed your budget and forecast.

The evaluation will help to pinpoint both strengths and weaknesses in the strategic and tactical plan. This will enable your company to adjust the appropriate areas and will serve as a guide when entering new markets. Keep in mind that your plans will not only vary from country to country, but from market segment to market segment. Therefore, it would be possible to successfully penetrate segment A in one country but have inappropriate strategies for segment B in the same country.

Stay Out Front in the Long-Distance Run

Having completed the Trial Run and implemented a Market Penetration program, you have probably come to the conclusion that the world is not such a big place after all. In terms of geography, there may be a lot of kilometers between you and your foreign buyer. However, the pace of communication, information transfer, and the immediate movement of funds through international banking linkages minimizes the impact of physical distance.

With Fast-Track Exporting, you have expanded your markets and made your company more profitable.

However, how do you maintain and improve your position in the global marketplace?

Your continued success will be impacted by the same basic factors that made you competitive in the domestic market. These include commitment by top management, producing the highest-quality product in the market and continuously striving to improve on that product, being the lowest-cost producer in the market, understanding and meeting the customer's needs, keeping in step with technological and other changes in the industry, and valuing and developing your human resources through education and training.

It is important to position yourself to compete in the global market of the future. Producers and service providers with the highest-quality product and the lowest costs will sell their product in every country on the globe. Internationalizing your company requires ongoing assessment of your company to be constantly aware of strengths and weaknesses, to evaluate international market opportunities in light of the full range of market entry strategies discussed at the beginning of Phase II, and to implement appropriate strategies.

Fast-Track Exporting Honor Roll

The Fast-Track Exporting Honor Roll was created to recognize exporters who have committed their companies to competing in the global economy, and who have used various techniques of fast-track exporting to achieve success and profit through export.

These Honor Roll companies are but a handful of the nation's successful exporters. They were recommended by export promotion organizations throughout the country or selected by us because they are instructive examples of how real life companies faced real life export issues and succeeded.

In the preceding pages of this book, we briefly introduced you to these Honor Roll companies through case examples that demonstrated how they used fast-track exporting techniques to enter Trial Run markets and proceed on to Market Penetration. Now we tell their full stories.

Amerex Corporation/Amerex Fire International

Location: Trussville, Alabama. **Founded:** 1971. **Employees:** 500. **First exports:** 1974. **Major products exported:** Hand-portable and wheeled fire extinguishers.

Amerex had no intention of expanding into export markets when it was approached by a competitor's Australian distributor. The competing company had been unable to deliver consistent supplies, so Amerex took advantage of the opportunity and became an exporter. The $40,000 in Australian sales that resulted that year became the basis of Amerex's international reputation for quality and service.

Inquiries began coming in from around the globe, and Amerex decided that its export efforts should become a separate component of its overall strategy for growth. Several new distributors were named for Denmark, Sweden, and Austria, and as a result of a poor selection in the Mid-East, Amerex learned that it was important to prequalify potential distributors prior to their selection.

A separate company, Amerex Fire International, Inc., was created in 1982 to handle all international business. It now sells to over fifty countries. A manufacturing facility has been established in Wales to serve the European market.

Marketing efforts to achieve international expansion consist primarily of participating in trade shows, advertising in trade publications, and distributing Amerex quarterly reports that not only show the company's past performance but also introduce new products. Trade shows often serve a dual purpose for Amerex Fire: product promotion and regional meetings for distributors from the area. Both its president and vice-president frequently attend shows around the world.

One obstacle that Amerex Fire has had to overcome is getting safety approval for its products in all countries. Usually, approval by a well-known U.S. insurance regulatory group has been sufficient to meet minimum safety standards required to sell fire extinguishers. But International Standards Organization (ISO) approval will be required to market in the European Community. To meet ISO approvals, Amerex has made a major investment to gain approval in the United Kingdom. With this approval, Amerex expects to have a significant advantage over its competitors in the European Community and the Commonwealth countries.

Amerex often looks to the USDOC for research assistance, and sometimes it goes directly to the commercial officers in posts around the world for help. It might, for example, request a photocopy of the section of the local Yellow Pages that deals with fire extinguishers in order to gather market information and a prospect list.

The advice the company gives to potential exporters is, "Go slow; make sure you have a quality product at a good price, and don't go out on a limb just because you get a few sales." Amerex almost learned this lesson the hard way. When Amerex Fire International was first looking at market potential in Africa, its vice-president and a colleague took a three-week trip to Nigeria. "It was 110 degrees in the shade," he recalls, "but when we finally came back home, there was a $1 million letter of credit waiting for us. We had met with the 'distributor' it was from, and everything—his business cards, letterhead, office—matched up and looked legitimate until we tried to call the bank that issued the LC. We found out that there was nothing there but a vacant lot!''

Anitec Image

Location: Binghamton, New York. **Founded:** 1981. **Employees:** 1,500. **First exports:** 1981. **Major products exported:** Graphic arts silver-sensitized film and paper and graphic arts chemicals.

Anitec Image has always considered itself a global company because it competes in markets where all its major competitors—companies such as 3M, Fuji, and Konica—have a strong international presence. Anitec's ambitious mission statement reads: ''To have the same market share for our products in all countries around the world.''

In order to achieve this mission, Anitec works according to the philosophy that all customers, regardless of where they are located, should receive the same high-quality product sold in the United States. The export market is never treated as secondary or as an outlet for excess capacity.

Anitec's first target markets were Western European countries because the European Community's high standard of living created a market for its products. Anitec's former parent company had established a manufacturing and converting facility in Belgium, which Anitec was able to acquire. Because of this facility, Anitec is perceived as a European company, and this gives it a marketing edge in Europe.

In each of the European countries where Anitec achieves a certain level of sales (approximately a 10–15 percent share), the company makes a commitment to that market by establishing subsidiary sales companies. The sales subsidiaries are staffed by local, native-language–speaking people who are brought on a regular basis to Binghamton for product training and technical updates. Expatriates are used only for high-level positions, and mostly in the area of finance. As a result of all these efforts, the European Community now makes up about 50 percent of Anitec's international sales.

After identifying its first target markets, Anitec looked at import and export statistics in other markets. If there was a significant amount of activity in graphic arts products, Anitec decided to enter. Word of mouth, people in the industry, local newspapers, trade publications, and on-site visits have been a means of locating distributors in these markets. The criteria used to select a distributor varies depending on the market, but a few things are consistent: The company looks for integrity, market knowledge, good reputation, ability to maintain a local inventory, and stable financial position. Anitec now sells in Latin America and Asia, as well as Australia, the Middle East, and Africa.

Anitec's personnel and management style reflects its commitment to exporting. Personnel with international experience are preferred; however, Anitec also trains existing staff to meet the demands of exporting. Management's style is "hands-on," gaining understanding of the company's markets and unique situations by traveling extensively. This allows it to respond more quickly and effectively when problems arise.

Globalizing Anitec has made the company not only more competitive in the face of tough competition but more stable. Because of global business cycles, negative factors affecting one market can be offset by positive factors in others. And that makes Anitec Image a stronger company in the long run.

ARTIST Graphics

Location: St. Paul, Minnesota. **Founded:** 1982. **Employees:** 150. **First exports:** 1984. **Major products exported:** High-resolution graphic controllers for IBM and compatible PCs and enhanced CAD software for use with the controllers.

ARTIST Graphics is a leading-edge company operating in a global market and in a fast-paced industry where competitors from the United States, Europe, and Asia can catch up to new product developments within a few months of their introduction. So in addition to being an innovator in technology, ARTIST Graphics has also had to develop a leading-edge global marketing strategy.

The company started to formulate its international marketing strategy when overseas inquiries began coming in as a result of advertisements in U.S. publications and the reputation ARTIST Graphics was building in the United States. Its goal was to become the world's leading high-resolution graphics company.

The best source of market information for ARTIST Graphics turned out to be the software firms with which the company worked, and in particular one U.S. firm that holds approximately 70 percent of the worldwide market. That company provided ARTIST Graphics with its sales statistics and shared some of its knowledge about the industry— including information about distributors.

With the insight provided by its industrial partners and information obtained through trade publications, ARTIST Graphics identified Germany as its first target. It also selected a "value-added" distributor, one with a strong presence in the market and that carried complementary products, offered expertise, emphasized strong customer technical support, and had a good dealer network. This distributor was impressed with ARTIST Graphics' quality products, its philosophy of delivering outstanding customer support—specifically its twenty-four-hour response time to all questions—and its ability to offer value-added features to software and hardware.

A major trade fair in Hanover, Germany, in 1986 allowed the company to broaden its European sales. As a result of that show and subsequent follow-up, a number of distributors were signed not only in Europe but throughout the world.

The next milestone in the company's international development came in 1988 with the opening of a sales and support office in England and, later, the establishment of a manufacturing, sales, and service facility in Dublin, Ireland.

Penetrating the Japanese market was another challenge. Research showed that the market potential was strong, but sales had been minimal. A trip to the market provided a crucial piece of information: The Japanese use a type of computer that is different from those used anywhere else in the world. ARTIST Graphics decided to design controllers and adapt and translate software that would be compatible with the Japanese computers. A Japanese distributor for the new products was signed. A company programmer, based in St. Paul but originally from Japan, now travels about six times a year to support the distributor and its customers.

Because export licensing has been one of the more troublesome aspects of its international operations, a full-time employee was assigned to this task. The process has been especially time-consuming when selling for re-export into Eastern Europe. However, the changes taking place in export licensing have prompted ARTIST Graphics to take steps to test this market. "A year ago we may not even have bothered to try."

Today, over 50 percent of ARTIST Graphics' sales come from outside the United States.

Benfield Electric Supply Company

Location: White Plains, New York. **Founded:** 1951. **Employees:** 100. **First exports:** 1976. **Major products exported:** A full line of electrical material from over 300 U.S. manufacturers.

Benfield Electric Supply Company had been doing good business since it was founded. So when the company decided to go into exporting, it committed itself to be as effective in export markets as it had been in the U.S. market. Benfield created a subsidiary, Benfield Electric International Ltd. (BEI), to handle its export operations.

BEI has found success by operating according to the philosophy that customer satisfaction comes first. And that means that the company must meet its customers' critical delivery requirements while relying on the performance of the manufacturers with which it works. BEI works to create customer satisfaction in a number of ways. Above all, it strives to provide fast, on-time, quality delivery. The quality of the final delivery is ensured through careful packaging. BEI uses heavy-duty materials, photographs the material and export markings for documentation, and provides detailed packing lists so that customers can manage their incoming product. "It is important to use whatever methods are necessary in packaging to avoid a dissatisfied customer who has lost time and money due to poor quality," says BEI's president. Any delay on the part of BEI can mean substantial losses to its customers and could cost BEI the relationship.

Building long-term relationships is another key to customer satisfaction. BEI's Japanese branch office, established in order to reach the major Japanese construction companies that operate around the world, offers an example of how providing customer satisfaction has helped BEI compete. Having a BEI employee on-site, meeting regularly with clients and establishing direct relationships with the parent offices where major decisions are made, has helped win contracts many times. Once, for example, BEI represented a Houston-based company bidding on a $3 million contract in Japan. BEI and the Houston firm could not afford a price war, so they had to compete on some other basis. BEI studied the product features and found that the long-run cost efficiency through energy savings should be emphasized to the Japanese company. BEI helped win that contract because of its understanding of Japanese priorities and the long-standing relationships built by its Japanese office.

Benfield uses research methods to identify markets and build prospect lists. Its library contains publications, such as *International Construction Weekly* and the *Clark Reports,* that announce major construction projects and name companies awarded projects. It receives sales leads from the international division of the New York State Department of Economic Development and has periodic meetings with the New York District Office of the USDOC to stay in touch with developments in the global marketplace.

In addition to BEI's attention to customer satisfaction, the company's flexibility has been key to its success. According to the company's president, "You have to recognize the differences in cultures and between individual customers. This will help you determine what your client is looking for—and what it will take to make the sale."

BEI is a recipient of the New York State Governor's Award For Achievement In Export (1989) and the President's "E" Award (1990).

Boboli International, Inc.

Location: Stockton, California. **Founded:** 1986. **Employees:** 2. **First Exports:** 1987. **Major products exported:** Boboli brand prebaked cheese crust, flour mix, and pizza sauce.

Gourmet pizza on an Italian crust with olive oil, mozzarella, and parmesan cheese baked right in. Sound good? The Japanese think so and buy thousands of Boboli's crusts every year.

When the original owners sold Boboli, Inc., they retained the rights to international distribution of the company's upscale prebaked cheese crusts, and Boboli International was formed to introduce pizza lovers overseas to the popular crust.

Since U.S. consumption of Boboli's product was closely tied to disposable-income levels, the new international company looked for foreign markets that met the profile of high disposable income and selected Japan as its first market. Boboli International decided to use the same marketing tool in Japan that had been successful in the United States: trade shows. The company participated in the U.S. Department of Agriculture (USDA) pavilion at the FoodEx show in Tokyo and gave away samples to visitors. The response was terrific and led to the company's first Japanese customer, the supplier of a large restaurant chain. After an initial period of exporting the prebaked crusts, Boboli licensed the baking of its crusts to the Japanese customer, with Boboli continuing to supply the flour mix. This reduced the customer's import tariffs from 30 to 15 percent and saved on transportation and storage costs.

The next target market was the United Kingdom. The company used the same marketing methods as in Japan and generated a good response but few orders. The main obstacle seemed to be that the U.K. distributors wanted to order in quantities too small for economical shipment. Boboli responded by locating a warehouse in the United Kingdom and appointing a food broker. This allowed distributors to place smaller orders, and the product began to sell well. The U.K. warehouse now also serves the company's distributors in France, Germany, Benelux, and Spain.

While there are no tariff barriers when shipping from the United Kingdom to other European Community countries, nontariff barriers do complicate matters. For example, the United Kingdom, like the United States, requires that all bread be made with vitamin-enriched flour. But in France and Belgium, vitamin-enriched flour may not be used. This means that Boboli must maintain double inventories in its U.K. warehouse, thus increasing its costs. "The European pizza market is behind the U.S. and Japan," says Boboli's president. "We've seen the business grow a lot in the past few years and expect it to continue. It's worth the extra inventory cost to be in Europe."

The USDA has been extremely helpful in helping Boboli market its products overseas. It has provided country surveys, trade leads, sponsorship of pavilions at foreign trade shows, label review and clearance services for compliance with foreign regulations, names of competitors, and so forth. "The USDA has great resources, which they are very happy to put to work for people," says Boboli's president.

Bondhus Corporation

Location: Monticello, Minnesota. **Founded:** 1964. **Employees:** 127. **First exports:** 1969. **Major products exported:** Nonpowered fastener tools.

The ability to make corporate growth and profitability compatible with employee growth and career satisfaction is one major factor leading to success for Bondhus Corporation. Another is the company's strategic pursuit of international markets and manufacturing opportunities.

The company began in a small shop (part of which was partitioned off as living quarters), and generated $2,000 in sales during its first year. By 1969, Bondhus was selling in all fifty states; orders began coming in from overseas, and the company began filling some export orders. By 1979, it had achieved close to 50 percent market share domestically and its president decided it was time Bondhus committed itself fully to international markets.

Bondhus began by targeting medium-size industrial markets, since such markets offered substantial sales potential but tended to have fewer and less aggressive competitors than the large markets. Market sizes were determined using GNP figures and industrial statistics; per capita income was factored into the analysis because Bondhus made the assumption that its labor-saving products would be more appealing in markets with higher labor costs. The company looks at, but does not rely on, USDOC trade statistics, since it feels that these data are highly influenced by historical relationships (e.g., trade between Commonwealth countries) that follow no logical business reason and because the data fail to account for domestic competitors.

Priority is given to the process of finding the right distributors. Sole distributors are used in all markets except France and Germany (where most distributors are too specialized either by product or geography to serve as sole distributors). Using telephone books, *Kompass* and other directories, commercial mailing lists, and USDOC services, a foreign market database of several hundred names is established. Next, letters and company information sent to potential distributors along with requests for information allow Bondhus to narrow the field of potential distributors. The next step is to visit the market to meet with the distributors, their customers, and the end users. These contacts provide information about needs and expectations and give Bondhus insights into the distributors' reputations. Such a visit lasts from two to four weeks.

Once a distributor is chosen, it takes additional research and skill to negotiate the agreement. "The distributors tend to want to do things their own way, saying, 'This is the way things are done in this country,' " says the company's president. But Bondhus believes that its end users are basically the same from one country to another and that many of the things learned in one market can be applied to another. "You have to spend some time to determine whether what they say is a fact or whether they are just being resistant to new ideas. You have to question the distributor. Sometimes they are right, and sometimes you find more effective ways of doing business."

Bondhus works very closely with its distributors to maximize sales. "We push them to work with us as a team," says its president. Distributors are invited to work with the company on annual joint marketing plans; a 10 percent bonus for product promotion is included if they participate. "The distributors own and run their own businesses, but it's almost like having our own sales office in the market," notes the president.

The company's international markets have grown to twenty-seven medium- and large-size industrial markets. In 1986, Bondhus opened a manufacturing facility in Barbados from which it can ship duty-free to the United States, Canada, Japan, and the European Community. Bondhus Corporation received the Presidential "E" Award in 1984 and the Governors Export Award in 1985 as a result of its success in international markets.

Bondhus plans to maintain its international focus, and has set its next international sales goal equal to 50 percent of its total sales.

Cambridge Products, Ltd./Naremco, Inc.

Location: Springfield, Missouri. **Founded:** 1956. **Employees:** 35. **First exports:** 1970. **Major products exported:** Patented livestock feed additives and supplements for poultry, swine, and cattle and a gentian violet mold-inhibiting product.

In the early 1970s, Naremco started getting inquiries from overseas companies interested in its products. "The men didn't want to answer the inquiries," recalls the former secretary/office manager and current vice-president who ran the company with her husband. "I'm the type of person who tries to respond to all the letters we receive." In the process of answering those letters, she broke trade and gender barriers at the same time.

One of the first letters she responded to led to a licensing agreement with an Australian poultry grower. The Australian company hoped that Naremco's mold-inhibiting product would help improve the health of its poultry. Naremco was ready to export in the quantities needed. But while the two parties were working out details of the sale, Naremco's vice-president received a letter from the agricultural agency of the Australian government telling her that Australia would not allow large imports of this product. The letter suggested that Naremco allow the Australian company to manufacture the product in Australia. With some assistance from within the company and minimal assistance from a lawyer, a licensing agreement was drawn up, and production began in Australia shortly thereafter. That relationship still exists today.

Naremco continued to receive inquiries from abroad as a result of advertising in U.S. industry publications, and in 1974, Naremco decided to approach exporting in a more structured way. Initially, an international division was established within the company, and later a subsidiary company, Cambridge Products, Ltd., was formed to handle exports. Today, Cambridge's exports account for about 15 percent of Naremco's total sales, and the company has customers in Australia, Asia, Central and South America, Canada, the Caribbean, the Middle East, and Europe.

Throughout the initial phases of its export program, Cambridge relied heavily on the USDOC. Each time an order came from a new country, the company called the USDOC District Office for assistance. "I've used practically all their services," says the vice-president. Cambridge also relies on its banks, which offers seminars on letters of credit and other finance tools. The Missouri International Business Office has also been very useful, supplying leads, helping to locate translators for large export shows, and bringing trade delegations to visit the company.

The biggest problem Cambridge has encountered in exporting is getting its product registered in the different markets. Also, once the product is approved, it is not always easy to protect the company's patent in a market. The company has found, however, that its strong trademark helps a lot when such problems arise. "Patent infringement can happen anywhere—even the United States," says the vice-president. "The best thing you can do to protect yourself is get a good patent attorney."

Cambridge believes that people are basically the same all over the world and should be treated with honesty and respect. It also believes in persistence and taking time to close a sale. "Exporting has been very challenging, but also very rewarding for our company."

James Clem Corporation

Location: Chicago, Illinois. **Founded:** 1982. **Employees:** 60. **First exports:** 1986. **Major products exported:** An impermeable geocomposite clay liner system for the water, mining, petrochemical, and waste containment industry.

The Clem Corporation was established to manufacture an invention of its founder. Since the new product lacked a developed market, some clout was needed to build recognition. So an agreement was signed with a major multinational chemical company giving it exclusive distribution rights in North America for five years. Unfortunately, the distributor failed to develop the strong domestic market necessary for sales growth. Something had to be done to improve the company's cash flow. However, because its contractual obligations barred Clem from selling its product in North America, it looked to the European market as its only source of survival.

With little money and no international experience, the company did not know where to start. It had heard about the USDOC, but was unsure about what could be done given its very small marketing budget. When it met with the USDOC Chicago District Office, three suggestions changed its perspective.

First, the USDOC suggested it try the Agency Distributor Service Program. Clem supplied product literature and information to the US-DOC, and the commercial officers of the embassy and consulates in target markets were able to supply the company with profiles of potential distributors. At $90 per country, this proved to be a cost-effective way of generating and determining market interest in the product. Further communication with the potential distributors helped the company gain valuable information about each country's natural resources, environmental regulations, and other information critical to its success.

The USDOC also suggested running an advertisement in a special edition of *Commercial News USA*. This publication, which goes to every American consulate and embassy in the world, generated 350 sales leads for an investment of $150.

Finally, the USDOC introduced the company to the International Business Division of the Illinois Department of Commerce and Community Affairs. Together, the representatives of these two agencies recommended an initial trip to the market and identified an important European trade show for the water and waste industries held in Amsterdam. Before the trip, new product literature had to be developed. All available cash was spent producing a four-page, two-color brochure in English, French, and German.

Although Clem did not close any deals on the first trip, the analysis of the information gathered from the trade show and contacts in the embassies, consulates, and Illinois trade office in Brussels helped the company decide to participate in a USDOC Match-Maker program in Italy. It was a risk, but since the consular post in Milan was able to prearrange seven appointments, the risk seemed worthwhile. The result was that the company met with eighteen different Italian companies, all of which requested distribution rights.

In selecting its first foreign distributors, Clem decided that it did not want to be involved with a huge company the way it had been in North America. It wanted its products to be priority items for its distributor, and it wanted a distributor that was knowledgeable about the industry and one that the company liked and trusted on both a personal and professional level. "We look for the perfect marriage," says the vice-president of Clem's international division, "because we don't want to end up in divorce court."

Six weeks after the Match-Maker trip to Milan, the first Italian distributor was appointed. Within nine months, over $400,000 of product had been sold in Italy. Although the company was not aware of it when it went to Italy, Clem later found that the soil resources of the country required that clay be imported for landfills to prevent leaching of polluted water into the soil. Clem's impermeable clay liner system achieves the same results at considerably lower cost. The Italian market now accounts for 50 percent of total international sales.

As the European market developed, competitors moved in, and Clem was forced to begin litigation in Germany, charging a low-cost competitor with patent infringement. It may have been possible to avoid the suit if the original patent had been written and translated more accurately. "The smartest thing you can do is to get a good international lawyer with a network of offices in your markets. You may never get into major litigation, but even structuring agent or distributor contracts is complicated in some countries. Good legal representation may be expensive, but its well worth the price paid," states the international division's vice-president.

Clem believes that participation in state and federal programs gave their company credibility with foreign distributors. Potential distributors could have confidence that the agency had determined that the American company was legitimate and could deliver on promises.

The James Clem Corporation was awarded the President's "E" award for exports in recognition of its outstanding contribution to the increase of U.S. trade abroad. "For the Clem Corporation, exporting forged an incredible path. The distance is long and the race is fast—the true marathon has begun."

Goguen Industries, Inc.

Location: Liverpool, New York. **Founded:** 1975. **Employees:** 45. **First exports:** 1988. **Major products exported:** Electronic components—air wound coils, surface mount coils, and molded tunable inductors.

"A journey of a thousand miles must begin with a single step." The president of Goguen Industries quotes Lao-Tzu to illustrate his commitment to exporting. Although he knows that his export markets will take a good deal of time and effort to build, he is looking toward the long-term growth of his company and the role that exporting will play in its growth.

While Goguen was probably the largest manufacturer of its product in the world, it was not exporting. It had been interested in doing business in Europe, since its major competitors were in Asia. So, in 1988, when Europe 1992 began to look as if it might become "fortress Europe," Goguen decided to move.

The president's first step was to call the International Division of the New York State Department of Economic Development. The latest copy of the division's *Export Opportunities Bulletin*, which had been coming across his desk on a fairly regular basis, prompted him to find out how the Division could help the company start up its export marketing efforts. The timing couldn't have been better. The Division was in the process of planning a catalog show in Barcelona, and for $750, Goguen Industries could send product literature and samples to be displayed at the international trade fair. "We didn't even have to attend," says the president. Through that initial show, Goguen located about twenty potential European representatives and narrowed the field by using the following criteria: Did the distributor sell a complementary product line to the same industry segment? Did it have at least ten employees? How were its bank and trade references? Did the U.S. consulates have any information on the distributor?

Goguen found that one of the major difficulties for the exporter was the representative's contract; it had to be well-structured and translated accurately. Since certain countries treat representatives as legal employees, if the representative is terminated, the company may be liable for up to a year or more in severance pay. Goguen Industries reduced the chance of such errors by agreeing, with a handshake, to a trial period. This gave both parties time to get to know each other and the market and to make an educated decision about a long-term relationship.

An extremely effective representative for the United Kingdom was found almost by accident through the second New York State trade show delegation in which the company participated. Goguen's president and the Briton in the booth next door started talking, realized their mutual interests, and ended up entering into a representation agreement. Today the United Kingdom accounts for nearly 50 percent of the company's international sales.

Subsequent visits to trade shows and target markets were key to the company's success. The president participates in nearly ten international trade shows each year. As a sign of respect and friendship, he always wears a lapel pin showing two flags: the flag of the host country and an American flag. He has learned conversational French and German and always knows at least a few words of the language, whatever country he visits. This kind of effort reflects well on the company, he says, and helps sell his product. He underlines this fact with a joke he hears in Europe: "If you speak three languages, you're trilingual. If you speak two languages, you're bilingual. If you speak one language, you're American."

Within one year—almost to the day—of that first visit to a foreign market, Goguen Industries won the New York State Governor's Award for Achievement in Export.

The only real problem Goguen Industries has encountered in its exporting efforts is its high transportation costs. It combats this problem by shipping its product to the United Kingdom for all of Europe. The U.K. representative then breaks up the shipment for its various continental destinations. This technique has resulted in a 25 percent transportation cost savings.

Goguen Industries' journey of a thousand miles has been supported by the commitment of its president and employees. They expect this commitment to help sustain the company's long-term growth.

International Diabetes Center

Location: Minneapolis, Minnesota. **Founded:** 1967. **Employees:** 60. **Major products and services exported:** Educational materials, training, and expertise for diabetic health care.

The International Diabetes Center (IDC) is a nonprofit organization, and its goal is to enhance the life and health of people with diabetes by applying the latest knowledge and technology to manage diabetes and its complications. The Center works with patients and health care professionals to achieve this goal through education (including materials development), research, and clinical care.

The IDC took on its international orientation in 1981 when it became the designated World Health Organization Collaborating Center in diabetes education and training. Requests and referrals from around the world began to increase. Health care professionals began to come more frequently from other countries.

"There is a great deal of interest in our programs, but as a nonprofit organization, we can't do everything," says IDC's executive director. Therefore, the requests from overseas have to be prioritized. The professionals trained at the IDC need credibility in their community and broad knowledge of the disease. They also need an entrepreneurial spirit because, in most cases, a great deal of change needs to occur to create a more effective health care delivery system for diabetics.

In Australia and Taiwan, the IDC helped establish programs, write materials, and supply other training tools based on the U.S. model of patient treatment. Since their establishment, the programs in Australia and Taiwan have been run entirely by the staffs of the foreign facilities.

The establishment of a diabetes treatment program in the Soviet Union, however, proved to be a major challenge and required the development of a new strategy for its international program. In 1988, the IDC initiated cooperation with the Soviet Union when the Minnesota Trade Office recruited the IDC to participate in a trade mission to Moscow. There, it made contact with people from the Central Institute for Advanced Studies, the organization in charge of all graduate work for doctors, and later entered into a five-year contract to assist the Soviets.

The IDC soon learned that the many differences in the cultures and health care delivery systems of the United States and Soviet Union would require considerable adaptation of the teaching process in order to achieve results. The IDC found that the most important difference is the patient-doctor relationship. In the United States, most of the responsibility for the day-to-day management of the disease rests with the patient. In the Soviet Union, on the other hand, the physician plays a much greater role. "In the U.S., we give patients sample menus and lists of foods with their nutrients; then the patient plans his meals; 95 percent of the disease management is done by the patient. In the Soviet Union, the doctor manages everything and the patient makes no decisions; the diabetic patient sees the doctor weekly. When we ask patients, 'What do you eat?' they consistently answer, 'What do you want me to eat?' " Cultural differences and such basic things as the availability of the right foods for diabetics have made the direct translation of U.S. methods for treating diabetic patients impractical in the Soviet Union.

The IDC has also had to cope with radically different approaches to health care in foreign countries. Soviet doctors, for example, are often frustrated by the lack of equipment and supplies, yet it is common practice for diabetic patients to stay in the hospital for three or four weeks. This practice would be viewed as totally unnecessary, and extremely costly, in the United States.

Thus, the biggest challenge facing the IDC in the Soviet Union and many foreign countries is to teach health care professionals how to develop "culturally appropriate delivery systems" within the context of the country's overall health care system and culture. Then the foreign physicians must develop their own patient treatment techniques within the context of their own unique delivery system. Exporting services is in many ways a greater challenge than exporting a product. The IDC has found the path to success in this field of endeavor.

Las Americas International

Location: St. Louis Park, Minnesota. **Founded:** 1987. **Employees:** 1. **First exports:** 1967. **Major products exported:** Dairy and beef cattle.

The first-class travelers on Las Americas' trips to Latin America are not the seasoned international type. They are usually Holstein dairy cattle on their way to a Mexican, Colombian, Costa Rican, or other Latin American ranch.

The company acts as one link in a chain that brings together midwestern farmers and foreign buyers who want U.S. cattle. The cattle are first purchased from farmers and brought to a large yard by a farmer who operates as a middleman. Las Americas, the exporter, then selects cattle according to the specifications of the foreign buyer. Sometimes, buyers from Latin America come to Minnesota to make the final selection from the Las Americas cattle prescreen. The company then works with them to arrange financing and transportation and to make sure that all documents are in order.

Las Americas builds its network of midwestern suppliers through several sources, of which word of mouth is perhaps the most important. Another source is the livestock industry specialist at the Minnesota Trade Office, who puts together *In Source,* a quarterly listing of cattle available for export.

Las Americas uses a number of means to locate foreign buyers. Many referrals come as a result of the company's reputation. It is also listed in the American Holstein Association's directory of exporters. Participation in two annual trade shows in Mexico gives Las Americas and its suppliers good visibility among potential buyers there. And periodic advertisements in the *Los Angeles Dairy Journal* reach markets throughout Latin America.

Commitment to quality exporting has been the key to developing a network of cattle suppliers and buyers for Las Americas. After more than twenty-five years of experience exporting cattle, clients of Las Americas' president have confidence in his ability to deliver the best products and services for their needs. The president often visits buyers' farms to see how they are managed, what kind of feed and other resources they have, and how the cattle will be used. This helps him understand precisely what kind of animal the buyers need. Trustworthiness and experience are his most valued assets, and his clients recognize this. A thorough knowledge of both the U.S. and Latin American markets, language, and culture have helped build this dependability.

The company uses Mexico's import permit as a buyer-screening tool. Because it may take from two weeks to two months for a buyer to receive the permit, Las Americas' president requests that his buyers complete this formality before he begins negotiation. Going through that process indicates that the client is ready and able to buy.

Pricing the cattle for sale to Latin America requires flexibility. Initial quotes are considered estimates only, since market prices and currencies fluctuate until the moment the deal is closed. Transportation, documentation, and health requirements are also a challenge. For example, U.S. truckers generally do not drive into Mexico, so the cattle must be unloaded from one truck and reloaded onto another at the border. All this must be completed relatively quickly, because the cattle can suffer serious health risks, even death, if the process takes too long.

Las Americas feels that its long experience in exporting cattle offers its customers the best animals for their purposes, greater security, and lower costs. In addition, the cattle get first-class service from the Midwest to Latin America.

LecTec Corporation

Location: Minnetonka, Minnesota. **Founded:** 1978. **Employees:** 45. **First exports:** 1986. **Major products exported:** Conductive, adhesive, and therapeutic disposable medical products that are highly compatible with skin—e.g., medical electrodes, TENS electrodes, medical/surgical tapes, and transdermal medications.

The philosophy of making the highest-quality product at the lowest cost and using the best available technology has, according to its chairman, helped LecTec Corporation become a world leader in its market niche.

When the company began looking at international markets, the USDOC helped it to optimize its resources. The first USDOC service the company used was the *Comparison Shopping Service*, which allowed it to study the cardiac electrode market (an instrument with which its product is used) in Germany, the United Kingdom, and South Korea. The *Service* answered questions about how well-developed the market was and how well-known certain product applications were. It also enabled LecTec to identify potential distributors and end users, supplying the company with enough information to begin to pursue those markets.

Next LecTec tried the Agent/Distributor Service (ADS). This, too, supplied considerable information, although at first glance it seemed negative. Six countries were selected for the distributor search, yet only one customer was finally located by indirect means. But because of the ADS, the company learned a valuable lesson: Export efforts should *not* be focused on those six countries. LecTec's price was too high because of the product's sophistication and a relatively undeveloped market.

The third and most directly beneficial USDOC service that LecTec used was *Commercial News USA*. For $150, it placed an advertisement that resulted in a nearly overwhelming number of inquiries. "We have advertised in a number of trade magazines, but nothing has come close to the response from our ad in *Commercial News USA*," says LecTec's director of international marketing.

LecTec stays in touch with its Minneapolis USDOC District Office so that it can take advantage of visiting trade delegations. For example, the company was visited by a group from Saudi Arabia when it came to Minneapolis. The USDOC gave LecTec information on each member of the delegation prior to its arrival, and the company was able to telex to set up appointments. In fact, LecTec takes every opportunity to invite prospective customers to visit its facility. "We have people coming through almost every other week these days. It helps people get to know us better." LecTec believes that this kind of marketing activity can be more effective and more economical than visiting foreign markets. Thus, the company never participates in overseas trade shows.

The USDOC District Office is also a source of such information as country market data, import duties, laws concerning distributors, and the medical system. When there are questions of protocol, the company calls the USDOC International Policy Office country desk officer in Washington, D.C., for advice.

LecTec also established alliances with world leaders in the medical field. For example, LecTec's advanced technology and participation in Minnesota's WorldMed Health Care Congress, where the company's chairman met the director of Siemen's medical division, helped LecTec win the right to supply, under private label, disposable products for Siemen's medical instruments. As a result, LecTec products are now sold in every country in the world but one. LecTec has also entered into an agreement with Biersdorf, the oldest tape producer in the world and a direct competitor in the U.S. market, whereby LecTec produces its product under private label for Biersdorf's distribution in the United States. Because of its technology, LecTec can turn out the lowest-cost, highest-quality product in the world, and this fact has led to a strategic alliance rather than competition with one of its biggest competitors. According to its president, LecTec is always looking for large companies that will take it into new markets.

LecTec's chairman believes that U.S. companies "must look beyond traditional ways of doing things, whether it be in technology or distribution, in order to succeed in world markets." And, in innovation, LecTec has excelled at home and abroad.

Little Giant Pump Company

Location: Oklahoma City, Oklahoma. **Founded:** 1941. **Employees:** 500. **First exports:** 1966. **Major products exported:** Fractional horsepower pumps such as sump pumps for sewage systems, effluents, and basements and pumps for air conditioners, refrigerators, the chemical industry, and medical applications.

Since it began exporting, Little Giant's philosophy has been to view the global market as a natural extension of its domestic market. Its first international sale came after an English distributor inquired about some of its products at a trade show in the United States. A successful agreement was eventually struck, and Little Giant began exporting into the United Kingdom.

The success of that first agreement pushed the company to look at other export markets. It first found representatives in Europe, then Asia, the Middle East, Africa, the Caribbean, and Central America—fifty-one countries in all. Agents are appointed in the smaller countries, and sole distributors are used in larger markets. In some cases, such as the United Kingdom, two distributors are appointed, with one handling consumer products and the other handling commercial products.

Since quality is Little Giant's selling point, its distributors must be able to provide after-sale service. But Little Giant is able to expect this commitment from its distributors because its warranty rate is extremely low—just one percent compared to 5–6 percent for many of its competitors. Little Giant managers visit with distributors at least once a year, either in Oklahoma or the foreign market. They find that face-to-face meetings are essential to building the relationship, reviewing business, and dealing with any service or training needs the distributors may have.

Little Giant supports its distributors in a number of ways. The company participates in about twenty-seven international trade shows each year, its primary source of sales leads. It also places advertisements in a number of trade publications, which also result in sales leads.

Little Giant has used a variety of means to research the markets it considers entering. The first step is usually to go to the USDOC District Office to look at trade statistics. If similar products sell in a certain market, a visit to that market is planned. Little Giant uses the USDOC's Agent/Distributor Service to locate distributors. Writing directly to the commercial section of the U.S. Embassy or Consulate in the areas being visited to set up an appointment with the commercial officer, it gets another perspective on how its products will sell. "The more specific I have been in my requests—letting them know about my product and the type of distributor I'm looking for—the more they have been able to help me," says Little Giant's vice-president. The company also contacts the American Chamber of Commerce in the cities visited, as well as local chambers of commerce. Both can sometimes set up appointments to meet with their members. The company also checks to see if the trade associations to which they belong have affiliates in the target country. Editors of trade publications can often refer the company to local companies. And when potential competitors have been determined, Little Giant finds out about their volume through a credit check.

Trying many ways of gathering information results in a cost-effective visit to the target country and allows Little Giant to make an educated decision when it goes into the market.

Mate Punch and Die Company

Location: Anoka, Minnesota. **Founded:** 1962. **Employees:** 200. **First exports:** 1986. **Major products exported:** High-speed punch press tooling and accessories for numerically controlled turret punch presses.

Entering the export arena has meant substantially increased sales for Mate Punch and Die Company. In fact, the company now expects that well over half of its growth in sales will come from foreign markets.

Mate made a conscious commitment to international development because orders had been trickling in from abroad for some time, proving at least some interest in its products. An international marketing director was hired to develop the international distribution network, and two extra order writers were added because of anticipated volume increases and time differentials. Instead of a formal export plan, an outline of Mate's marketing strategy was developed. It covered such things as pricing, distribution, product return policy, currency policy, promotion, and protection of intellectual property.

Mate targeted Europe and Canada as its initial markets and used the USDOC Agent/Distributor Search Program to identify potential distributors for Spain, France, Italy, and Germany. In the United Kingdom, the company bought a mailing list of metal fabricators and hired a student to work out of her home calling the over three thousand companies on the list. From this, it was able to identify 220 high-potential clients. A local salesperson was hired to call on them. Mate also advertised in national business journals and contacted national trade associations. After establishing distribution in Europe and Canada, it went on to establish distributors in Mexico, New Zealand and Australia, Singapore, and the Far East.

Pricing for foreign markets was one of the first challenges faced by Mate Punch and Die. The key was to learn about its competitors' price, quality, delivery, and service for each market, because these factors varied widely from market to market. To do this, it called on well-established distributors, and even potential customers.

Since the goal of Mate's pricing strategy was to gain market share, and since Mate offered a premium product, prices were set just below the market leader's price. It prepared end-user price lists for each market and supplied them to distributors, who received a discount from the price list. Mate saw considerable success using this strategy. However, it soon found that its distributors were increasing the prices (and their margins) and printing their own price lists. To regain control of the market, Mate started using "netto" pricing, which meant that Mate set its netto prices close to what the market would bear and sold its product to its distributors at the netto prices. This allowed the distributors to determine their own margins and set their own market prices. There are other benefits to using this system. When the product is imported showing an end-user price with a discount to the distributor, the distributor pays customs duty and VAT on the full end-user price, not on the discounted price actually paid. But with netto pricing, the costs of duty and VAT are lower and result in savings to the distributor. One final advantage of netto is that it eliminates haggling over discounts and prices.

Quality and delivery are Mate's primary Market Penetration tools for gaining market share. Since Mate's philosophy is to make it as easy as possible for the customer to acquire its product, Mate quotes in eight different currencies and accepts the exchange risk itself. Mate also opens up toll-free 800 telephone numbers in its major markets with direct access to its home office, where the telephones are staffed during European business hours by language-proficient customer service personnel. "We want to get a high-quality product to the door faster than the local competition," says Mate's international marketing manager.

If the order is under $1,000, Mate generally ships the first order on 30-day open account. A credit check takes place during the initial thirty-day period, and if the customer is creditworthy, an ongoing open account is established. For larger orders, the company delays shipment until a credit check can be completed and a judgment regarding risk can be evaluated.

In addition to increasing sales, another benefit of exporting has been an improved product. Because of the different requirements of European machines, Mate had to redesign its tooling process. For example, Mate now uses a universal lock washer fastening system that does not require screws or threads, thus satisfying both the metric and imperial tooling users' needs.

Mate has become more flexible and better able to meet the challenges of the global market because of its export program and the commitment of its owners and employees.

Murdock, Inc.

Location: Comptom, California. **Founded:** 1953. **Employees:** 485. **First exports:** 1980. **Major products exported:** Custom-formed sheet material aircraft parts, Murdock-designed hot press machines, and tooling for fabricating and assembling aircraft parts.

When Murdock, Inc., began exporting, its first ventures into international markets were not really a planned attack. "I don't know whether we decided to export or whether it was decided for us," says the director of international sales. "A major Japanese company contacted us, and soon we had our first international sale."

After that initial sale, Murdock made a conscious decision to develop exports. It could see that its industry was changing. National airlines were growing, especially in some of the less-developed countries, creating many new opportunities to sell aircraft parts and machines to aircraft manufacturers.

Because of top management's commitment to support the export program, exports now account for 10–19 percent of the company's total sales. That support is crucial to convincing its export customers that Murdock can support their requirements from a continent away. "The most important thing we do is to go see the customers in person—anywhere. It is expensive, but very rewarding," says the director of international sales. Murdock finds that this type of service helps make it competitive even where strong national preferences exist.

The company has used several export promotion organizations in its international marketing efforts, including the USDOC and the California State World Trade Commission. For example, the company's participation in the Paris Air Show with the Trade Commission was an important first step on the company's road to building export sales.

Discerning different strategies for different markets is important to Murdock's effectiveness. In most markets, Murdock uses direct sales. But in France, it has operated very successfully through a licensee with a great deal of credibility among the large manufacturers who represent potential clients. The United Kingdom, like France, also tends to be very nationalistic in this industry. The U.K. company Murdock chose to work with as a licensee has a strong reputation in the industry and had good technology similar to Murdock's.

"In these cases," says the director of international sales, "it was much easier for us to go to the host country and propose a licensing agreement to an established manufacturer than to try to start from scratch in that market." Murdock looks for licensing partners with complimentary technology, production ability, established marketing channels, a good reputation in the industry, and partners it can trust. While Murdock does not set sales objectives for the licensee, it does have biannual meetings to discuss business and the industry.

In Japan, Murdock built on its initial success using direct sales. With the help of quality representatives, Japan became Murdock's major export market at 50 percent of export sales. The representatives in Japan act as intermediaries, helping with negotiations and communications, making sure that expectations between parties are clear. In 1989, Murdock decided to further improve its position in Japan by entering into a joint venture with its representative and a medium-size Japanese steel company, Nippon Yakin. Nippon Yakin had developed a new type of lightweight stainless steel that can be formed using Murdock-designed technology. Nippon Yakin saw the joint venture as a chance to develop a market for the new product by leveraging Murdock's existing connections in the industry, and Murdock saw a way of expanding its market and overcoming many of the nationalistic, language, and cultural barriers present in Japan. Each of the three parties shares in the ownership of the new company, and each party brings something different to the table. Murdock supplies the equipment (the presses), technical know-how, and some capital. Murdock's representative in Japan offers his highly developed marketing channels and a good reputation, opening valuable doors for the new joint venture. Besides bringing its new lightweight stainless steel and the majority of the start-up capital to the joint venture company, Nippon Yakin brings its Japanese identity. This is very important because larger companies generally prefer not to subcontract to non-Japanese firms.

While the joint venture will be producing some products that compete with the products manufactured in California (formed parts), the venture company will give Murdock the chance to have much broader and deeper market penetration in Japan.

For both licensing and joint venture agreements, lawyers played only a minor role. The agreements are simple, written in English (not "legalese"), and are really based on a gentleman's agreement. Counsel for all parties reviewed the agreement after it was agreed upon.

Murdock's planning and creative use of marketing strategies have helped the company continue to grow and be successful both in the United States and around the world.

Northwestern Steel and Wire Company

Location: Sterling, Illinois. **Founded:** 1879. **Employees:** 3,000. **First exports:** 1989. **Major products exported:** Finished steel and wire products.
[See case write-up in the Introduction.]

nView Corporation

Location: Newport News, Virginia. **Founded:** 1987. **Employees:** 30. **First exports:** 1987. **Major products exported:** Liquid crystal display panels and remote control keyboards for personal computers.

"Stability, consistency, and persistence" is nView Corporation's philosophy when it comes to global business. The company has adhered to the philosophy since it made the initial commitment to exporting the year it was founded. Today, between 30 and 40 percent of total sales go primarily to Europe, South America, Canada, and Asia.

"Our first moves into international were proactive in the sense that we responded aggressively to interest generated by our products." Much of that initial interest was generated when nView participated in a major trade show for the computer industry in Boston. The company received numerous requests for international distributorships, and a number were soon signed.

Many of nView's original distributor relationships are still intact today. The company credits part of its success with its distributors to its outstanding support of them, from the training of the sales and technical service personnel to promotions, printed material, and trade shows. To get the most out of its participation in trade shows, both in terms of distributor support and locating new distributors, nView has worked with both the Virginia international trade department and the USDOC. The company finds that going to trade shows under the state or national banner gives it more visibility. These organizations also help with some of the details and paperwork necessary for show participation, which nView finds a real time-saver.

nView has also found the USDOC to be helpful in researching and understanding its markets. *A Basic Guide to Exporting* has been one of the company's most valuable reference sources. And frequent communication from the USDOC District Office, generally through newsletters, helps the company stay tuned to changes in current markets and potential openings in others. To analyze its current distribution of the company's international resources and to gain a more rational allocation of its resources, nView called upon the statistical services of the USDOC.

nView considers its freight forwarder to be the most valuable of its export services. The freight forwarder completes some of the export documentation and presents the required papers to banks for payment of letters of credit. It also provides information to help nView evaluate transportation, warehousing, and other options. "They do a good job for us," says the general sales manager, "and it's not worth the headache for us to try to fill that function at this point."

nView doesn't want to "take over the world," just achieve solid growth and consistent performance. So far, that has been a winning formula.

Redcom Laboratories, Inc.

Location: Victor, New York. **Founded:** 1978. **Employees:** 220. **First exports:** 1978. **Major products exported:** Telecommunications switching equipment.

Redcom Laboratories, Inc., specializes in niche markets, and its strategy has been to provide unique products for unique applications.

The company's president recognized that certain types of customers were being turned away by large telecommunications firms. These were the smaller customers with projects located in areas that are sparsely populated or remote, experience extreme weather conditions, or have unique requirements for applications in traditional areas. Redcom was formed to make products designed to meet the telecommunications needs of just such customers. Since extremes of weather and areas of sparse population are found around the globe, exports now make up nearly 40 percent of Redcom's annual sales.

But making unique products with unique applications is costly. "We spend proportionately more money on engineering than on any other part of our company," says its president. "By viewing the world as our marketplace, we find we can spread some of the cost and gain some volume advantage." When a market does become more mature and competitors begin to move in, Redcom is still able to compete on the basis of quality, quick turnaround, and a decision-making process that can be faster than in a large company.

The remote areas that Redcom serves around the world have special needs, and its products are designed for those needs. The systems have to be able to function at 50 degrees Celsius above or down to zero. They must be able to operate with minimal disruption when power sources are inconsistent. And they must be very reliable. "When you have to reach an area by dog sled or hire a helicopter at $500 an hour, reliability takes on a whole new meaning," explains Redcom's president.

Patience and persistence in international markets gives Redcom good results. Since Redcom's president is well-known after thirty-five years in the industry, he actively participates in conferences and trade association activities that promote the company's products. Redcom's reputation for quality generates referrals from previous customers, and these are a major source of business. The company also advertises in relevant trade magazines and attends many trade shows in areas such as Japan, Singapore, the Philippines, and Geneva.

As Redcom's president sees it, the real problem for exporters is being able to afford doing international business. Companies have to be prepared to spend some money up front for marketing. Visits have to be made to the target markets. As Redcom's president says, "You can't fly coach. You'll be too tired and your clothes will be wrinkled when you get off the plane. You have to be prepared to meet people as soon as you land."

Systems Center, Inc.

Location: Reston, Virginia. **Founded:** 1981. **Employees:** 750. **First exports:** 1982. **Major products exported:** Network software products, systems software products, and relational database products for IBM and compatible computers.

Systems Center (formerly VM Software) got into the international arena because its U.S.-based multinational customers' needs extended across the Atlantic and around the globe. This meant that the company had to establish overseas offices in order to provide truly effective support for its customers. Therefore, ten support representatives were set up in countries the company considered key to its growth. Today, Systems Center sells its products in fifty-five countries.

As the company's international sales grew, an international sales group was formed, and foreign sales increased by more than 390 percent in three years, contributing 31 percent of the total company revenues.

One reason for the international group's success has been its exceptional support of its representatives. "There are a lot of good companies with good products," says Systems Center's director of international operations and agent sales. "But the best representatives in foreign markets will pick and choose. They'll only do business with the companies that make it easy for them to succeed." In order to help its representatives succeed, company managers visit them to build long-term partnerships and to assist the representatives in closing sales. Also, all representatives, both domestic and international, who exceed the "Sales Quota Club" expectations are paid overachievement bonuses. The company also meets with its representatives to establish joint business plans for the coming year, and these plans are incorporated into the overall plan for the international group.

In spite of all its success and winning the President's "E" Award for exporting, the international group still finds that it helps to set expectations within the company. "We have to be sure to let people in the financial management department know how long it takes to get paid internationally, for example. And the people in shipping need to know that there are a few more forms to fill out when you send something to Dublin rather than Dallas."

Wahl Clipper Corporation

Location: Sterling, Illinois. **Founded:** 1919. **Employees:** 400. **First exports:** 1920s. **Major products exported:** Hair clippers and trimmers for professional and consumer use.

[See case write-up in the Introduction.]

The Witt Company

Location: Cincinnati, Ohio. **Founded:** 1887. **Employees:** 210. **First exports:** 1985. **Major products exported:** High-quality, fire-safe painted and galvanized metal waste receptacles and ash urns including the corrugated steel trash can on which it holds the original patent.

Since celebrating its centennial in 1987, the Witt Company has achieved an outstanding 51 percent growth in overall sales. But Witt is not relaxing as it enjoys its success. "From a long-term planning perspective, we need to look at a number of alternatives for growth, including making this a more international company," says Witt's president. "The market is far from saturated here, but we see internationalizing as a way to flatten out business cycles and create new opportunities."

In its initial phases of exporting, Witt set up a relationship with a South Carolina-based trading company. The trading company took title to the goods, accepted the credit risk, and assumed responsibility for transportation and other administrative duties involved with exporting. The marketing activities of the trading company, however, were mostly confined to responding to inquiries rather than undertaking more active promotions. Pricing, too, was generally left to Witt. Still, the trading company helped build Witt's exports to about 1.5 percent of total sales.

As internal expertise increased, Witt felt that it was necessary to learn more about international markets for its products in order to achieve greater control over the growth of the company's export sales. Resources that were particularly helpful included the publications *Export Market Planning for Small Manufacturers* (distributed by the Greater Cincinnati World Trade Association and the USDOC District Office) and *Business America* and the seminars offered by the Association and the USDOC. One of the company's most important sources of information has been other manufacturers within the industry (i.e., companies making related but noncompeting products); they have helped Witt acquire a better sense of the market, needed advice, and distributor references.

The Ohio International Trade Development Office has also been a valuable resource given that the Witt Company has decided to focus its efforts on the European Community. Ohio's six-person office in Brussels helps identify potential representatives and customers.

Witt chose the European Community as a target market because of the relative ease of doing business there and the strength of the economy and because the most recent and strongest interest from prospective customers has come from Europe.

Visiting the target markets has provided a lot of market information and helped the company's president discover just how much there is to learn, especially about the importance of cultural factors. According to Witt's president, "My travels have underscored the importance of having good follow-up in the language of your customers if at all possible."

Witt Company's long-term plans will likely include taking the company from being a basic manufacturer to developing a more value-added, design-oriented product line. Witt feels it cannot lose by exploring international markets, because "even if we don't come out with big sales, we will have learned more about our end users' quality needs and taste in design." For Witt, learning and growth have been part of a century of successful business.

Appendix A

Selected Resource Organizations

Federal Organizations

The recommended general reference book for federal export promotion organizations is *Exporter's Guide to Federal Resources for Small Business* (see Appendix B).

The following is a selected list of federal departments and agencies responsible for export promotion programs.

Agency for International Development (AID)

Office of Small and Disadvantaged Business Utilization (OSDBU), 320 21st Street NW, Washington, D.C. 20523-0069 USA. Telephone: 703-875-1551.

Export-Import Bank of the United States (Eximbank)

Headquarters: 811 Vermont Avenue NW, Washington, D.C. 20571 USA. Telephone: 202-566-8990.

Office of the U.S. Trade Representative

Headquarters: 600 17th Street NW, Washington, D.C. 20501 USA. Telephone: 202-395-3230.

Overseas Private Investment Corporation (OPIC)

Headquarters: 1615 M Street NW, Washington, D.C. 20527 USA. Telephone: 202-457-7200.

U.S. Department of Agriculture (USDA)

For program information and specific contacts within the Foreign Agriculture Service, order *Food and Agriculture Export Directory* (see Appendix B).

☐ *Economic Research Service*, 1301 New York Avenue NW, Washington, D.C. 20005 USA.
  • Agriculture and Trade Analysis Division, Room 732, 1301 New York Avenue NW, Washington, D.C. 20005 USA. Telephone: 202-786-1700.
  • Commodity Economics Division, Room 1024, 1301 New York Avenue NW, Washington, D.C. 20005 USA. Telephone: 202-786-1822.
  • Information Division, Room 228, 1301 New York Avenue NW, Washington, D.C. 20005 USA. Telephone: 202-786-1504.

☐ *Foreign Agriculture Service (FAS)*, Room 5071-S, Washington, D.C. 20250-1000 USA.
  • Export Credits Division, Room 4071-S, Washington, D.C. 20250-1000 USA. Telephone: 202-447-6301.
    —Commodity Credit Corporation, Room 4071-S, Washington, D.C. 20250-1000 USA. Telephone: 202-447-3224.
  • Commodity and Marketing Program Division, Room 5089A-S, Washington, D.C. 20250-1000 USA. Telephone: 202-447-4761.
    —AgExport Services, Room 4647-S, Washington, D.C. 20250-1000 USA. Telephone: 202-447-7103.
  • Foreign Agriculture Affairs, Room 5092-S, Washington, D.C. 20250-1000 USA. Telephone: 202-447-6063.
  • Information Division, Room 5092-S, Washington, D.C. 20250-1000 USA. Telephone: 202-447-7115.
  • International Trade Policy Division, Room 5057-S, Washington, D.C. 20250-1000 USA. Telephone: 202-447-3935.
    —Food Safety Office, Fifth Floor-S, Washington, D.C. 20250-1000 USA. Telephone: 202-382-1312. (Temporary address.)
    —Trade and Economics Information Division, Room 6506-S, Washington, D.C. 20250-1000. Telephone: 202-382-1293.

U.S. Department of Commerce (USDOC)

For specific program contacts within the USDOC, order *USDOC Telephone Directory* (see Appendix B).

☐ *Bureau of Export Administration*, Room 3898B, Washington, D.C. 20230 USA.
  • Export Counseling Division. Telephone: 202-377-4811.

☐ *International Trade Administration*, Room 3850, Washington, D.C. 20230 USA.
  • International Economic Policy (country desks), Room 3864, Washington, D.C. 20230 USA. Telephone: 202-377-3022.
  • Trade Development (industry desks), Room 3832, Washington, D.C. 20230 USA. Telephone: 202-377-1461.
  • U.S. and Foreign Commercial Service, Room 3804, Washington, D.C. 20230 USA. Telephone: 202-377-5777.
☐ *Other Offices*
  • National Institute of Standards and Technology, A629, Gaithersburg, Md. 20899 USA. Telephone: 301-975-4040.
  • Office of Metric Programs, Washington, D.C. 20230 USA. Telephone: 202-377-3036.

U.S. Small Business Administration (SBA)

Office of International Trade, 1441 L. Street NW, Washington, D.C. 20416 USA. Telephone: 202-653-7794.

U.S. Trade and Development Program

Headquarters: Room 309-SA-16, Washington, D.C. 20523-1602 USA. Telephone: 703-875-4357.

Private Organizations

American Management Association, 135 West 50th Street, New York, N.Y. 10020-1201 USA. Telephone: 212-586-8100.
American National Standards Institute, 1430 Broadway, New York, N.Y. 10036 USA. Telephone: 212-354-3300.
Business International Corp., 215 Park Avenue South, New York, N.Y. 10003 USA. Telephone: 212-460-0600.
Foreign Credit Insurance Association (FCIA), 40 Rector Street, 11th Floor, New York, N.Y. 10006 USA. Telephone: 212-306-5000.
International Bank for Reconstruction and Development (World Bank), 1818 H. Street NW, Washington, D.C. 20433 USA. Telephone: 202-477-2001.
U.S. Council for International Business, Inc., 1212 Avenue of the Americas, New York, N.Y. 10036 USA. Telephone: 212-354-4480.
World Trade Center Association, Inc., Suite 7701, One World Trade Center, New York, N.Y. 10048 USA. Telephone: 212-313-4600.

Foreign Government Organizations

Japanese External Trade Organization (JETRO), 1221 Avenue of the Americas, 44th Floor, New York, N.Y. 10020 USA. Telephone: 212-997-0400.

Appendix B

Selected Resource Materials

The following resource materials include publications, videos, database reports, on-line services, computer databases, and other items that have been referred to in the text.

More information about the resource materials may be obtained by writing or calling the contact following the resource title. The contact and cost of resource materials were based on the latest information available at the time of compilation. However, this information is always changing and should be confirmed before ordering.

Many of the publications available through the U.S. Government Printing Office (USGPO) are also available from the relevant departments and agencies. If you submit an order to the USGPO, do it well in advance of the date you will need the materials.

Agent/Distributor Service (ADS) ($125 per country). USDOC District Office.
AgExporter ($11 per year). USDA Foreign Agricultural Service, Room 4642-S, Washington, D.C. 20250-1000 USA.
AgExport's Trade Leads.
- Newsletter (weekly) ($75 annually). USDA Foreign Agricultural Service, Room 4647-S, Washington, D.C. 20250-1000 USA. Telephone: 202-447-7130.
- On-line ($300–$500 per year). Agridata Resources, Inc., 330 E. Kilbourn, Milwaukee, Wisc. 53203 USA. Telephone: 800-558-9044.
- Dialcom, Inc., 600 Maryland Avenue SW #307W, Washington, D.C. 20024 USA. Telephone: 202-488-0550. Also published in abbreviated form in *Journal of Commerce.*

AID Consultant Registry Information System (ACRIS) (free). AID, OSDBU, Washington, D.C. 20523-1414 USA. Telephone: 202-875-1590.

AID Importer Lists (free). AID, OSDBU, Washington, D.C. 20523-1414 USA. Telephone: 202-875-1590.

AID Procurement Information (free). AID, OSDBU, Washington, D.C. 20523-0069 USA. Telephone: 202-875-1590.

Background Notes on the Countries of the World Series. Periodically updated ($1 for single country copy, $14 per year for updated country notes). USGPO, Washington, D.C. 20402 USA. Telephone: 202-783-3238.

A Basic Guide to Exporting ($8.50). USGPO, Washington, D.C. 20402-9329 USA. Telephone: 202-783-3238.

Business America. Bi-weekly ($49 annual subscription). USGPO, Washington, D.C. 20402 USA. Telephone: 202-783-3238.

Business International: Indicators of Market Size. Annual ($75). Business International Corp., 215 Park Avenue South, New York, N.Y. 10003 USA. Telephone: 212-460-0600.

Buyer Alert. USDA Foreign Agriculture Service, Room 4647-S, Washington, D.C. 20250-1000 USA. Telephone: 202-382-8533.

Commercial Agency ($15). ICC Publishing Corp., Inc., 156 Fifth Avenue, New York, N.Y. 10010 USA. Telephone: 212-206-1150.

Commercial News USA ($250 per product advertising insertion). USDOC District Office.

Comparison Shopping Service ($500–$1,500). USDOC District Office.

Correct Way to Fill Out the Shipper's Export Declaration (free). USDOC, Bureau of Census, Washington, D.C. 20233 USA. Telephone: 301-763-5310.

Country Information Kit ($10–$45). Overseas Private Investment Corporation, 1615 M. Street NW, Washington, D.C. 20527 USA. Telephone: 800-424-6742.

Country Marketing Plan. Series. USDOC District Office.

Culturegrams. Country series ($25). Brigham Young University, Publication Service, 280 HRCB, Provo, Utah 84602 USA. Telephone: 801-378-6528.

Custom Statistical Service ($25 and up). USDOC District Office.

Discover Dollars in Drawbacks ($11). NCITD-International Trade Facilitation Council, 350 Broadway #205, New York, N.Y. 10013 USA. Telephone: 212-925-1400. Fax: 212-941-0371.

Doing Business In. Country series (free). Price Waterhouse, Publications

Coordinator, 1251 Avenue of the Americas, New York, N.Y. 10020 USA. Telephone: 212-489-8900.

Do's and Taboos Around the World. 1988 ($10). John Wiley & Sons, 605 Third Avenue, New York, N.Y. 10158 USA. Telephone: 212-850-6000. Fax: 212-850-6088.

Economic Bulletin Board. On-line service ($25 annual fee plus 5¢–10¢ per minute connect time). USDOC National Technical Information Service, 5285 Port Royal Road, Springfield, Va. 22161 USA. Telephone: 703-487-4630.

European Marketing Data and Statistics ($185). Gale Research, Inc., Book Tower, Detroit, Mich. 48277-0748 USA. Telephone: 800-233-4253.

Exhibitions 'Round the World ($30). Croner Publications, Inc., 211-03 Jamaica Avenue, Queens Village, N.Y. 11428 USA. Telephone: 718-464-0866. Telex: 425-329. Fax: 718-464-5734.

Export Administration Regulations. Periodically issued and continually updated ($87). USGPO, Washington, D.C. 20402 USA. Telephone: 202-783-3238.

Export Contact List Service (ECLS) Available on labels, printouts, text diskette ($0.25 per listing, $10 minimum order), USDOC District Office.

Export Guide to Europe ($130). Gale Research, Inc., Book Tower, Detroit, Mich. 48277-0748 USA. Telephone: 800-223-4253.

Export Information System (XIS) Product Reports (free). SBA District Office.

Export Licensing Checklist for Temporary Exports (free). USDOC Bureau of Export Administration, P.O. Box 273, Washington, D.C. 20044 USA. Telephone: 202-377-8731.

Export Manuals. The term refers to the following publications: *Exporters' Encyclopaedia; International Trade Reporter; Export Reference Manual; Official Export Guide; Reference Book for World Traders.*

Exporters' Encyclopaedia ($485 annual subscription with update and hotline service). Dun's Marketing Services, 3 Century Drive, Parsippany, N.J. 07054 USA. Telephone: 800-526-0651.

Exporter's Guide to Federal Resources for Small Business ($4). USGPO, Washington, D.C. 20402 USA. Telephone: 202-783-3238.

Exports by Mail (free). USDOC Bureau of Export Administration, P.O. Box 273, Washington, D.C. USA. 20044 USA. Telephone: 202-377-8731.

Export Yellow Pages (free). USDOC District Office.

Express Mail International Service Guide (free). U.S. Post Office.

Federal Express Worldwide Service Guide (free). Federal Express Corporation, Box 727, Memphis, Tenn. 38194 USA. Telephone: 800-238-5355.

Food and Agriculture Export Directory (free). USDA Foreign Agriculture Service, Room 5920-S, Washington, D.C. 20250-1000 USA. Telephone: 202-447-7937.

Foreign Agriculture. Annual ($12). USDA Foreign Agriculture Service, Room 4642-S, Washington, D.C. 20250-1000 USA.

Foreign Agriculture Trade of the U.S. (FATUS). Bimonthly ($21 annually). USDA Economic Research Service, P.O. Box 1608, Rockville, Md. 20849-1608 USA. Telephone: 800-999-6779.

Foreign Buyer Lists ($15 per list). USDA Foreign Agriculture Service, Ag Export Services, 4647-S, Washington, D.C. 20250-1000 USA. Telephone: 202-447-7103.

Foreign Consular Offices in the U.S. ($4.75). USGPO, Washington, D.C. 20402 USA. Telephone: 202-783-3238.

Foreign Economic Trends and Their Implications for the United States (FET). Country series ($55 annual subscription). USGPO, Washington, D.C. 20402 USA. Telephone: 202-783-3238. Single country copies available from USDOC District Office.

Foreign Market Research Service ($10 and up for printout, $12 for text diskette). USDOC District Office. Includes *Country Marketing Plan Series*, *International Market Research (IMR)*, and *International Market Information (IMI)*.

Foreign Sales Corporation (Free). Price Waterhouse, Publications Coordinator, 1251 Avenue of the Americas, New York, N.Y. 10020 USA. Telephone: 212-489-8900.

Going International ($10). Copeland Griggs Productions, 302 Twenty-Third Avenue, San Francisco, Calif. 94121 USA. Telephone: 415-668-4200. Fax: 415-668-6004.

Going International. Video series. "Bridging the Cultural Gap," "Managing the Overseas Assignment" ($100 per video rental fee). Copeland Griggs Productions, 302 Twenty-Third Avenue, San Francisco, Calif. 94121 USA. Telephone: 415-668-4200. Fax: 415-668-6004.

Guide to Agencies Providing Foreign Credit Information (free). Foreign Credit Insurance Association (FCIA), 40 Rector Street, 11th Floor, New York, N.Y. 10006 USA. Telephone: 212-306-7020.

Guide to Documentary Credit Operations ($19). ICC Publishing Corp., Inc., 156 Fifth Avenue, New York, N.Y. 10010 USA. Telephone: 212-206-1150.

Guide to Drafting International Distributorship Agreements ($26). ICC Publishing Corp., Inc., 156 Fifth Avenue, New York, N.Y. 10010 USA. Telephone: 212-206-1150.

Highlights of U.S. Export and Import Merchandise Trade FT900 Supplement. Monthly ($120 annual subscription, $10 single issue). USDOC Bureau of the Census, Room 2179, Washington, D.C. 20233 USA. Replaced FT990 in 1989.

Incoterms 1990 ($19). ICC Publishing Corp., Inc., 156 Fifth Avenue, New York, N.Y. 10010 USA. Telephone: 212-206-1150. Telex: 661-519.

Interdata. Importer mailing lists. Interdata, 1480 Grove Street, Healdsburg, Calif. 95448 USA. Telephone: 707-433-3900. Fax: 707-433-8920.

International Directories in Print ($175). Gale Research, Inc., Book Tower, Detroit, Mich. 48226 USA. Telephone: 800-223-4253.

International Directory of Importers. Regional series ($125–$225 per region). International Directory of Importers, P.O. Box 788, Healdsburg, Calif. 95448 USA. Telephone: 707-433-3900. Fax: 707-433-8920.

International Exhibitors Handbook ($175). International Exhibitors Association, 5103-B Backlick Road, Annandale, Va. 22003 USA. Telephone: 703-941-3725. Fax: 703-941-8275.

International Mail Manual ($14 semiannual subscription). USGPO, Washington, D.C. 20402 USA. Telephone: 202-783-3238.

International Marketing Data and Statistics ($185). Gale Research, Inc., Book Tower, Detroit, Mich. 48233-0748 USA. Telephone: 800-223-4253.

International Market Research (IMR). Industry/country series ($10 for summary report, $12 on text diskette). USDOC District Office.

International Trade Fairs and Conferences Directory ($55). International Trade Fairs and Conferences Directory, 366 Adleaide Street E, #339, Toronto, Ont. M5A 3X9 Canada. Telephone: 416-264-1223. Fax: 416-364-6557.

International Trade Reporter: Current Reports. Weekly ($816 annual subscription). Bureau of National Affairs, 1231 Twenty-Fifth Street NW, Washington, D.C. 20037 USA. Telephone: 800-372-1033.

International Trade Reporter: Export Reference Manual. Updated weekly ($524 annual subscription). Bureau of National Affairs, 1231 Twenty-

Fifth Street NW, Washington, D.C. 20037 USA. Telephone: 800-372-1033.

International Tradeshow Directory ($175). Tesar Communications, 97A Chestnut Hill Village, Bethel, Conn. 06801 USA. Telephone: 302-792-8237.

International Trade State and Local Resource Directory. State series (free). SBA Office of International Trade, 1441 L. Street NW, Washington, D.C. 20416 USA. Telephone: 202-653-7794.

Journal of Commerce ($205 annual subscription). Journal of Commerce, 110 Wall Street, New York, N.Y. 10005 USA.

Key Officers of Foreign Service Posts ($5). USGPO, Washington, D.C. 20402 USA. Telephone: 202-783-3238.

Kompass. Country series ($85–$349). Trinet, Inc., 9 Campus Drive, Parsippany, N.J. 07054 USA. Telephone: 800-367-3282.

Market Backgrounders Country Series (free). USDA Foreign Agricultural Service, Room 5920-S, Washington, D.C. 20250-1000 USA. Telephone: 202-447-7937.

Metrication for the Manager ($16). American National Metric Council, 1620 I. Street NW #220, Washington, D.C. 20006 USA. Fax: 202-659-5427.

National Trade Data Bank. CD-ROM series ($360 annual subscription, $35 single issue). USDOC National Technical Information Service, 5285 Port Royal Road, Springfield, Va. 22161 USA. Telephone: 703-487-4630.

Official Export Guide ($349). North American Publishing Co., 401 N. Broad Street, Philadelphia, Pa. 19108 USA. Telephone: 215-238-5300. Fax: 213-238-5457.

Outlook for U.S. Agriculture Exports. Quarterly ($19 annual subscription). USDA Economic Research Service, P.O. Box 1608, Rockville, Md. 20849-1608 USA. Telephone: 800-999-6779.

Overseas Business Reports (OBR). Country International Marketing Information Series ($14 annual subscription). USGPO, Washington, D.C. 20402 USA. Telephone: 202-783-3238. Single country copies available from the USDOC District Office.

P.I.E.R.S. (approximately $360 per monthly report). Journal of Commerce, 120 Wall Street, New York, N.Y. 10005 USA. Telephone: 212-425-1616.

Reference Book for World Traders ($115). Croner Publications, Inc., 211-03 Jamaica Avenue, Queens Village, N.Y. 11428 USA. Telephone: 718-464-0866. Telex: 425-329.

Schedule B: Statistical Classification of Domestic and Foreign Commodities Exported From the United States ($77 annual subscription). USGPO, Washington, D.C. 20402 USA. Telephone: 202-783-3238.

Showcase USA (Free new product section and regular rate advertising). Sell Overseas America, 2512 Artesia Blvd., Redondo Beach, Calif. 90278 USA. Telephone: 213-376-8788. Fax: 213-376-9043.

Statistical Yearbook. Annual ($75). United Nations Publications, Room DC2-853, Dept. 701, New York, N.Y. 10017 USA. Telephone: 212-963-8302.

Statistics and Outlook Report. Commodity series ($19 annually). USDA Economic Research Service, P.O. Box 1608, Rockville, Md. 20849-1608 USA. Telephone: 800-999-6779.

Survey of Foreign Laws and Regulations Affecting International Franchising ($140) American Bar Association, 750 N. Lake Shore Drive, Chicago, Ill. Telephone: 312-988-5555.

System for Tracking Export Licenses (STELA) (free). USDA, ITA Automated Information Staff, Room 3898, Washington, D.C. 20230 USA. Telephone: 202-377-2753 (for information), 202-377-2752 (for application status).

Trade Directories of the World ($70). Croner Publications, Inc., 211-03 Jamaica Avenue, Queens Village, N.Y. 11428 USA. Telephone: 718-464-0866. Telex: 425-329.

Traveler's World Atlas and Guide ($6.95). Rand McNally & Company. Available at bookstores.

Ulrich's International Periodicals Directory. R.R. Bowker, 245 West 17th Street, New York, N.Y. 10011 USA.

Unz & Co. Catalog for International and Domestic Shippers (free). Unz & Co., 190 Baldwin Avenue, Jersey City, N.J. 07306 USA. Telephone: 800-631-3098.

Unz & Co. Export Management Control System ($70 for ten folders). Unz & Co., 190 Baldwin Avenue, Jersey City, N.J. 07306 USA. Telephone: 800-631-3098.

USDOC Telephone Directory ($11). USGPO, Washington, D.C. 20402 USA. Telephone: 202-783-3238.

U.S. Export and Import Merchandise Trade FT900. Monthly ($120 annual subscription, $10 single issue). USDOC Bureau of the Census, Room 2179, Washington, D.C. 20233 USA. Telephone: 202-763-5140.

U.S. Exports: Schedule E Commodity by Country FT410 (replaced by U.S. Merchandise Trade FT925 in 1989). Available at USDOC District Office.

U.S. Exports of Domestic and Foreign Merchandise EM545. Monthly printout ($125 annual subscription, $25 single month). USDOC Bureau of the Census, Room 2179, Washington, D.C. 20233 USA. Telephone: 202-763-5140.

U.S. Merchandise Trade FT925. Monthly ($300 annually, $30 single copy). USDOC Bureau of the Census, Room 2179, Washington, D.C. 20233 USA. Telephone: 202-763-4100. Replaced FT410 in 1989.

U.S. Trade Reports (free). USDA Foreign Agricultural Service, Room 6506-S, Washington, D.C. 20250-1000 USA. Telephone: 202-382-1295.

World Chamber of Commerce Directory ($24). World Chamber of Commerce Directory, P.O. Box 1029, Loveland, Colo. 80539 USA. Telephone: 303-663-3231.

The World Is Your Market (free). USDOC District Office.

World Market Atlas. Annual ($385). Business International Corp., 215 Park Avenue South, New York, N.Y. 10003 USA. Telephone: 212-460-0600.

The World's Largest Market: A Business Guide to Europe 1992. AMACOM Books, 135 West 50th Street, New York, N.Y. 10020 USA. Telephone: 518-891-1500.

World Tables. The World Bank, 1818 H. Street NW, Washington, D.C. 20433 USA. Telephone: 202-477-1234.

World Trade Center Network. Your nearest World Trade Center *or* World Trade Center Associations, Inc., One World Trade Center, Suite 7701, New York, N.Y. 10048 USA. Telephone: 212-313-4600. Fax: 212-488-0064.

World Traders Data Reports (WTDR) ($100 per report). USDOC District Office.

Index

[Italic page numbers refer to figures and tables.]

263